RENEWALS 458-4574
DATE DUE

WITHDRAWN
UTSA LIBRARIES

History in Practice

History in Practice

LUDMILLA JORDANOVA

A member of the Hodder Headline Group
LONDON
Co-published in the United States of America by
Oxford University Press Inc., New York

First published in Great Britain in 2000 by
Arnold, a member of the Hodder Headline Group,
338 Euston Road, London NW1 3BH

http://www.arnoldpublishers.com

Co-published in the United States of America by
Oxford University Press Inc.,
198 Madison Avenue, New York NY 10016

© 2000 Ludmilla Jordanova

All rights reserved. No part of this publication may be reproduced or
transmitted in any form or by any means, electronically or mechanically,
including photocopying, recording or any information storage or retrieval
system, without either prior permission in writing from the publisher or a
licence permitting restricted copying. In the United Kingdom such licences
are issued by the Copyright Licensing Agency: 90 Tottenham Court Road,
London W1P 0LP.

The advice and information in this book are believed to be true and
accurate at the date of going to press, but neither the author nor the
publisher can accept any legal responsibility or liability for any errors or omissions.

British Library Cataloguing in Publication Data
A catalogue record for this book is available from the British Library

Library of Congress Cataloging-in-Publication Data
A catalog record for this book is available from the Library of Congress

ISBN 0 340 66331 6 (hb)
ISBN 0 340 66332 4 (pb)

1 2 3 4 5 6 7 8 9 10

Production Editor: Wendy Rooke
Production Controller: Priya Gohil
Cover Design: Terry Griffiths

Typeset in 10/12pt Sabon by Phoenix Photosetting, Chatham, Kent
Printed by Arrowsmiths Ltd, Bristol
and bound by MPG Books Ltd

Library
University of Texas
at San Antonio

What do you think about this book? Or any other Arnold title?
Please send your comments to feedback.arnold@hodder.co.uk

For all my students –
past, present and future

Contents

Postscript:

List of illustrations

Preliminaries

Opening statements such as this one are designed to offer acknowledgements for help received in the preparation of the book and to set the scene for what follows. By its very nature, a project like this one incurs many debts. Since, strictly speaking, I have no formal qualifications in the discipline of history, as it is conventionally defined, beyond a secondary school examination taken in 1966, I am especially grateful to those who encouraged my aspirations to be a 'proper' historian: Roy Porter, Gillian Sutherland, Peter Searby, Joyce Appleby, Charles Webster and the members of the appointments committee at the University of Essex who, in the summer of 1979, offered me a post in a very special department, focused on comparative history. I stayed at Essex for close to 14 years and the experience of teaching and thinking about history in a comparative context was a formative one. I was particularly inspired by Leonore Davidoff and Steve Smith, and by Jordan Goodman from whom I learned how exciting economic history can be. I shall always be grateful for the time I spent in the History Department at the University of York between 1993 and 1996, not only for the wonderful students I had the privilege to teach there, but for the intellectual companionship it offered. In particular, I thank John Bossy, Chris Clark, Geoff Cubitt, Simon Ditchfield, Mark Jenner and Jane Rendall from whom I learned so much. I am no longer in a history department, although I continue to think of myself as a historian. Such a situation serves as a constant stimulus to reflect upon both the discipline of history and its relations with other, closely related disciplines.

It is not possible to do research in the usual sense when preparing a general book about a field of study. Everything concerning our experience and study of the past is potentially relevant and hence I am drawing on all aspects of professional life, especially teaching and informal contacts with fellow historians. I have, however, been able to interview a number of historians who work in fields distant from my own and I would like to thank them most warmly for sharing their ideas with me: Joyce Appleby, Steve Church, Peter Garnsey, Rachel Klein, Mark Mazower, Richard Rathbone, Carole Rawcliffe, Ulinka Rublack and Steve Smith. I appreciate Jo Beighton and Christopher Gartner talking to me about the school history education they received in Germany. For their assistance in the preparation of this volume, including reading drafts and making constructive suggestions, I am indebted to Patrick Finney, Alix Jordanova, Christopher Wheeler, Andy Wood and an anonymous reader. Alix and Andy have been exceptionally helpful to me – it is a pleasure to acknowledge their input. Warmest thanks to Anthony Knights both for doing the bulk of the work on the glossary and for much kind support, and to Alix Jordanova for preparing the index. Many people responded generously and patiently to my questions – I thank them all.

It was Christopher Wheeler of Arnold Publishers who suggested I might like to write this book, and I have greatly appreciated his support, encouragement, sound advice and patience throughout. I was heartened by three anonymous readers' reports on the original proposal, which has remained the blueprint to which I have worked subsequently. I owe a quite special debt to my agent Derek Johns for his guidance.

Authors inevitably rely a great deal on those closest to them when preparing a text. As I hope they know, my friends mean a very great deal to me. My daughters, Alix (now a fledgling historian) and Zara, have been a constant source of pleasure and inspiration. On the domestic front, I could scarcely function without Margaret Gibson, my 'angel in the house'. At the University of East Anglia, I am particularly indebted to the members of the informal eighteenth-century visual culture research group, to my friends in the School of History, and to my colleagues and students. As the dedication indicates, I owe most to the students, with whom, since 1971 when I started supervising in history and philosophy of science at Cambridge, I have been able to think about the practice of history in many different guises. There are so many impediments in universities now to creative teaching, thinking and writing that our contacts with students are increasingly governed by the need to save time and conform to bureaucratic norms. The pressure for so-called radical teaching efficiencies has created a climate in which the complex processes whereby academic staff enable others to learn are no longer given their due. The strongest defence of teaching rests on the inseparable claims that it fosters research and reflection and that it stimulates thinking about how human beings behave and represent their behaviour. It is also fun. I thank my students most warmly for everything they have taught me.

These acknowledgements have begun to set the scene for the book that follows, and I would now like to turn to that task more directly, beginning with my own intellectual background. After secondary school, my first meeting with history was through studying the history and philosophy of science in the late 1960s. While this field was certainly concerned with the past, at that time it was driven by an agenda set largely by the natural sciences. Encountering history in the company of philosophy was significant – the combination allows the critical analysis of ideas to be central to historical practice. While undertaking doctoral research on the French biology of the late eighteenth and early nineteenth centuries, I started to become aware of the possibility of a closer integration between history and the history of science, without being at all sure what this would entail. I have been greatly influenced by others who, more sure-footedly, pursued these possibilities. As a result of their endeavours, the history of science and of medicine are now much more integrated with general history, although they remain distinct sub-fields, which are frequently pursued by those with some training in the sciences or medicine.

One of the big developments in the history of science has been 'science and literature', which brought literary critics, with their distinctive assumptions, methods and goals, into close contact with historians of science. This encounter with text-based approaches has been enormously important to me. So too was the 'discovery' of anthropology, which historians of science made in the late 1960s and the 1970s. It enabled them not only to value other belief systems that were, by modern standards, 'unscientific', but to appreciate the power of simultaneously maintaining a critical distance from, while sympathetically entering into, other cultures. For me this remains the kernel of historical practice. Much later I started thinking about the objects and images that are produced in the course of scientific and medical activities, and this led me to art history. Like the history of science, the history of art is a separate field with its own journals, professional associations and intellectual frameworks. Art, like science, carries an aura that sometimes acts to discourage its full contextualisation, yet both domains can only be understood if placed in a rich historical context. This constitutes an important project, since everyone in the past used their visual experience, the traces of which, accordingly, afford general historical insights. All these areas may be distinct, but they have much to learn from each other, and the terrain they inhabit is not neatly packaged up to meet modern disciplinary distinctions. These interdisciplinary experiences inform my ideas about the discipline of history, which, I shall argue, possesses nonetheless its own distinctive character.

The periods on which I have worked also shape my view of history. The vast majority of my work has been concerned with the second half of the eighteenth century and the first half of the nineteenth century, although I have worked a little on adjacent eras. At Essex I was involved with some early modern survey teaching, and my interest in that ill-defined period was extended by the strong group of early modernists at York. I am intensely conscious, however, of never having studied ancient or medieval history. I hope that some of the concerns of historians working on much earlier periods are nonetheless reflected in this book. By the same token I have tried to think about contemporary history. In ways I explore in Chapter 5, we have all sorts of mechanisms, conscious and unconscious, for shaping and imagining the past. These privilege some times, themes and approaches and marginalise others. The models each historian finds appealing have a great deal to do with 'their' period, as well as with their own political, social and economic views.

The pursuit of history is, whether practitioners choose to acknowledge it or not, a political occupation. For the entire time I have been doing historical work, politics has loomed large in every aspect of it, from the relationships between the wider political world and research undertaken, to the micro-politics of academic institutions and of sub-fields. It seems to me not just natural but proper that professional energies should be concerned with the most cherished values out of which politics is built. Thus, I am proud to call myself a feminist historian, because thinking about gender relations, their history and their future from a woman's perspective has been a central part of my life. All this occurs in specific contexts that may accurately be called political. I make this point about the pervasiveness of politics for historians partly because any book about the practice of history has to tackle the question of 'bias'. All human beings have biases of one kind or another and to pretend otherwise is simply dishonest. There is no such thing as unbiased history, but there is such a thing as balanced, self-aware history. Bias becomes a problem when it prevents historians from being judicious and from having a measure of creative, critical distance from their work. For historical writings to be informed by our passions and values is not just inevitable, it is good in that it lends them energy. But passions and values should also be constantly subjected to scrutiny; they need to be tempered by evidence – for a conviction to be heartfelt need not imply it is unreflexive. It is pointless to hold up an ideal – unbiased history – which is simply unobtainable.

I am setting the scene in this way because *History in Practice* argues for the importance of knowing an author's position. Those who are curious about mine could start with the Postscript. Naturally there is much about any writer that can never be known, sometimes for lack of evidence, and always because of the complexity of the unconscious. Readers still need to know, more or less, where an author is coming from. I have been indicating here not only where my own interests and enthusiasms lie, but also my methods of working. Closely bound up with this is my imagined audience. I have deliberately tried *not* to imagine myself writing for my peers, but for, on the one hand, general readers and, on the other, students. Those who teach courses on historiography and related areas will, I hope, read the book, but it is not primarily aimed at them. Furthermore, it is best read as a series of interconnected arguments, and taken as a whole. I am not conveying information but working through ideas. One reason for treating the volume as an entity is connected with the manner in which I have proceeded in writing it: I started at the beginning and developed the ideas in the sequence in which they will be read. Brief examples serve to amplify key points; other examples would have done equally well.

A few further words of explanation are in order at this point. *History in Practice* is designed to provoke the reader to think about the processes through which the kind of knowledge called 'history' is made and used. It leaves much unresolved because there are no simple resolutions to most of the questions I pose. The discipline is intriguing precisely for this reason. It is also a vast domain and I make no pretence to cover everything – that would be absurd. I can only apologise for the book's limitations and hope that these are understood for what they are: human frailty combined with an unwillingness to pretend to experience and knowledge I do not possess. I have therefore used examples with which I am familiar. I have also sought to provide positive rather than negative instances to illustrate key points. In the relative privacy of the seminar or tutorial we can dismantle the work of others and see how it might be done otherwise, but in a work of this kind explicit criticism of named historians is out of place.

In explaining the type of arguments that follow, it is best to be perfectly open about what this book does *not* do. For instance, it is not about the philosophy of history, which examines the nature of arguments, the use of concepts, theories and evidence, and evaluates these abstractly. Inevitably we will touch on these issues, especially in Chapter 4, but they are not the centrepiece of the book. Nor am I responding to the challenge of post-modernism or of any other theoretical framework. Although I hope to convey how the practice of history has changed in recent years, I am not defending the discipline or engaging with particular theoretical issues. *History in Practice* is not a handbook that tells readers how to be better historians, do research more effectively or get published. It would be wonderful if it raised the awareness of those starting out as historians, but it does not contain recipes for improvement. Finally, it is not a history of history; no attempt is made in the pages that follow to provide a narrative overview of the ways in which either history writing or the historical profession have changed over the centuries.

History in Practice has three goals: to give readers a sense of the issues in the discipline; to place the field in a wider context; and to sketch in what historians actually do and how and why they do it. Thus it is more an 'anthropology' of history, in that it tries to make sense of the practices and ideas of a distinct group of people, without being overly prescriptive about what historians ought to do. Yet it is not an ethnography – a detailed account of directly observed behaviour – for it works at a more general level than that term implies. I allow myself to speculate a little about the future of history in the concluding statement, which will set out priorities for the field as I see them. This book does not ignore the question of standards. I believe that it is both possible and essential to discriminate between 'good' and 'bad' history. So, the interest in an 'anthropology' of history should be taken as meaning not simple observation, but a sympathetic account of what doing history is all about, which includes critical evaluation as an integral part of the enterprise.

There are two last points that need to be addressed here. The first arises directly out of remarks I have already made about my own background. For me it is important that we avow, in so far as this is possible, what our interests, prejudices, working assumptions and so on, are. I have already indicated that this will only ever be a partial account, because our unconscious investments are so complex. Often people talk about these problems in terms of 'bias', which I find unsatisfactory, largely because it erroneously implies the existence of *un*biased judgements, which individuals produce through the exercise of conscious control. I have searched for other vocabularies through which to speak about the values historians hold. I do not believe that all value judgements are equally OK, or that all accounts of the past are equally valid. In a book of this kind it is necessary to make generalisations which cannot be supported by voluminous footnotes. Thus it is all the more important that the means by which opinions have been arrived at are as transparent as possible. The second point – about the book's apparatus – follows directly from this. By 'apparatus', I mean the supports for my arguments. References for the small number of direct quotations are always given in footnotes, which also make the general claims of the text a little more concrete. The further reading includes items that I have found relevant in writing the book and that will offer readers further insights into the themes with which it deals. Accordingly it is divided into sections reflecting the organisation of the text.

I would like to suggest a metaphor through which *History in Practice* may be approached. Perhaps it can be understood as a sketch map – an apt metaphor if history is a field – which helps in finding one's way around, locating basic markers and also appreciating the terrain.

L. J.
Norwich
July 1999

Introduction

HISTORY AND DISCIPLINES

The word 'history' has a number of meanings, and a wide range of connotations, some of which are charged with intense emotion. We use it to invoke the authority of precedents, to refer to what is no longer relevant, to endow objects with value and status, and to mobilise longings for better worlds. Since one of the main meanings of history is simply 'the past', then almost any association with past times can be transferred to 'history'. Yet there is another rather different way of defining history: as the *study* of the past. In this sense history is an academic discipline. What is implied by calling something an academic discipline? Chapter 1 seeks to answer this question.

I have already stated that *History in Practice* has three main aims: to convey a sense of the issues in the discipline; to place the field in a wider context; and to indicate how historians actually practise. These aims already imply some of the answers to the questions 'what is an academic discipline?' and 'what is the nature of history in particular?' My first aim implies that fields share intellectual preoccupations, and in this sense they are communities built around ideas of one kind or another, where members are constantly conversing, in their writings as much as in their direct contacts. One result of this is that publications are never free-standing, although they are often seen this way, but rather are parts of elaborate conversations with other historians, living and dead. They are also conversations with governments, political parties, interest groups and so on. As this book will constantly make clear, publications work at many different levels, so that, in addition to participating in conversations, they stake out territory for their authors, speak to contemporary concerns, and contribute to the creation of imaginative frameworks through which the past is felt, as well as thought about.

The second aim, to place the field in a wider context, implies that disciplines, like those who practise them, cannot be seen as isolated; in reality there are no ivory towers in which academics and their productions exist detached from the world. In recent decades the practice of history has become ever more bound up with politics, with the popularisation of history, with ideas of heritage, and with the changing priorities of nation states. The demands of intellectual rigour, to which all disciplines are subject, are not incompatible with extensive engagement with a wider world. The study of history is intimately bound up with social, political and economic institutions, such as museums, the educational system and government. It is equally closely connected with cultural life, that is, with television, fiction, drama, poetry, radio, film, art and so on. For centuries elites have recognised that the past is usable, as a resource, an instrument through which it is possible to persuade, cajole and moralise. Groups that have felt themselves to be subordinate, oppressed or marginal have taken up the same tools, hence the development of oral history, labour history, black history and women's history, of history from below and 'subaltern studies'.[1]

My third aim, to indicate what historians actually do, implies that the discipline of history is best understood as a set of practices, rather than as, say, a constellation of beliefs or theories, or a stable body of subject matter. History is indeed about what historians do. This formulation is not circular, as might at first sight appear. Rather it signals that there is no essence of the discipline, which is made up of what members of the community agree will count as such. Through the institutions that regulate academic disciplines in a variety of ways, conventions are formed about who counts as a historian and what counts as academic history. Of particular importance in this respect are schools, universities, professional groupings, government bodies and specialised publishers. This is not to say that disputes do not constantly arise. They occur precisely because, on the one hand, our investments in how the past is interpreted are so great, and, on the other, because our interests in it are so diverse. They also arise because there are never clear boundaries around academic subjects: these are imposed on the 'raw' materials, in a manner that reveals more about scholars and scholarship than about the past itself. Nonetheless most people who earn their living as historians agree on what the general rules for generating sound knowledge of the past are – for the selection, use and citation of sources, for example – and disputes frequently revolve around whether these have actually been followed. Beyond that historians differ on academic matters as much as they do on political ones. They are

1   *Subaltern Studies* was the name of a series of books produced from 1982 in India. They promoted, from a radical and theoretical perspective, a form of people's history that addressed power relations from the point of view of the colonised. The determination to use the past for fresh purposes has been widespread: see, for example, the introduction to the magazine *Amistad* (1970) which attacks the '"intellectual" racism' of, among other things, the teaching of American history. It published material suitable for use on black studies courses. Cf. F. Krantz, ed., *History from Below*, Oxford, 1988.

united, not by the *content* of what they believe, but by their commitment to the importance of studying the past, by their participation in shared activities, and by their conviction that certain ways of proceeding produce reliable historical insights. Thus the discipline of history is a complex array of practices, and these practices are underpinned by an infrastructure. Just as modern societies need to be understood in terms of the structures, such as transport, banking and health services, which enable them to function, so academic disciplines need to be placed in the context of their support systems and institutional bases, and it is to these that I now turn.

INFRASTRUCTURES

There are a number of elements that need to be distinguished in the infrastructure of history: training; professional organisations; government agencies; employment; marketing; and the dissemination of ideas and information. There is, inevitably, some overlap here – for example, schools and universities are places of training and employment, and in most countries they interact extensively with government agencies. Nonetheless it is useful to distinguish these areas in order to be able to think about them as clearly as possible, since they give rise to distinct issues. Before discussing these elements in more detail, two general points need to be made. The first serves to draw attention to the *variety* of ways in which individuals, groups and nations use, shape and respond to the infrastructure of intellectual life. Historians make choices, to belong to one professional association rather than another, for example. In Britain we have two main national organisations: the Historical Association, founded in 1906, which embraces both professional and amateur historians, and the Royal Historical Society, founded in 1868, which elects to the Fellowship those with scholarly publications on historical topics. Decisions about joining such bodies express an individual's assumptions about priorities in the study of history and how they are best expressed. Many, including myself, would see populist and scholarly organisations as complementary. Neither organisation, however, is as politically up-front as the American Historical Association (AHA), founded in 1894, a huge and powerful body, which publishes the prestigious and widely-read *American Historical Review* (1895).[2] Issues around gender, race and class, both as subjects within history and as professional matters, have been foregrounded by the AHA, as they have been by many historical organisations in the United States. The British organisations,

2 Dates after journals indicate the year in which the first part appeared.

A Brief Overview of the AHA

The American Historical Association (AHA) is a nonprofit membership organization founded in 1884 and incorporated by Congress in 1889 for the promotion of historical studies, the collection and preservation of historical documents and artifacts, and the dissemination of historical research. As the largest historical society in the United States, the AHA serves as the umbrella organization for historians. In this role, it conducts an active scholarly and professional program for historians interested in every period and geographical area. Among its 15,000 members are faculty at secondary schools and two- and four-year colleges and universities, independent historians, and historians in museums, historical organizations, libraries and archives, government, and other areas.

American Historical Association Mission Statement

In 1889, the U.S. Congress chartered the AHA, charging it to act "in the interest of American history, and of history in America." One hundred years later, a review committee defined the mission emerging from this charge as service to history professionals (defined as individuals with graduate degrees or some formal training in history) who practice history either in teaching or research or both. Teaching was defined quite broadly, to encompass "a wide range of efforts at communication and dissemination in varied settings -- museums and historic sites as well as classrooms -- and involving the use of visual materials and artifacts as well as words." Research was defined as "the uncovering and exchange of new information and the shaping of interpretations.... The profession communicates with students in textbooks and classrooms; to other scholars and the general public in books, articles, exhibits, films, and historic sites and structures; and to decision-makers in memoranda and testimony.

AHA

1.1 Extracts from the American Historical Association Web-site
Most profesional organisations now use the internet to publicise their activities. The format, visual style and content chosen convey a great deal about their self-image. In the case of the American Historical Association, the emphasis is on its government mandate, its broad constituencies, the professional services offered to members, and the public significance of history.

while they seek to represent the interests of historians broadly defined, are considerably less political and often more traditional – the Royal Historical Society will have its first ever woman president only in 2000, for instance. In one sense the History in the Universities Defence Group (HUDG), which was founded in the Thatcher years, is more 'political' than the other national organisations in Britain, in that it engages directly with government policy, claiming to speak on behalf of university historians as a whole. Yet it is not partisan, in the sense of espousing party-political lines, not least because this would be divisive, and hence weaken HUDG's position. So, not only do individuals make choices, but historians in different countries exercise their choices in markedly different contexts.

One element referred to above was the dissemination of ideas and information, and this includes the press. Daily newspapers in France devote considerable space to historical issues. When the prominent historian Fernand

Braudel died in 1985, a number of papers discussed him and his contributions at considerable length – far greater coverage than is imaginable in Britain or the USA. Nonetheless, books about history, especially biographies and anything to do with heritage matters, are widely reviewed in British newspapers and magazines. Thus, when we think about the practice of history in France, we should bear in mind the larger environment, especially the on-going, passionate debates about revolutionary traditions, which partly account for the distinctive French preoccupation with the past and those who recount it.

The second point follows directly: while there is considerable room for individual choice and collective manoeuvring, attitudes to history are nonetheless strongly shaped by institutional structures and the ideologies that go along with them. We can illustrate the point by thinking about attitudes towards Germany and Japan, especially in those countries that won the Second World War. National stereotypes have proved extraordinarily persistent, and they manifest themselves in a number of forms, from imitating accents to huge generalisations about a nation's character and culpability, and a reluctance to learn certain other languages. While some might say that this is no more than popular prejudice, I would reply that such feelings are reinforced by institutions such as schools, newspapers and the media, especially by the film industry, which, in the years following the war, constructed, using visual images, language and music, a quite particular set of responses to the events of 1939–1945.[3] Such values, selectively reinforced by the infrastructure of the discipline, have real consequences for the manner in which history is practised. *Styles* of education, which go far beyond the *content* of history syllabuses, play an extraordinarily important role in setting the most basic terms through which children think about and imagine the past.

EDUCATIONAL SYSTEMS

The study of history is an important part of most educational systems. It is identified as a major subject in conventional curricula, and this is because in most countries knowing about the past is valued as, on the one hand, an important component of a well-educated mind, and on the other, a source of useful insights for the modern citizen. Later on I shall examine the idea of 'lessons from history', which underlies many educational arguments about why the subject should be widely taught, and which is often invoked as a

---

3 See, for example, J. W. Chambers and D. Culbert, eds., *World War II, Film and History*, New York, 1996.

MARTIN COULBERT

1.2 'Company F, 55th Virginia Infantry Regiment', an American Civil War re-enactment group, at Saffron Walden, UK, 1998
The re-enactment of battles has become a popular activity for participants and audiences alike. Yet such performances offer limited historical insights given that they are highly selective and have been purged of most risks. They reveal how parts of the past can remain alive for a long time and how seductive the idea is that we can experience it vicariously.

major defence of the field. I am referring to widespread assumptions about the value of school history here because the vast majority of the population first encounters the subject at school. Ideas about the past, the degree of interest it holds, and the esteem given to those who study it, are subsequently further shaped by the mass media, especially by newspapers, historical fiction, film and television.

The educational system also trains historians. In this respect it is less a purveyor of governmental and general ideological values than the structure that determines what the next generation of teachers and researchers will be like. For some, school history is simply part of the furniture, for others, it is a preparation for a career. The history taught in schools changes with historical fashions, and responds to political imperatives. For example, it is only relatively recently that school history has given less weight to political history, and that it has communicated a wider range of historical styles, including reminiscence and oral history. The shift towards studying direct testimony places heavy stress on the notion of empathy with historical actors. The concept of living history, of dressing children up in order that they can behave more like people in the past 'really' did, has a marked effect both on general attitudes to history and on the way historians think about their professional activities. Re-enactment is promoted in museums, and hence is related to public history, which will be discussed in a later chapter. There is a simplistic literalism here, which needs to be seen in the context of broader educational trends. These imply that the past was not really foreign and they mobilise superficial notions of historical accuracy. They also make assumptions about class and about historical agency, for example, by advocating listening to a wider variety of accounts – those of so-called 'ordinary' people, rather than to those of elites, who were far better placed to record their views in enduring forms. The implication is that history is not just made by those in charge but by those with less overt power. Going along with this are a number of more subtle shifts of ideas about the ownership and use of the past. The idea that groups, especially non-elite ones, own their past and need to engage with it as a means of constructing more satisfying identities in the present, is now pervasive, and quite evidently it is political at its core, as is clear in the concern with post-colonial identities. It is sustained and popularised by organisational structures, which convey values through the teaching of history. These are contentious matters and we shall encounter them in many different forms in the pages that follow. Are female historians uniquely well placed to study women's history, or can men do it too? Is the study of Jewish history in the post-Holocaust world to be undertaken by Jews alone, or can it be legitimately undertaken by any interested historian regardless of background?

Educational systems do not speak with one voice. In Britain, which has a legally enforced national curriculum, the teaching of history is also used to explore concepts of nationhood, which operate in tension with people's history. An interest in nationhood tends to return politics and political leaders to centre stage, and to approach the past teleologically via the nation state, which then becomes the goal towards which earlier processes are seen as leading. Hence modern nation states are presented as the norm, the proper state of affairs, and this assumption is not only sustained by history teaching in schools and universities, but is also propagated by activities outside education, such as the organisation of sporting events and international diplomacy. School history sets in place basic notions about the past, thereby defining the terms in which both the general public and historical professionals think about the subject.

The contrast between Britain and the United States is instructive here. The persistence of the British monarchy and its highly controversial nature, especially over the last decade, sustains an extraordinarily high level of popular interest in kings and queens of all periods, one result of which is a strong association between nation and monarch. Notions of citizenship are not particularly strongly promoted, nor are the complexities of ethnic and regional identities across the British Isles given prominence. Admittedly some, like 'the Irish question' are unavoidable, but the point remains that persistent tensions between, say England and Wales, are accorded no priority in the national curriculum.[4] In the USA, by contrast, where political identity is predicated on a conscious act of nation-creation, which made the subjects of imperial Britain into citizens of an independent new republic, the history of the nation is presented quite differently and far more explicitly in terms of citizenship. However strong the cult of presidents may be, it differs markedly from the British obsession with their monarchs. How ethnic identities are to be understood historically is an increasingly explosive question, which is constantly being rehearsed at every level of American society. These processes are only beginning in Britain and the rest of Europe.

However hot a political topic the teaching of history in schools is, university courses have a considerably more far-reaching effect on the values, attitudes and intellectual frameworks of professional historians. Furthermore, what is taught in universities varies dramatically within and between countries – far more, I would venture, than in the sciences, and possibly even more than in other humanities subjects. These variations indicate where some of the

---

4   'One of the longest-running and most intractable issues in British politics
    [which] revolved around land, religion and the political conflicts from these':
    J. Gardiner and N. Wenborn, eds., *The History Today Companion to British
    History*, London, 1995, p. 423. The phrase, 'the Irish question' was commonly
    used in the nineteenth century: see, for example, Karl Marx and Friedrich
    Engels, *Ireland and the Irish Question*, London, 1971, a collection of their
    writings over several decades; and Joseph Chamberlain, *Home Rule and the
    Irish Question: A Collection of Speeches Delivered between 1881 and 1887*,
    London, 1887.

main issues lie in the discipline of history at the moment. The following variables would seem to be the most important: the periods and countries covered; the balance between primary and secondary sources; the degree to which teaching is organised thematically; the extent to which it raises openly political and theoretical issues. Naturally these relate to the *content* of history, but they also relate to its organisational framework, and they do so in three main ways. First, institutions of higher education possess administrative mechanisms for approving courses that staff wish to offer. Within both the formal and informal cultures of these institutions some subjects are deemed suitable, and others unsuitable, for teaching to undergraduates. We can immediately appreciate how important these mechanisms are when we notice that many history departments held out for a long time against offering courses in women's history, and many in Britain and Germany still offer nothing on race and ethnicity or on oral history. It is significant that 'new' subjects are seen as threatening, and that organisations find ways not just of resisting them but of presenting them as less intellectually demanding, as overly modish, in fact as not 'proper' history. I put new in inverted commas because sometimes, as in the case of women's history, the subjects are not in fact new at all. Professional historians have been writing on this subject for as long as there have been professional historians. What was 'new' about women's history was its overt association with a populist women's movement, that is with second-wave feminism, which posed a threat to the academy that is still being worked through. Feminism remains a contested term, and gender relations continue to be a site of social, economic and political conflict. Nonetheless, as more women and men who are sensitised to these issues get academic jobs, and precisely because gender matters are debated so widely, the composition of committees changes, and proposals that would previously have been seen as way out are accepted. I am not saying that curriculum innovation is automatically 'good' and resistance to it 'bad'. However, curricula do need to change and mobilise fresh energies, and the manner in which this is resisted illuminates cherished assumptions within a discipline and an institution. At the same time, change always brings costs and valuable perspectives can be lost in the process.

The second way in which organisations shape the content of history, the provision of resources, is particularly relevant to university-level teaching. New areas of history demand extra resources, such as tapes, CDs, computing facilities, videos, slides, new books and periodicals. Yet, despite increasing participation rates, it seems that the boom time for education is over worldwide. This is not to say that governments are less committed to education, and certainly their rhetoric to this effect remains strong, but recent shifts in the world economy have squeezed spending in this area, and many countries are working with infrastructures, such as libraries, that are weak by any standards. Even 'first-world' countries are concerned to keep budgets for education under tight control, while also seeking to improve the general skill levels of their populations. 'Skills' here means literacy, numeracy and analysis, as well as an ability to use information technology efficiently. There are many ways in which computers have come to play a part in the practice of history, and their provision has become a major component within history's infrastructure. The internet, by providing access to library catalogues and holdings worldwide, interactive web-sites, and huge amounts of information, has become a particularly significant part of that infrastructure. At the same time there is an expansion of the sheer *amount* of history being produced, with more journals and books in circulation than ever before. The result is intense pressure on resources, and, although so far this has probably not prevented the introduction of new fields or courses, it does shape the experience students have of working at more advanced levels. Especially significant in this respect is the degree to which students have access to both primary and secondary sources – the most effective university-level education involves experience of using wide ranges of both types of material.

The third way in which organisational issues inform the content of history concerns 'demand'. General shifts have certainly taken place in the last years of the twentieth century as a result of which the ideologically charged language of the market has become dominant; they are particularly marked in higher education. Education policies have changed along with the rhetoric. History is in the marketplace; the point applies to universities as much as to, for example, publishing. Courses do ultimately respond to student demand, which itself is shaped by prior educational experience, by career opportunities, by personal commitments and by the political environment. The more universities offer open choices to students, who are in effect putting together customised degree schemes, the greater the impact of 'the market' will be. Naturally, perceptions about career choices are particularly relevant here, and there seems to have been a general trend in higher education towards vocational subjects, presumably due to increased pressure on employment opportunities. Yet choices are not only driven by instrumental demands; for example, there has been a general decline of interest in economic history, despite it being high on 'relevance' to many careers, whereas there is increasing demand for courses on culture in general and the mass media in particular, where related careers are dramatically oversubscribed. Humanities students may now be increasingly sceptical about quantitative methods, and lack the skills to master them, but there is also a sense that economic history is less exciting and cutting-edge than other historical areas. We can note these trends and try to explain them, but historians should also be mounting strong intellectual arguments to demonstrate the importance of subjects, such as economic history, which are perceived as less alluring. In a state of anxiety about their income, institutions sometimes allow less fashionable fields to decline, precisely because they do not seem to be what students want. However, if such areas are promoted vigorously within departments and universities, this can often shift patterns of demand.

Academic disciplines work, then, within elaborate organisational frameworks, by which they are shaped. And these frameworks, although they have the inertia of institutions behind them, are also subject to change. Many different types of change affect academic disciplines: a good example of the point is the naming of departments and degree-level courses. History is currently taught under many umbrellas, some of which do not even have the word 'history' in their titles. The rise of area studies, where history, along with other humanities and/or social science disciplines, is applied to a specific geographical region, is a case in point.[5] This trend is indicative both of alterations in which parts of the world are thought worthy of specialised investigation, and of changes in the relationships between history and other disciplines. The surge of interest in the Soviet Union during the Cold War is a noteworthy phenomenon, and Russian studies brought together historians, linguists, sociologists, economists and political scientists. Despite renewed conflicts with far-reaching implications in areas formerly part of the Soviet Union, Russian studies as a field has shrunk. In area studies the kinship between history and other disciplines tends to come to the fore. For the purposes of area studies, such as American studies, Latin American studies and so on, history is one of a range of approaches, which are complementary. Generally language teaching, which is otherwise declining in the context of history, is part of the package. Outside Germany, German history is a relatively small field, especially in the English-speaking world, partly because the language is not widely taken up. This is an ironic situation given the huge interest in twentieth-century Germany. Nonetheless, there are strong attempts to promote some more 'exotic' languages, especially when, like Japan, the areas in which they are spoken are politically and economically powerful – African languages, for instance, have not exercised similar appeal. The appeal of languages and geographical areas

5 It is important to remember that the names used for these areas can be misleading, not just by virtue of their inaccuracy – evident, for example, in the way 'Russia' and 'America' are commonly used – but also by virtue of the way in which they lump diverse societies together, as is the case with 'Africa' and African studies.

needs to be seen in a wider cultural context, which, through art, music and literature, shapes aesthetic preferences. These general responses affect the practice of history.

Gradually, since the Second World War, those parts of the world that are both politically sensitive and economically significant – Russia, Africa, Latin America, Asia – have come under the area studies approach. Which areas are favoured at any given moment depends in part on patterns of colonial development – the current interest in both India and the Caribbean among British scholars reveals much about the ways in which those zones entered the national consciousness, often through family memories and traditions, coming as much from a sense of guilt as from pride. Both areas have, through patterns of emigration, become a presence in our social life. Hence, which geographical areas seem important for scholarly work depends on where you are standing. To historians in Britain the notion of 'British studies' seems rather odd: the *Journal of British Studies* (1962) is an American publication, which publishes important articles on British history. Each country tends to privilege its own history, although the degree of reflexiveness involved is quite variable. Yet to designate an area suitable for inter-disciplinary studies implies a tinge of exoticism; hence area studies are not based on our own region but on zones that are already 'other' in some way. Area studies are by no means uniformly distributed across universities, and tend to be found in institutions already committed to inter-disciplinary work, and sensitive to the political imperatives behind historical scholarship. They can also be a form of international relations, with the country or region being studied offering funding incentives and, through cultural diplomacy and institutes, promoting conferences and exhibitions that bring the attention of scholars elsewhere to that particular part of the world. By these means geographical regions can be promoted as interesting, and worth visiting and trading with, that is, as players on a world stage.

Many universities still have separate history departments and teach degree courses in history that would be more or less recognisable to students from earlier generations. Yet the organisational environment has changed markedly. In countries such as the United States, which have for a long time had a modular approach to degrees together with mechanisms for preventing early specialisation, the idea of studying one field as an undergraduate for 3 or 4 years is foreign. A more focused model persists in many European countries, including Britain. Although most British courses are modular, few rules exist to prevent specialisation, so that in practice students rarely take the range of options, within history and across disciplines, that students in North America do. One British concession to over-specialisation is joint degrees involving history and another discipline, which were particularly fashionable in the 1970s. Although they appear superficially to break down barriers between disciplines, in practice the two disciplines are mostly taught in parallel rather than being integrated, hence conventionalised disciplinary boundaries remain more or less intact. Nonetheless, organisations are increasingly encouraging inter-disciplinary ventures; at least there is much rhetoric to this effect.

Another significant development is the tendency in recently founded institutions to put different humanities disciplines together in general departments called 'Humanities', 'Combined Studies' or even 'Theoretical Studies'. Distinguished historians may well be teaching under such rubrics, although what they do is not necessarily signalled as 'history'. This fosters a thematic approach rather than a descriptive one. A course entitled 'Early Medieval Europe' or 'Early Modern Spain' would exemplify the latter approach. Often thematic courses are enticing because they cut the historical cake in fresh ways, thereby encouraging students to consider new approaches and unfamiliar angles. 'From the Cradle to the Grave' looks at demography and family life over several centuries, while 'That's Entertainment' presents a social history of commercial entertainment in a single country over two hundred years.[6] Many institutions offer courses on 'Revolution', which encourage students to consider both the similarities and differences between, say, France in 1789 and Russia in 1917: in other words, to think comparatively. This allows students to become more analytical about the relationships between economic difficulties and political protest, about what makes regimes weak, about charismatic leaders, about politically active classes, about theories of revolution and so on. Yet, if themes are taken out of context, if feminist movements are not placed in the context of other attempts at political reform, for instance, or if the scientific revolution of the seventeenth century is not compared with other intellectual and social changes of the period, partial vision results. Of course the same arguments apply to descriptive courses, where countries, regions or periods are too often taken as self-evident and treated in isolation from one another, and a privileged place is given to political developments as if these somehow *are* the history. The ideal situation is to have a mixture of courses and approaches, which is precisely what the very large North American departments of history achieve. But for most institutions this is simply not possible, and their ethos, organisation and approach to disciplines will determine the overall approach taken to the teaching of history.

6   I have taken these examples from the School of History, University of East Anglia, UK.

So far I have sketched in some of the parameters which determine how the educational arm of the discipline is organised, and I have stressed that within these the variations are huge. However, across most countries, there are common elements in the ways in which professional life is organised, and these apply to history as to other subjects – the centrality of the school curriculum, the need for most school teachers to have a university degree and a teaching qualification, and the existence of a system for research training, which qualifies people to teach at more advanced levels, government involvement in funding and in standards, and professional bodies that bring historians together for conferences, lobbying and publication.

ORGANISATIONS FOR HISTORIANS

Many different types of organisation exist to help historians in some way or another, from local ones that promote the use of archives in their area to international ones that sponsor huge meetings of professionals from all over the world. Since the levels of specialisation have increased so markedly in most fields in recent years, the proliferation of organisations is hardly surprising. It reflects both the wide range of people, professional and amateur, with an interest in the subject, and the expansion of jobs related to history not just in educational institutions, but in government, the media and museums. Rarely do such organisations have a single function; they exist to promote ideas and people, and they become especially significant when resources are limited. Professional bodies have particularly varied functions, some of which are more openly acknowledged than others. They often protect the interests of a field, for instance, by expressing an opinion on proposed changes in government policy. They serve to bring that field to the notice of peers, scholars in cognate disciplines, and sometimes the general public. Frequently they sponsor journals, so that in some sense the journal represents and thereby becomes one public face of the professional grouping or learned society. By such means they help to define what counts as 'history', so that articles published in the *American Historical Review* or the *Transactions of the Royal Historical Society* (1876) come under the remit of 'history'. This function is especially important when fields are changing and new sub-fields grow up – being able to get an article on a 'new' topic into an established journal means more than the publication of an individual piece: it signifies something about definitions of history. New organisations and journals are instruments of legitimation, endowing their founders with 'career capital'. Thus professional bodies help to define their disciplines; they also create communities, and a concomitant sense of being part of an intellectual network, by means of conferences, newsletters and other publications.

It follows then that many people come to see themselves as historians, not just by earning a living and/or publishing, but by belonging to groups that affirm their occupational identity. Along with this go more directly professional functions, such as networking to make contacts that help secure jobs, assist in publication and develop careers. Some societies advertise jobs and see it as their role to ensure that institutions do not cut 'their' subject, that the best young scholars are appropriately placed, and that women and minorities get a fair crack of the whip. Professional bodies, in other words, help historians develop an ownership of their subject, to debate issues, to promote a general sense of the value of history and to forge their identities in the process. We can see these working in presidential addresses and inaugural lectures, when distinguished members of the field have a chance to address their fellows, and lay out key issues. Many members will strongly identify with those figures and use their words to affirm or adjust their own sense of themselves as historians, just as many may disagree and will clarify their identity by contrast. All these processes are characteristic of the ways in which professional middle classes establish and maintain their positions.

It can be quite expensive to join a professional body and some can only be joined by invitation or by submitting one's name for election. Since they have a variety of roles, there is considerable variation between them according to which ones are predominant. New fields and scholars who fear they may be marginal are especially reliant on groups of like-minded people running conferences, perhaps publishing proceedings, and generally publicising their activities in order to achieve respectability and legitimation. Some such groups see themselves as radical and oppositional, for example, the Oral History Society in Britain and the group that founded *Radical History Review* in the United States; they strive for a public voice and some sort of recognition. The recognition of peers is just as important as recognition by governments, universities, funding agencies and so on. Historians need to affirm the value of what they do by bonding with the like-minded, and then show the wider world the nature of our achievements. Knowledge is shared, and displayed, in professional bodies and thereby the quality of what is done is, hopefully, improved. But the more subtle functions, such as networking, bonding, affirming and so on are just as significant. It is vital that these bodies have one or more public faces; they stand at the interface between highly specialised forms of knowledge production and the wider world.

PUBLISHING

History, like other disciplines, relies on the open dissemination of findings, and hence it is closely bound up with and dependent upon publishers. The general assumption is that for something to count as knowledge, whatever the field, it has to go through a series of evaluations and checks, such that authors are felt to be somehow accountable to their readers. At the most basic level this is why scholarly works have footnotes and bibliographies, so that their claims can be verified by those who wish to do so. Footnotes also indicate the range of sources the author has consulted, and it is open to critics, such as book reviewers and referees for journals and books, to argue that authors have missed important categories of sources, or misread those they have consulted. This is why undergraduates are taught how to evaluate evidence and to provide full citations for quotations. That at least is the theory; in practice the situation is rather more fluid. Who you are certainly has an impact on publication, especially if earlier publications have been successful. But what, we must ask, does 'successful' mean in this context? It can mean that many people have read and used the item in question, or that it has been highly influential upon the work of others. Scepticism is important here given that many 'bestsellers' are hardly read and have achieved that status by exceptionally aggressive marketing, and supposedly objective indicators, such as citation indexes, can be misleading. In any case, we should distinguish between commercial and critical success, and then acknowledge that a number of communities pass judgements on any particular publication – peers are one such. So when we are told that a book is 'good' or 'bad', careful probing is called for.

It is well known that 'names' or 'stars' find it easier to publish. In book publishing little work is refereed totally 'blind', that is, with the referee having no idea at all of the author's identity. Some publishers, like a number of journals, do still seek to do this, but my impression is that much is published that has not gone through these procedures in their most rigorous form. In any case, effective operation of the blind refereeing system depends on a number of factors, such as the genuine impartiality of readers, which is inevitably hard in one's own field, while those who work in more distant areas may not be able to pick up problems. The system also depends on authors being willing to accept the need for any changes suggested. More prosaically it depends on authors genuinely disguising their identity when writing, which is in fact quite hard to do, although it is somewhat easier for younger scholars who have not already published a great deal and are less established in networks. Give-away signs like 'this is based on my thesis' or 'see my earlier article on . . .' can be difficult to eliminate totally. My hunch is that the most prestigious journals still operate this system as strictly as possible, given the inevitable difficulties I have mentioned, such as the existence of relatively small and closed scholarly communities. Even so, it does not follow that articles rejected by prestige journals are 'worse' than those they do publish. For instance, rejects may fail to conform to the house approach to history or be on subjects the editor and/or editorial board do not happen to find particularly interesting. Hence simple claims to quality in scholarship need to be viewed sceptically. Nonetheless the goal of transparency – openness in relation to sources, approaches, decision-making and interpretation – remains important.

We can put these points in a different way by mentioning the continued importance of patronage, including in publishing. Most institutions connected with history see themselves as meritocratic, but it does not follow that patronage is unimportant. In a competitive world selection is necessary, and in any case it is impossible for selection criteria to be perfectly rational. It is well known that in obtaining academic jobs the referees are of crucial importance – are they powerful in the field, do they write for lots of people and risk devaluing their currency, do they really know the candidate, are they generally respected? The same considerations apply in publishing, where historians will often recommend those whom they wish to promote, such as their own doctoral students, to a particular publisher, just as they will encourage them to speak at conferences, make sure that they get invitations to address the research seminars of other departments, and meet influential scholars. Series of books edited by one or a small group of historians is one particularly clear way in which patronage can be exercised at the same time as a field is shaped. Many university presses have such series, which indicate academic priorities.[7] Among academics these points are commonplace; they are less familiar to undergraduates, who often take a publication at face value, without thinking about the patronage relationships involved, which have a real bearing on what is published, who is publishing where, and how the work is promoted. That is why informed readers turn first to the preface and acknowledgements of any work, where the author generally indicates who their most significant mentors and teachers were, and how they place themselves in a field.

Publishing is a huge and complex industry, which operates at an international level. While the details of the composition and functioning of this industry are not strictly relevant here, it is vital to bear in mind the diversity of presses that publish history books, and to have some understanding of their

7 Cambridge University Press has a number of series in its history lists which
   nicely illustrate the points I have been making.

different commercial and intellectual goals and their distinctive lists. They occupy specific niches in the market. While no publisher can ignore commercial factors, many, especially of the long-established university presses, continue to undertake costly and or highly specialised publishing ventures that other companies simply would not be prepared to entertain. A good example of this is the *New Dictionary of National Biography* for Britain, which is being heavily subsidised, and undertaken under the auspices of Oxford University Press. It is a huge project for two main reasons: the range and numbers of individuals have been expanded – many more women are now being included, for instance; and, in taking account of modern scholarship, there is a great deal of new material to be processed. There are other approaches to producing reference books: for example, Routledge publish a number, which are not as ambitious as the new DNB, but which are bought extensively by libraries and sometimes put into paperback.[8] On the whole, Routledge tend to keep books in print for a relatively short time and to publish in areas of wide immediate interest. Publishers develop market niches and their choices have a considerable impact on the content of what is published, especially on how books are used within the educational system.

When people think about educational publishing, the notion of a textbook springs readily to mind. While these are used a lot in schools, and at all levels in the sciences, law, economics and medicine, their role in the study of history, especially at university level, is considerably more problematic.[9] Four key assumptions typically underlie textbooks: that there is stability in a subject over time; that in different locations more or less the same subject matter is being taught; that it is appropriate to feed students 'pre-digested' material; and that there is sufficient consensus on key issues to make such volumes viable. Commercial considerations permitting, textbooks can be revised and updated regularly, although it is hard to imagine that this could be done more often than every four to five years. And even so, the basic premises of the work would remain the same. There is a certain innate conservatism in the very notion of a textbook, not just in terms of content, but in pedagogic philosophy. Textbooks can be rather distant from primary sources and, although some include short extracts, this is unsatisfying to more advanced students. There are document collections, which can be very useful, especially when they

8 Particularly relevant here is the *Companion to Historiography*, a collection of 39 essays edited by Michael Bentley and published in 1997. Routledge have published many companions, including those on the history of science and the history of medicine.

9 V. Berghahn and H. Schissler, eds., *Perceptions of History: International Textbook Research on Britain, Germany and the United States*, Oxford, 1987.

contain material otherwise unavailable to those without the relevant language. Nonetheless textbooks present a viewpoint, which, by the very nature of the genre, readers are discouraged from contesting, whereas a monograph, that is, a specialised scholarly work presenting the findings of original research to those who are pretty expert already, can evaluate diverse approaches to a subject, and acknowledge the depth of intellectual divisions, even if, in the end, it puts a particular case with a distinctive type of authority. Many monographs are pitched at a level that undergraduates find difficult. Because textbooks generalise, synthesise and seem to speak with authority, they can be somewhat bland. Since they seek to be fair and uncontentious, the sparkle, the sense of what the stakes are in divergent views of the past, sometimes gets lost. It is important to recognise the special form of publication that they constitute, often making their publishers a great deal of money, and to develop the critical skills to evaluate them. Textbooks need to be understood in terms of professional structures and disciplinary infrastructures.

We can usefully compare textbooks with survey histories. Textbooks are written expressly for a defined educational level and purpose. Surveys, which typically cover significant swathes of time and a range of topics, may become textbooks, but can be more polemical.[10] As with textbooks, the reader has to take a great deal on trust in reading any survey history – that the examples have been well and carefully chosen, that the author has not simply followed what others have claimed or been uncritically reliant on secondary sources, that they have taken account of recent research and approaches and so on. Some historical surveys come to wield huge influence. An excellent example of these points is the clutch of books by Eric Hobsbawm: *The Age of Revolution* (1962), *The Age of Capital* (1975), *The Age of Empire* (1987) and *The Age of Extremes* (1994). These have become established and venerated, although the perspective from which they were written, that of a committed Marxist, is one with which only a limited number of readers sympathise. So, what makes a particular book become a standard? There are no simple answers to this question, but it must be posed if we are to think at all critically about historical publications, and by extension about how views of the past gain acceptance and change.

We shall return to these issues throughout the book, but they need to be mentioned here for two reasons. First, there are many different genres of historical writing, and each has its own place in the publishing industry and is

10 For example, Paul Johnson's *The Birth of the Modern: World Society 1815–1830*, London, 1991, is definitely a survey, despite its narrow time-span, and it is also polemical. It can easily be used in teaching, but is certainly not a textbook.

an important element in the infrastructure of history. We need some understanding of the differences between genres of writing, and more particularly of how they win over readers. Second, publications are never received in isolation, and often, when they gain acceptance, it is because they fit in, mesh with other assumptions about the past. To return to the example of Eric Hobsbawm, you do not have to be sympathetic to Marxism to be convinced of the power of economic forces. Although his books are not narrowly economic, they are built around distinct phases of capitalism. Economic history may not be perceived as the sexiest field within history, but many historians, like members of the general public, are at heart economic determinists. It may well be that the revival of interest in his books over the last few years says more about attitudes to wealth and consumption than about the so-called decline and death of Marxism.

At the other end of the accessibility scale are learned journals, which usually come out several times a year and publish specialised articles on new research. In practice historical journals are incredibly diverse, with some publishing pieces that are recherché by any standards, while others, such as *History Workshop Journal* (1976) and *Radical History Review*, contain many types of article including 'think pieces', obituaries, and responses to exhibitions, precisely in order to respond to all aspects of 'history' and to keep their audiences as wide as possible. They also publish research articles, but the whole style of these journals is designed to open up diverse historical issues and to avoid narrow, elitist exclusivity. Many journals place no a priori limits on the subject matter of articles – anything 'historical', interpreted broadly, is eligible: *Annales* (1946), and *Past and Present* (1952), for example. But others have narrower agendas, to promote research into a given country, region, field or period: *Journal of Italian History* (1978), *French History* (1987), *Journal of Pacific History* (1965), *Journal of Historical Geography* (1975), *Social History of*

OPPOSITE: *1.3 Instructions to Contributors,* German History
      Each academic journal has a more or less distinctive style, to which
      layout, typeface, and type of footnotes make a contribution as do
      subject matter and historiographical preferences. Each journal uses
      different publishing conventions, generally laid out as a set of rules in
      each issue or available on request. It can prove extremely time-
      consuming for scholars to make sure that each time they submit an
      article to a journal they have abided by the house rules. Note that in
      the case of German History *these cover issues such as the assignment of*
      copyright.

INSTRUCTIONS TO AUTHORS

1. Submission of typescripts

Three copies of each typescript should be sent to the Editors, together with the originals and two photocopies of any statistical tables and maps.

The Editors will notify authors as soon as possible about the acceptability of a paper, but will not enter into correspondence about papers considered unsuitable for publication. Neither the Editors nor the publisher accept responsibility for the view of authors expressed in their contribution. Authors may not submit to *German History* a typescript that is under consideration elsewhere.

Articles should be between 7,000 and 10,000 words in length.

2. Typescript layout/disks

All material should be on A4 or quarto paper, in double-spaced typing, and on one side of the page only. Ample margins should be left. Each page of the typescript should be numbered. In Notes and Reviews, all material should be incorporated into the text: there should be no footnotes. In articles, footnotes should be numbered consecutively and placed together in double-spaced typing on a separate page or pages at the end. In Notes and Reviews, the author's name should appear at the end on the right-hand side, with his/her institution on the left. In articles, the author's name and institution should appear at the beginning, immediately under the title. Quotation marks should be single; double quotation marks should be used only to indicate one quotation within another.

Disks should only be provided after the manuscript has gone through all the review and editing stages when the data should be copied on to a clean newly formatted disk. Each disk should be identified by the first author's name and article title and give details of the hardware and software used.

3. Illustration

All maps, diagrams, figures and graphs should be submitted in the form of completed artwork suitable for reproduction. They should be separate from the typescript (with a list of captions on a separate sheet), but their place in the text should be marked.

No illustration (*including caption*) will be given more space than the text area of the journal page, i.e. 191 mm × 112 mm. Figures should ideally be drawn for a reduction of one-third, i.e. 3:2.

4. Tables

Tables should be typed on separate sheets. Indicate in the margin of the text where the tables should be placed.

5. References

These should be kept to the minimum. Books are italicized (underlined in typescript), e.g. F. L. Carsten, *Princes and Parliaments in Germany* (Oxford, 1959). In second and subsequent references to a work, an abbreviated title should be adopted, e.g. Carsten, *Princes*, p. 72. A reference to an article in a periodical should include (after the author's name and the title of the article and the title of the journal) the volume number (arabic), data in brackets, and relevant page numbers, e.g., 'The False Joseph II', *Historical Journal*, 18 (1975), 467–95.

6. Copyright/offprints

In submitting a paper to *German History*, an author recognizes that, on its acceptance for publication, its exclusive copyright shall be assigned to the Germany History Society and operated on the Society's behalf by the publisher. In consideration of this provision, the publisher will supply the author with 50 offprints of his/her paper. (Offprints of reviews are not supplied.) The publisher will not put any limitation on the freedom of the author to use material contained in the paper in other published works of which he/she is author or editor. It is the author's responsibility to obtain permission to quote material from copyright sources.

7. Alterations to articles

Any amendments or corrections should be sent to the Editors (or Review Editor) as soon as possible after any author receives notification of acceptance for publication of his/her article. Because of the high cost of correction, the Editors reserve the right to reject alterations in proof. To avoid delays in the production of the journal, contributors will be asked to return their proofs promptly. Proofs are not sent to authors of reviews.

Medicine (1988), *Le Moyen Âge* (1888), *Seventeenth Century* (1986) or *Victorian Studies* (1957). The huge proliferation of fields, sub-fields and associated periodicals does pose a number of problems connected with the fragmentation of knowledge and audiences. For any given piece of research, what is the appropriate audience? This question is made quite pressing by research assessment exercises, by trends towards inter-disciplinary history,[11] and by the relative difficulty of getting work accepted by the general historical journals, many of which enjoy high reputations, but since they cover the whole of history, receive huge numbers of submissions and have to be extraordinarily selective. Since journals are presented as the latest thing, students are often surprised at how long it takes for the whole process to occur from initial submission to final appearance, which includes refereeing, making revisions suggested by referees, having the revisions accepted, checking proofs and so on, and that assumes the first journal contacted accepts the piece! One to two years is not uncommon. Constraints, such as word limits, that are imposed by the article format, as well as by each individual periodical, mean that this is a genre with strong conventions, although these are invisible to the uninitiated. At the same time, periodicals are often the place where intellectual disputes can be slogged out, precisely because they come out several times a year, and often encourage this type of exchange.[12]

Many other types of publication bear on the practice of history, including those designed for broader audiences, such as magazines and newspapers. In many countries it is quite common for academic historians to write accessibly about current affairs in order to bring out the historical issues implicit within them. Book reviews appear in many forms, and they can generate exceptional heat, since they are one of the places where strong opinions can legitimately be expressed; these are unavoidably somewhat personal given that they are directed at named authors. From the publishers' point of view, the more controversy the better; from the authors' point of view, attacks on their work or reputation are exceptionally painful. It is vital to remember the diversity of publications and their audiences, the range of ways in which history is presented to a larger public, and the complexity of the publishing infrastructure.

---

11 The *Journal of Interdisciplinary History* was founded in the United States in 1970.
12 For example, *Social History*, 23, 1998, 325–30 for a heated exchange prompted by a conference report. The *American History Review* encourages debate through thematic fora, e.g. special issue entitled 'Forum: Histories and Historical Fictions', 103, no. 5, 1998.

RESEARCH

So far in this chapter I have referred to 'research' as if it was self-evident what this term meant. In fact it is rather loose and under-determined in its meaning. One implication of the term 'research' is the discovery of fresh materials and novel insights. Originality is supposed to be an important element. Yet it is often unclear to what extent research is original, given the huge amount of history being written in so many different places. So how is it possible to assess the degree of originality involved? Material on the internet is particularly hard to evaluate. And is 'research' primarily about the investigative process, through which sources are gathered and read? What about the process of writing, through which interpretative frameworks are developed? Any new materials or information by themselves are not particularly significant; rather it is the ways in which they are used and connected up with previous accounts that really matter. Although previously unstudied public records are released regularly, only rarely do newly available archives change historical assessments radically. Sometimes this is simply because of the information they contain, but more often historians have to work extremely hard at making sense of such evidence, and a good deal of research effort is expended on finding theories, concepts and approaches that will do the business.

Although it is potentially misleading to think of historical research in terms of 'data', the phrase 'raw data' is nonetheless revealing. It suggests the importance of preparation, cooking and digestion, and that is precisely what writing, together with the thinking and puzzling that precedes it, does. In fact, as we shall see, sources are rarely 'raw'. These issues are clearly central to the skills historians deploy, which will be discussed in the final chapter, but they also bear on the infrastructure of a discipline which, to be called a discipline at all, has to support research. There are three main ways in which research is made possible: by institutions, mainly but not exclusively of higher education, giving their staff time, money and library facilities specifically in order to undertake research; by dedicated organisations, either governmental or charitable, giving grants to individuals, groups or institutions to defray the costs of research; and by individuals using their own time and resources. Thankfully 'private scholars' still exist and many of them do very distinguished work indeed. The first two forms of support for research come with strings attached. Sometimes these are overt: for example, most grant-giving bodies expect transparency both in terms of financial management and regular reports. Universities may impose fewer overt conditions, but pressures connected with research assessment exercises and other markers of status, or indeed with non-research duties, significantly affect what and how much research is done. Access to primary materials is a major issue, although the possibility of downloading more and more resources from the internet may make a difference eventually. Yet historians also depend on other kinds of sources, such as archives, many of which have never been microfilmed or transcribed, and some have not even been fully catalogued. The costs of travelling to work on sources of which there are no copies, and of photography, should not be underestimated.

It is evident that historians who work close to great library collections are at a tremendous advantage. This is why large, rich universities in 'new' countries, such as Canada, the USA and Australia, have pursued active acquisitions policies, generating in the process some of the finest rare book and manuscript collections in the world. Yet even the greatest libraries have their limitations, and historians who work on parts of the world that are distant from their own, poor or politically unstable, probably have the hardest time; furthermore, these tend to be the areas of which the 'developed' world is most ignorant. They include much of Latin America, of Asia (especially central Asia), and a significant proportion of Africa. Of course such historians face other problems – the unfamiliarity of readers with the basic historical and geographical contours of their area, language difficulties, and the need for special interpretative tools and frameworks – that go far beyond the questions of infrastructure with which we are primarily concerned here. Yet the lack of resources for some types of history and the failure to recognise their importance, maybe even a sense of their threat or irrelevance, are related. It is usually more comfortable to work on and read about situations with which we are already familiar from direct experience. This would include, for instance, the distant history of one's own country or region, where intervening political lineages, social issues, buildings, music and so on act as bridges between then and now.

BRIDGE

Most of this chapter has been concerned, as is much of the book, with the discipline as it is practised within specialised institutions, and hence with professional history of one kind or another. The discipline is increasingly fragmented and specialised, yet it covers such broad terrain that those inside it tend to forget how inaccessible most of it has become. The view from inside is indeed only a partial view. The leisure industry, for example, supports the endeavours of historians, through theme parks, museums and galleries, popular publications, films, television and radio, and all those shops that market the past. It may surprise some readers that I used the word 'support' above.

IRONBRIDGE GORGE MUSEUM TRUST

1.4 Ironbridge Gorge

Ironbridge Gorge is a spectacular site, which combines natural beauty with an engineering feat. The varied displays and activities available to visitors, while they work hard to offer historical insights, are nonetheless carefully manicured versions of 'the industrial revolution'.

I do not mean to imply that these admittedly diverse branches of the heritage and leisure industries expressly set out to contribute to the discipline of history, although many in museums and galleries certainly do see their roles in this way.[13] I am suggesting that these industries are inevitably connected with the ways in which the past is conceived and studied. Indeed they materially contribute to it. One particularly pertinent example comes to mind – Ironbridge Gorge in Shropshire, England, described as 'the birthplace of the industrial revolution' and now a United Nations World Heritage Site. It is simultaneously a successful commercial enterprise, a significant area for industrial archaeology, and a vast display connected with a defining process for British identity. Such a venture depends upon the industrial revolution being 'remembered' with interest, as a phenomenon that could occasion visual pleasure and general curiosity, indeed as a heritage issue. This is a relatively recent phenomenon, as is the growth of interest in industrial archaeology. No doubt restored pumping engines have long exercised a particular appeal, perhaps akin to that of steam trains, but Ironbridge is a completely different phenomenon. This trend is closely connected with a growth of interest in the history of everyday life that is being carefully packaged. I do not want to claim that one came before the other; leisure industries and academic disciplines are subject to similar social forces. But I do assert that whether the past is presented in documentary terms or openly fictionalised, the heritage industry too is part of an infrastructure, helping to make available and promote ideas, words, objects, images and buildings that contribute to a widely diffused sense of the past. Academic disciplines exist in these larger contexts, and this is most obviously the case with history. Yet 'history' is also a huge idea, with many facets, and in Chapter 2 we shall attempt to map these more precisely, especially with respect to their content and approaches.

13 The notion of a 'heritage industry' is associated with Robert Hewison's highly polemical 1987 book of that name. Like many commentators, he perceives close connections between museums, the practice of history and contemporary culture. Cf. R. Samuel, *Theatres of Memory*, 2 vols. London, 1994 and 1998.

THE DIMENSIONS OF A DISCIPLINE

Academic disciplines have a number of dimensions, and so far I have dealt with one of them – the organisational base or infrastructure, which is similar for most fields. I have alluded to the other dimensions of a discipline and called them its content. But the content of history is not as straightforward as it seems. In a way, the past is the content of history, but this concept is so vast and inchoate that it hardly helps us to be clearer about the dimensions of the discipline. We can observe that, in general, disciplines tend to be composed of methods, approaches, theories and bodies of knowledge. Superficially, defining history as a body of knowledge appears attractive; it fits well with the fact that a great deal about the past is known, and with the existence of accumulated wisdom about how to make sense of it. There are two problems with this formulation, however. First, it assumes a finite field with relatively clear boundaries. 'History' includes so much, and has such fluid edges, that the idea of a delimited *body* of knowledge is not really appropriate. Second, it fails to take account of the radical differences between accounts of the past that historians give. To the extent that historians share anything, it is less an intellectual corpus than a combination of a commitment to the value of historical study and a shared sense of how relevant sources should be handled. To be sure, we produce historical knowledge, but there is no body of historical knowledge that underpins the whole field. Knowledge implies intellectual stability. Although this is indeed present for historical fields that have been studied over long periods of time, the discipline is made up of hugely diverse areas and it is currently addressing a wide range of topics, such as sexuality, which have not been studied systematically before. So, given the size of the discipline and the diversity of historical practice, defining its content as a body of knowledge is unsatisfactory.[1]

---

1 We can illustrate the point by trying to imagine what a short dictionary would be like that was called simply *A Dictionary of History*, in the manner of a dictionary of chemistry or of sociology: for example, J. Daintith, ed., *The Oxford Dictionary of Chemistry*, Oxford, 1990; N. Abercrombie et al., *The Penguin Dictionary of Sociology*, third edition, London, 1994.

Perhaps, then, there are characteristic methods and approaches? History is a notoriously eclectic discipline methodologically speaking; as a result, it uses a wide range of approaches and is constantly drawing on other disciplines. While I want to suggest that there is something distinctive about the discipline, we do not, I think, get any further in our discussion of its *content* by pressing on its methods. So what about theories? This is a difficult issue. The phrase 'theories of history' refers to claims both about what has determined temporal change and about the basis for the entire discipline, and it has a dated ring to it. Most professional historians are deeply sceptical that there can be any one way of explaining change. The range of cases such a monolithic interpretation would be expected to apply to is simply too vast for a single theory to possess sufficient explanatory power. In this respect the discipline of history is totally unlike the natural sciences; they possess bodies of theory *and* knowledge without a mastery of which one cannot be said to practise them at all. In thinking about the content of history we must turn elsewhere. I propose that we look to two other dimensions of the discipline – its sources, and the manner in which it is divided up. This chapter pays particular attention to the intellectual organisation of history and to the assumptions about historical practice implicit within it. One of the most characteristic features of the discipline is the elaborate, overlapping classifications of the types of history it contains, which, as specialisation proceeds apace, become ever more complex. It is precisely because history covers so much territory that navigational aids are required. In any case, a subject of this size has to be divided up and we need to understand what underlies those divisions, appreciate how and why they change, and examine the nature of the constituent parts.

BASIC MATERIALS

The starting point for this chapter must be the basic materials of which history is composed. Although historians use disparate sources, their engagement with their chosen ones is so fundamental a part of historical practice that it must be considered early on in our discussions. Before going any further, however, I must make two preliminary points. The first concerns serendipity and sources. Many sources have survived accidentally. They are always vulnerable to mishaps such as fire and flood, they have often been destroyed wilfully, and simple neglect accounts for a great deal of loss. Furthermore many sources have been created with no particular view of their permanence in mind. Although most institutions have deliberately sought, with an eye on the future, to generate accounts of their activities, many other areas of human life are less self-conscious. Even where there have been attempts to leave records for posterity, they remain vulnerable. Of course there have been countervailing forces, and documents that promise rights, rewards and recognition have been preserved by many social groups, who often put them to quite different uses from

JAMES E. YOUNG

2.1 Statue of Anne Frank, by Mari Andriessen, in the Westermarkt, Amsterdam
This statue, with its flowers, suggests that Anne Frank is a 'living' figure for many
people today. The figure by Mari Andriessen at the Westermarkt in Amsterdam
emphasises Anne Frank's youth. James Young discusses Anne Frank's memorials in
the collection of essays he edited: The Art of Memory: Holocaust Memory in History.

those their originators intended. Nonetheless, there is a significant element of serendipity involved in the survival of historical sources, which extends even to official papers. What does survive and is used by historians by that very token wields influence, yet it can be unclear how it fits into larger patterns. This should be known as the 'Anne Frank' effect, after the Jewish girl who hid from the Nazis in Holland during the Second World War. Her diary became a bestseller in many languages, to the extent that she became an icon and a legend. It only became known much later how carefully the diary had been edited and how profoundly this determined readers' responses.[2] Since her diary was first published, many other first-hand accounts have been found, providing a whole new context in which a source that was once seen as exceptional must be interpreted. The passion of the debates about Anne Frank and her legacy provide a vivid sense both of the weight sources carry and of their accidental nature.

The second point extends the theme of the accidental quality of sources. The motives for leaving a permanent trace are hugely diverse, and it is one of the historian's tasks to reconstruct them in so far as this is possible. Relatively few were constructed with future historians in mind; many were produced in settings where academic disciplines did not exist, and they largely stem from the messiness of lives as they are lived – and that includes institutions and arms of government. These points are obvious, but there is no harm in reminding ourselves of the anachronism of taking sources and making them work for the discipline of history as it has been developing over the last hundred years or so. To put the same point differently – in the sources themselves, there is little or nothing of what we know as 'history'. In this respect history differs from law and music, where the sources and the discipline share some kind of mental framework, and from the natural sciences where the distinctions between sources (nature) and the operations performed upon them are relatively clear. The match between history and its sources is considerably less clear, but the latter nonetheless constitute a major element of the former's content. The sheer diversity of sources is one of the discipline's most notable features.

Historians rely heavily on written evidence, although objects and images can be equally relevant. Written evidence is found in many different forms –

---

2   Anne Frank, who was from a Dutch Jewish family, kept a diary between 12 June 1942 and 1 August 1944, when she and her family were discovered by the Nazis. Only her father survived the war. See D. Barnouw and G. van der Stroom, eds., *The Diary of Anne Frank. The Critical Edition*, New York, 1989. The Foreword mentions the controversies surrounding the diary, esp. pp. ix–x.

PUBLIC RECORD OFFICE IMAGE LIBRARY

2.2 Magna Carta, 1215
This is a legendary document, yet is hardly visually appealing. It can be invested with
special status only through references to further information and elaborate
interpretation. Once an item has acquired mystique, however, people want to see the
original, although it is unclear precisely what first-hand visual inspection adds to their
understanding. Magna Carta's mythic status in English history has been sustained over
a long period of time, so that it has become a historical relic in its own right. It could be
said, however, to lack the immediate human interest of many sources.

too many to characterise in general terms since any trace of the past is potentially a useful source for historians. When we talk about sources, it is conventional to divide written ones into 'primary' and 'secondary'. Primary
sources are taken to be original documents, raw materials, direct evidence of
the era being studied, while secondary sources are those created by historians
and other commentators upon the past. Hence, writings *about* the past, which
are what most students and non-professionals rely on, are generally considered secondary sources in that they result from the study of and reflection
upon another type of material that was produced *in* the past – primary
sources. Hence Magna Carta, the charter of liberties granted to the English
people by King John in 1215, is, according to this distinction, a primary source,
while a book *about* Magna Carta is a secondary one.[3] Medievalists use chronicles a good deal; these were often compiled retrospectively, mainly by monks,
who were doing them for a patron and hence for a purpose.[4] Such monks are
a bit like historians, using documents to construct an account determined by
circumstances. Yet we value their accounts as primary sources, since they were
so much closer to the worlds they chronicled than we are, providing along the
way testimony to their own attitudes and values. So, in one sense, medieval
chronicles are primary, in another secondary, sources. There are many
instances where materials shift their status between being a primary and a secondary source. For example, a project on the development of the historical
profession would use writings about the past, conventionally designated secondary sources, as primary sources. E. H. Carr's *What is History?* is for a student of twentieth-century attitudes to the study of history, of E. H. Carr's
oeuvre or of recent British historians, a primary source. Similarly, when Roy
Porter wrote a book on Gibbon, the great eighteenth-century historian of the
Roman empire, his primary sources were Gibbon's own writings and those of
his contemporaries about him.[5] The *content* of the original sources Carr or
Gibbon used would be relatively uninteresting; rather it would be the way they

3 J. C. Holt, *Magna Carta*, second edition, Cambridge, 1992, is both a primary
   source in that it contains medieval texts, and a secondary source in that it
   contains historical arguments and editorial comments related to them.
4 Some chronicles, such as that by Jocelin of Brakelond (1173–1202), are more
   personal. This case illustrates some of the complexities of sources; the only
   complete manuscript dates from the mid to late thirteenth century. Recent
   editions, i.e. those used by most students, are translations, divided into
   chapters 'in order to facilitate its use by modern readers'. These are highly
   mediated texts: Jocelin of Brakelond, *Chronicle of the Abbey of Bury St
   Edmunds*, translated with an introduction and notes by D. Greenway and J.
   Sayers, Oxford, 1989, p. xxiv.
5 R. Porter, *Edward Gibbon: Making History*, London, 1988.

worked that was in focus. Like all historians, these authors relied on the findings and ideas of commentators; this rather common situation indicates that too rigid a distinction between primary and secondary sources is pointless. A certain collective moralism surrounds historians' use of sources, with primary ones being regarded as somehow 'better' and reliance on secondary sources being deemed weak. This is because the former are considered to lie closer to the past. There is nothing inherently wrong with using mixtures of primary and secondary works, so long as the status of different types of sources for a given project is made clear. We shall explore this issue further in Chapter 4.

So, the very terminology 'primary' and 'secondary' can be misleading, and the ways in which this is so needs to be made perfectly explicit. The words I have used in relation to primary sources should have indicated the difficulty. Terms such as 'original', 'raw' and 'direct' imply a special kind of authority that comes from first-hand testimony, from closeness to the events themselves. At a simple descriptive level this may be true – a description of a tomb or a plot of land by someone who has seen them is likely to be more reliable than a second-hand account. But this is a relatively trivial form of accuracy, and next to it we have to consider the possibility that those bearing direct testimony are also interested parties, who shape the evidence even as they are recording it. This may happen either consciously or unconsciously or from a combination of both factors – being very close to something can also mean that you see it less clearly. Thus the division between primary and secondary sources can be treacherous. Much of the historian's skill consists of being able to imagine how sources are constructed and using those very processes, as well as their manifest content, to reach sensible conclusions.

The materials from which history is made are, therefore, diverse and we need to be able to appreciate the richness and the limitations of each type. One characteristic of outstanding historical scholarship lies in the creative and self-aware use of the complexities of evidence. This involves conveying to readers something of the processes by which sources have been produced, so that they are not presented as static documents with self-evident authority, but rather emerge as layered assemblages that testify in a variety of ways. Although these skills are taught in universities, they begin to be properly acquired only at doctoral level, leaving undergraduates to receive historical evidence extensively pre-packaged.[6] As a result, the ways in which evidence has been found,

---

6 There has been a decline in (primary) source-based undergraduate teaching,
   which is where these issues are best broached. However, these skills are
   emphasised in areas of history, such as ancient and medieval history, where
   the sources themselves are of a distinctive kind. My point is that this
   approach should be routinely applied to secondary sources too.

selected and used, how authors have chosen a particular genre to write their work up in, which audiences they have targeted and the tacit assumptions upon which their work rests, tend to be obscured. A critical reader needs to be able to think through these issues, and one obvious first step is to ask what kind of history any given piece of writing constitutes. Before discussing kinds of history further, I want to acknowledge the less tangible ways in which sources inform historical accounts. We can best speak of these in terms of the emotional responses historians experience when working with their sources, and especially those upon which they rely most heavily. These responses are complex and certainly cannot be summed up in a few words, and yet they infuse everything historians do. Such persistent historical perfumes, which elicit quite individual responses, are not to be understood as good or bad. They should not be romanticised, but they must rather be acknowledged, discussed and, where possible, evaluated as inherent in the practice of history.[7]

KINDS OF HISTORY

The first point to note when thinking about kinds of history is how varied are the criteria by means of which the discipline is divided up. One of the main ones, according to *period*, goes right to the heart of the field because it works with notions of causality and time, which are central to historical explanation; these issues will be discussed in a separate chapter. Other criteria include: *methods* – for example, oral history and demographic history; *theories*, such as psychohistory; *places* – urban history, the history of specific regions, countries, or continents, for instance; *type of human being* – women's history, history of childhood, Jewish history, labour history; and *institutions* – church history, history of public policy or welfare states, for example. These are not mutually exclusive categories; each historian probably thinks of themselves and their work in terms of more than one. But, largely through journals, such types of history do define fields, and historians are constantly classifying each other in these ways, which are dense with political meaning and central to identity construction. Thus, a historian who worked on the schooling of girls in the nineteenth century could be a social historian, a historian of education, a women's historian, a feminist historian or a historian of the country in question. They might use different labels for different purposes, but the one that expressed most precisely what they felt was the core of their intellectual iden-

7   I have had a go at this issue in *Nature Displayed*, London, 1999, ch. 1, using a rather different vocabulary.

tity would be highly significant. Each of the possibilities just given carries distinct political as well as intellectual connotations.

The most familiar division of the discipline, however, is not according to any of these criteria. Indeed it is quite a challenge to work out precisely what the force behind this most conventionalised of distinctions is. I refer to the notion that there are three basic kinds of history – political, social and economic. Do we regard these as levels of analysis, as complementary aspects of a society, or as distinct phenomena? What do you do about the fact that the boundaries between them are evidently blurred and yet they seem to be 'right', 'natural' or 'obvious' categories?

It is not difficult to see some of what lies behind the separation out of political history. Most obviously, for a long time countries have generally been led by individuals, together with small elites, in many parts of the world. Thus, 'politics' is easily identified and is often seen as what really counts. Since successful monarchs, military leaders and so on not only displayed charisma but explicitly invited their subjects to identify with them and to see the person and the political identity as different facets of the same coin, these forms of power can readily be described. Leaders reinforced their position by the panoply of symbolic forms, such as coins, that supported a political order in whose name war was made and laws enacted. The notion of political history as a distinct kind of history appeals to common sense. Although it is often claimed these days that there could be a political history of just about anything, that is, a history that focuses on power relations, the connotations of 'political history' as the history of rulers, governments and dominant groups remains strong. It remains, in effect, history from above. A related assumption is that this type of history is totalising – it unifies a given historical situation by giving priority to state-centred phenomena. As a result, we are encouraged to comprehend a whole era, a whole area, via its politics – indeed phrases such as 'the age of absolutism' reinforce the point. There are historians who want to retain the specific flavour of political history by retaining its connotations of *high* politics and by resisting the idea that political history can be applied to any facet of a society. Diplomacy, military activity, constitutions and local government would all come under the rubric 'political history' as conventionally defined, yet these are less fashionable topics now than they were only a couple of decades ago. In the case of military history, popular interest endures, but this is scarcely reflected in the courses offered by most universities.

Military history illustrates a number of points about kinds of history in general and about political history in particular. The phrase itself suggests the detailed discussion of wars and strategies, battalions and battles. This is what continues to elicit great interest among the general public – the re-enactment of battles and the transformation of their sites into 'heritage' locations are further manifestations of that interest. These phenomena are 'political' in that wars, especially in the modern era, are generally waged by or on behalf of states, the leaders of which are closely involved in their execution. Typically they involve large numbers of fighters, who are enlisted in the name of politically powerful institutions – such as king and country, nation, the republic, the church. The polity in question has to offer further support – economic and moral at least – in modern times coordinated by governmental organisations. At first sight, nothing could be more political. The history of these phenomena can be written in many different ways, however. These will not necessarily be of the kind suggested by the term 'military history', as Paul Fussell's *The Great War and Modern Memory*, a study of soldiers' responses to the First World War, demonstrates.[8] This hugely successful and influential book found another way of talking about the war, from the bottom up and with an attention to texts. The proliferation of fiction about that particular war is a well-known phenomenon. Pat Barker's *Regeneration* trilogy, based on an exceptionally rigorous use of archives, prompts further reflection on the boundaries of history, war and politics.[9]

A strong commitment to political history conventionally defined has to be justified by the idea that politics is a special class of human behaviour, which may be distinguished analytically from social and economic phenomena. Yet the merest reflection suggests that politics, even of the most elite kind, always was bound up with more general prosperity, with sources of revenue, such as taxation, and with forms of expansion, such as imperialism. Thus, while many economic phenomena, such as the operation of local markets and of household economies, have relatively little to do with high politics, it is hard to imagine politics not depending in some way on the nature and sources of the wealth of elites and rulers. Inevitably, the more that societies possess structured institutions, the easier it is to separate out different kinds of histories. Thus, we could argue that political history is to be defined principally in terms of the apparatus of government, statecraft and their modes of operation. In

8   New York, 1975. Cf. his *Wartime: Understanding and Behaviour in the Second World War*, New York, 1989.
9   P. Barker, *Regeneration, The Eye in the Door,* and *The Ghost Road,* London, 1991, 1993, 1995; examples of what could be called the 'new military history' may be found in *War in History* (1994). On the distinctiveness of medieval warfare, see P. Contamine, *War in the Middle Ages*, Oxford, 1984. On another whole type of war, see R. Asprey, *War in the Shadows: The Classic History of Guerrilla Warfare from Ancient Persia to the Present*, revised edition, London, 1994. On the stakes in how war is written about, see J. Keegan, *The Battle for History. Refighting World War Two*, London, 1995.

societies that lack such defined structures, the notion of political history would accordingly become considerably more fluid and in fact might not serve any useful role at all. Presumably it would simply refer to the study of the most powerful people within the society in question.

We now need to note another problem with the tripartite political/social/economic model. 'Social' is an adjective whose related noun is 'society'. I use the word 'society' when I want to invoke a sense of a totality. I can thereby avoid using more loaded and historically specific terms, such as nation, which carry culturally and chronologically specific connotations. Naturally, I am not claiming that the term 'society' is totally neutral, only that its long-established use in the social sciences as an inclusive term for a structured collectivity, without specifying the precise form it takes – nation, tribe, city state, ethnic grouping – makes it handy for historians. Yet the very concept of 'society' is considered by some to be ideologically loaded. Society does indeed express something more than country, region and area, which do not imply any sense of humanly based cohesion, since diverse peoples can find themselves in geographical proximity to each other. 'Society' implies the existence of repeated patterns and motifs, indeed of coherent connections between constituent elements – coherent, that is, to those who study them. We need a *relatively* neutral word to evoke one type of unit that historians and social scientists study, and it is reasonable to suppose that aspects of that unit are linked to each other, that patterns emerge when groups of human beings live, work and reproduce together – the existence of such patterns is in fact what makes historical generalisations possible.[10]

How, then, can social history, if it is the history of societies, apparently refer to only *one* of their aspects? One possibility is that 'social' has taken on specialised meanings, thereby losing some of its inclusiveness.[11] So, what, in practice, does social history include?[12] The question can be tackled in three ways:

10 Concepts, such as community and tradition, that we might consider in this context, carry their own histories and baggage. Historians use them in diverse ways and for a variety of purposes; sometimes, given the emotional connotations of both community and tradition, these are quite manipulative. Cf. E. Hobsbawm and T. Ranger, eds., *The Invention of Tradition*, Cambridge, 1983. Always indispensable in these matters is R. Williams, *Keywords*. London, 1983.
11 Williams, *Keywords*, pp. 291–5. His discussion applies to the English term 'society'; it goes without saying that the connotations of such significant words are language-specific.
12 Among the main journals in the field are: *International Review of Social History* (1956), *Journal of Social History* (1967), *Histoire Sociale–Social History* (1968), and *Social History* (1976).

we can see social history as an approach rather than denoting particular subject matter; we can seek a distinctive set of topics that it addresses; and we can understand it in relation to other kinds of history, for example as a sort of remnant. If social history is an approach, then it can be connected with the conviction that the lives of ordinary people, not just elites, should be studied; that weight should be given to lived experience; that complex relationships between people, no matter of what kind, should be explored; that whatever phenomena societies throw up should be investigated historically. That is, taking its cue from social theory, it examines structures and patterns across societies. According to this reading, social history *is* inclusive in its methods and approaches, and the relationship between social and society seems relatively coherent.

If social history is a particular set of topics, then there is indeed a problem. Most topics have political and economic dimensions, so what kinds of human behaviour are inherently 'social'; presumably those with *less* politics and economics in? On this reading, social history might become the history of leisure and family life, which is precisely how some of its critics see it. Here 'social' means interactions between people and groups of people, especially in daily life and of the masses. To my mind, if we define social history in this way, the connections between 'social' and 'society' become confused. The concept 'society' begins to lose its inclusiveness, and it is hardly logical to claim that some human activities are more 'social' than others. The third definition of social history is as what was left over from other more defined, and possibly more prestigious, forms of history – precisely a remnant. By this account, it is *not* the history of politically powerful elites *nor* of forms of government, *nor* is it about the operations of the economy and its supporting institutions. Here the links between 'social' and 'society' are at their most fragile, since there is no attempt to conceptualise them at all. Rather 'social' comes to mean ordinary in its pejorative sense: what is mundane, unremarkable, insignificant, especially for national or world trends.

I do not think there can be a simple definition of social history, and indeed, as the field has developed, there have been persistent confusions and heated controversies over precisely these issues. This is not to say that social history is incoherent, rather that its key concepts, which I take to be 'society' and 'social relations', have been constantly contested both because they originally emerged out of specific theoretical models and because these models were highly politicised. Marxism, to take a model central to social history, contained assumptions about how societies worked – for example, about the fundamentally exploitative nature of class relations. Some commentators obviously worried that social history was really social*ist* history, while for many of its exponents that was precisely its allure![13] The most rigorous social historians have continued to debate the theoretical and conceptual issues raised by 'society' and its cognates.

HOLISTIC HISTORY

One possible way of overcoming the problems I have been discussing would be to embrace *histoire totale*, that is, a more explicitly holistic approach to the past, which is often associated with the French 'Annales' school.[14] The *Annalistes* were open to thematic history, to studying a wide range of human phenomena, and to collaboration with other disciplines, hence their intellectual embrace was notably generous. One problem such an approach throws up is what the focus of historical analysis should be – a community, a town or a region. Can *histoire totale* be done thematically – could you write the total history of an idea, an object or an occupation? The most celebrated example of this approach is Braudel's magisterial study of the Mediterranean.[15] He took a geographical region as his focus. It is a region with a rather special history, one that could be considered pivotal not just for the development of Europe but for the relationships between Europeans and other parts of the world – the orient, Africa and, in due course, the New World. Furthermore, Braudel worked with distinct historical levels and with a generous time span, a *longue durée*, and this helped him to solve what is always the most challenging problem for large-scale projects – how to establish a clear and coherent framework through which a book can be organised. Braudel's whole approach to history is inclusive – the environment, economics and social structures as well as 'events, politics and people' – and this led him to distinguish between different types and paces of change.[16] Those who take a relatively short period

13 *History Workshop Journal* was originally subtitled 'a journal of socialist historians'. On British traditions of social history, see A. Wilson, ed., *Rethinking Social History: English Society 1570–1920 and its Interpretation*, Manchester, 1993.

14 The famous journal *Annales: Economies, Sociétés, Civilisations*, changed its name at the end of 1993 to *Annales: Histoire, Sciences Sociales*. P. Burke, *The French Historical Revolution: The Annales School*, Cambridge, 1990.

15 F. Braudel, *The Mediterranean and the Mediterranean World in the Age of Philip II*, 2 vols., London, 1972 and 1973, first published 1949. An excellent discussion of the question of focus is B. Gregory, '*Is* Small Beautiful? Microhistory and the History of Everyday Life', *History and Theory*, 38, 1999, 100–10.

16 These traits are also evident in Braudel's three-volume *Civilization and Capitalism 15th–18th Century*, London, 1981, 1982 and 1984.

as their object of study will be unable to attend to those shifts that take place extremely slowly, hence decisions about the length of time to be covered automatically give priority to some kinds of phenomena and explanations over others. The shorter the time covered, the more limited are the historian's options. Defenders of micro-history point out the advantages of small-scale work, for instance in recreating everyday lived experience. A notion such as *histoire totale* helps historians to think about questions of scale and focus, and about the entailments of choices concerning the kinds of history we practise. When 'second-wave' social history got off the ground in the 1970s, it did not go down the path of *histoire totale* but of highly focused thematic or community studies on relatively restricted chunks of time.[17]

In its most rigorous form, *histoire totale* like *longue durée* history is little practised now. Yet the ideals they embodied are not altogether dead. There are small numbers of historians who are deliberately trying to write for wider readerships, for those outside the academic world, and who are seeking to make their books a good read. This is a significant trend in a number of respects. For example, it exemplifies a 'revival of narrative' to use Lawrence Stone's phrase, an interest in telling stories with which readers can identify.[18] Simon Schama's books are an example of this trend. His *Citizens*, published to coincide with the bicentenary of the French Revolution in 1989, examines the Revolution from the point of view of its participants. It is neither a political history nor a social history but a mixture of whatever is available in order to show what it was like to be there. It is not *histoire totale* in the sense that Braudel's works are. But it is embracing, wide-ranging, trying to move out of rigid categories, such as political history, which, in the case of the French Revolution, would involve charting the changes in regime, the nature of revolutionary leadership, the legislation introduced, the military campaigns and so on. Precisely because it does not address such matters, the book could be criticised for lacking a sense of the structural elements that made up the Revolution.

17 It may be helpful to think about micro-history in this context, which takes limited geographical areas in order to study as many aspects of them as possible. P. Burke, ed., *New Perspectives on Historical Writing*, Cambridge, 1991, ch. 5; E. Muir and G. Ruggiero. eds., *Microhistory and the Lost Peoples of Europe*, Baltimore, 1991.
18 L. Stone, 'The Revival of Narrative: Reflections on a New Old History', *Past and Present*, no. 85, 1979, 1–24.

Here, as in Schama's other books, there is an emphasis on culture and on themes that can be traced in many different forms.[19]

To the extent that holistic history is still being practised now, it takes two principal forms: biography and cultural history. I will return to cultural history shortly. Although biography could be understood as a literary genre, it is far more than this. Taking a person as the unit of analysis is to adopt a quite particular historical approach, one that emphasises individual agency and sees the subject as a point at which diverse historical forces converge, while taking the span of a human life as a natural period of time. Biography can cut across arbitrary divisions between historical fields and approaches. There are two pre-requisites for a viable biography – its subject must command more than specialist interest and there must be sufficient material available. Admittedly the second pre-requisite restricts the field somewhat, although it should be remembered that sources do exist for a surprisingly wide range of biographical studies. Nonetheless, it is worth noting how many influential figures destroyed or heavily censored their papers, and how many relatives have either done the same or refused historians access to privately held materials.

The nature of biographical writings has changed markedly over their long history. Whereas leaders – especially political and military ones – used to be favoured, and most subjects were given hagiographic treatment, in recent years biography has become the vehicle for sophisticated historiographical approaches, including psychoanalytical ones.[20] The critical evaluation of a life is now more acceptable and biographies remain extremely popular with general readers. In a single individual's life we see many factors at play – the expected political, social and economic ones, of course, but also education, kinship and friendship networks, leisure activities, reading, work and so on. In this way, reconstructing a life can be a form of *histoire totale* on a limited scale. It tells a story according to a pattern which most people find satisfying – a life story has an intuitive appeal that should not be sneered at. Whereas biographies used to be thought of as conventional and frumpy, it is now

19 S. Schama, *The Embarrassment of Riches: An Interpretation of Dutch Culture in the Golden Age*, London, 1987; *Citizens: A Chronicle of the French Revolution*, London, 1989; and *Landscape and Memory*, London, 1995. For different kinds of (*longue durée*) narrative, see R. Fletcher, *The Conversion of Europe: From Paganism to Christianity AD 371–1386*, London, 1997; and R. Porter, *The Greatest Benefit to Mankind: A Medical History of Humanity from Antiquity to the Present*, London, 1997.
20 S. Baron and C. Pletsch, eds., *Introspection in Biography: The Biographer's Quest for Self-Awareness*, Hillsdale, N. J., 1985.

becoming clear how rich in historical insights they can be.[21] Furthermore, a key feature of all historical writing is made manifest in them – the desire, even the need, to identify with our objects of study. The process of identification is facilitated when those objects are people, with whom one has to engage both intellectually and imaginatively.

So far in this chapter I have been addressing three points. The first is that history is so huge, in terms of its subject matter, its sources and its scope that it has to be divided up in order to make it manageable. The second is that there are many different ways of accomplishing this; all contain significant assumptions, which shape the historical writings that result. Third, precisely because the divisions between different kinds of history are problematic and arbitrary, there have been attempts to write about the past in a more satisfying manner. I have characterised these as holistic and given the example of biography. I have also suggested that cultural history, which is now enjoying an unprecedented vogue, is another manifestation of the wish for forms of history which recreate the range of experiences and imperatives to which all human beings are subject. Cultural history has shown itself to be open to a variety of theoretical perspectives that place the nature of human consciousness at the very heart of scholarship. In this case the coherence or sense of wholeness that is sought by a number of historical traditions is found in human mental processes, since all historical phenomena are mediated by them.[22] Now we should turn to very different ways of slicing up the historical cake.

FRESH FIELDS

Many new fields of history have emerged since the Second World War, and at first sight this looks like the result of processes of fragmentation and specialisation. There is certainly some of this involved – the expansion of

21   It is no coincidence that the history of science – a field in which the relationships between life and work are highly contested – should have produced some outstanding, and controversial, biographies: R. Westfall, *Never at Rest. A Biography of Isaac Newton*, Cambridge, 1980; G. Cantor, *Michael Faraday: Sandemanian and Scientist. A Study of Science and Religion in the Nineteenth Century*, Basingstoke, 1991; A. Desmond and J. Moore, *Darwin*, London, 1991; E. J. Browne, *Charles Darwin: A Biography, vol. 1: Voyaging*, New York, 1995. See also, M. Shortland and R. Yeo, eds., *Telling Lives in Science: Essays on Scientific Biography*, Cambridge, 1996.

22   R. Chartier, *Cultural History*, Cambridge, 1988; L. Hunt, ed., *The New Cultural History*, Berkeley, 1989.

higher education, for instance, has increased not only participation rates but also the numbers of university teachers. Not all teachers of undergraduates have had to do research, but now the trend is precisely in this direction, as teaching becomes valued less than research and as institutions compete for status and resources. In the humanities research is a matter for individuals, hence it is experienced as what is most properly one's own, even as a species of private property. It goes without saying that the academy is also committed to sharing knowledge freely and openly, and hence tensions constantly arise between this rather utopian goal and the need for researchers to make claims about originality in their research, which can be damaged if they pass findings around too freely before anything is published. The development of new fields can be seen as one way of creating distinctive niches, via specialisation, for the ever increasing numbers of historians. But there is another way of approaching the matter. New fields do not have to be seen just in terms of splitting a subject up to serve the interests of its practitioners; sometimes their formation is motivated by political concerns that require objects of identification.

The development of women's history is an excellent example of the complex investments in new fields. Historians have long been interested in women and specifically in whether women have a distinctive social role and hence history. This much is clear in eighteenth-century writings, which preceded the interest in the rights of women that is characteristic of the 1790s, and the growth of movements to reform women's legal and social status of the nineteenth century.[23] Yet the main impetus for women's history as a distinct field did coincide with 'second-wave' feminism, when more women were trying to make academic careers in institutions that were heavily male-dominated. To this extent the development of women's history could be seen as a move that served the interests of aspiring female historians. Yet many of the early pioneers of this phase of women's history were men, and there were no guarantees that the new field would provide employment for women – in fact there are still very few jobs designated as women's history positions in the UK, despite the fact that many people consider themselves to be working in the field. There are a lot more posts in the USA, where academic life built on politicised identities has been considerably more successful. In many parts of Europe, women's history is a tiny and somewhat marginal field compared to

23   J. Rendall, *The Origins of Modern Feminism: Women in Britain, France and the United States 1780–1860*, London, 1985.

more conventional historical areas, although it has gained significant ground in Scandinavia. [24]

Two other closely related issues were involved in the efforts to establish women's history as a recognised field – issues that come up in many new areas built around identity politics. The name 'women's history' implies recognition of the value of the category 'women' for the purposes of historical research. It constitutes a form of legitimation, not just for an academic activity, but for the group that is its focus. Giving value is a political process, and women's history endows with significance both women and those who study their past. The second issue brings us back to identification. Having a separate field facilitates the identification of historians with those they study, and, by extension, the identification of their readers with women in the past. It also helps historians build up their own identities in dynamic interaction with both their academic peers and political movements with shared concerns. Similar processes have been at work in the development of black history, which, like women's history, makes an important contribution in furnishing role models and acting as a vehicle through which painful experiences can be understood historically. Inevitably new fields also raise ethical issues – should historians apportion blame retrospectively, should they seek out and celebrate people who can be used as role models, should they seek to change present-day values by retelling the past? These are difficult questions, which are impossible to answer in general terms, since much depends on the context in which they arise. It is inevitable that new fields of study will be doing complex cultural work, and by that token they are likely to be controversial. Precisely because they contain demands – pay attention to this social group, recognise oppression, take my point of view seriously – they are felt to be threatening, strident and lacking in solidity by those working within well-established areas of history. To my mind a good example of these points, which brings out the complexities to which I am alluding, is the history of childhood.[25] This area of history has arisen in the context of unprecedented interest in psychoanalysis and child abuse; there is a particularly high moral ground to be occupied here. Given that there are relatively few direct testimonies from children themselves,

24 Relevant inter-disciplinary journals include, *Signs. Journal of Women in Culture and Society* (1975) and *Women. A Cultural Review* (1990). Those with broader remits, such as *Gender and History* (1989), publish a great deal on women. See also the *Journal of Women's History* (1989) and *Women's History Review* (1992).

25 See, for example, P. Ariès, *Centuries of Childhood*, Harmondsworth, 1973; G. Scarre, ed., *Children, Parents and Politics*, Cambridge, 1989; C. Steedman, *Strange Dislocations. Childhood and the Idea of Human Interiority 1780–1930*, London, 1995.

the opportunities for slippery forms of identification are particularly great. The feelings of both those who promote and those who resist new fields are to be taken seriously, although it is rarely possible for all the stakes involved to be openly acknowledged. Such conflicts are probably unavoidable, although they can and should be conducted with as much humanity and understanding as possible.

RIJKSMUSEUM, AMSTERDAM

2.3 'The Sick Child' by Gabriel Metsu (c. 1665)
Simon Schama used considerable amounts of visual evidence in The
Embarrassment of Riches. *Francis Haskell offered a persuasive critique of his*
approach, using this Dutch painting from the seventeenth century as an example.
Historians are often tempted to treat 'realist' images as windows onto past worlds.

Historical research stems from many impulses, and historians are often deeply emotionally engaged with both their subject matter and their approaches. This makes for high levels of commitment, which are not amenable to rational analysis, and for an intolerance towards those who do not share one's values and may even be opposed to them. Greater tolerance and respect for deep commitments is required, which might be easier if historians were more accustomed to speaking openly of their emotional investment in their work. Yet openness can be extraordinarily hard to achieve given the depth of political divisions among practitioners of the discipline. In these situations it is vital to be able to turn, dispassionately, to evidence and to firm ideas about its appropriate use, which involves both ethical and intellectual considerations. The alternative is trying to fight the matter out in terms that are ultimately unresolvable because they rest on matters of *belief* and not of *evidence*. Yet since beliefs are so important, there are bound to be conflicts. The extent of French collaboration during the pro-Nazi Vichy regime, which was established in 1940, is an interesting example. Feelings on the subject continue to run high – the very notion 'collaboration' implies moral taint, all the more so in what is widely regarded as a 'just war'. It is remarkable that the museum dedicated to the history of the French resistance in Lyon manages to handle the issue extraordinarily well, partly by presenting a great deal of evidence while acknowledging its emotional power.[26] Although I have linked these matters with the development of new fields, this is simply where they are most obvious; they arise in traditional areas too, especially where participation in political regimes now widely condemned is at issue. More generally, when fields change and the maps of a discipline are redrawn, then occasions arise for reflecting upon settled assumptions.

GEOGRAPHICAL BOUNDARIES

So far, when taking examples of sub-fields, I have used those which bring to the fore categories of human beings that claim special attention, and elicit special forms of identification: women, blacks, Jews, children and so on. I could have chosen other examples: workers, gays or slaves, for instance. But history can also be divided up according to other criteria. I want now to consider some of these and four in particular: regions, approaches, themes and

26 The museum is part of the Centre d'Histoire de la Résistance et de la Déportation; a catalogue of their permanent exhibition, edited by S. Zeitoun and D. Foucher, was published in 1997.

theories. After the political/social/economic schema, the most common division is by place, which often involves an area that is now a nation state. We should note, however, that less professionalised forms of history pay particular attention to local areas, to regions that are considerably smaller than nation states, often of long-standing in terms of their names and boundaries, and administratively important when it comes to organising records and archives.[27] In part this reflects the vitality of amateur local history and the strength of local pride. Equally it reveals long-standing scholarly traditions in which the past of a delimited area is examined by archaeologists, antiquarians, genealogists and architectural historians, as well as by 'historians'.

Countries are taken as obvious units of analysis, despite the fact that national boundaries are rarely neat at all. We can make the obvious point about disputed and changing borders, and add that within national boundaries questions of language use, ethnicity, religion and regional variations may be so contentious that any sense of unity becomes exceedingly fragile. For French, Chinese, German, Mexican or Italian history to be meaningful notions, historians require conceptual frameworks that hold disparate phenomena together. To lump historical processes together because they occurred in areas we *now* name France, China and so on, is intellectually weak. Accordingly, it is possible to return to the unifying effect of political structures, and argue that if there is a single governmental apparatus, head of state, and systems for law, healthcare, education and so on, then it is meaningful to speak of Greek history, Spanish history, Egyptian history and so on. Historians are becoming increasingly attentive to the complexities of just these issues. Yet at undergraduate level they are rarely raised, and many students take courses in French history without being aware either of the complexities of 'France' or of the ways in which prior assumptions about 'France' shape the work that is carried out. It is frequently taken for granted that French history is characterised by the existence of a strong state, hence areas where this was resisted, ineffective or simply not operative are played down. (It is equally surprising how often France means just Paris.) In contrast, British historians until recently have tended to imagine that during the period of French absolutism, Britain was characterised by a weak state apparatus. Revisionism on these issues strikes at the very heart of a sense

---

27 C. Phythian-Adams, *Re-thinking English Local History*, Leicester, 1987, puts local history in a broad intellectual context and considers local/national relationships. Cf. A. Wood, *The Politics of Social Conflict: The Peak Country, 1520–1770*, Cambridge, 1999.

of national identity.[28] In the British case this has involved the idea that we are *laissez-faire* at heart, although there is considerable evidence to the contrary from many historical periods. Yet this invented self-image still sets the terms in which (some) history is practised, and it is significant, I suspect, that few of the great theorists of the state have been British.

The problem is that we think of places as self-evident – geography is simply there – and tend to neglect the intricate historical processes through which they have been constructed. The point applies not just to countries but to all the geographical units that historians use.[29] The solution is to pay more attention to the ways in which these were defined and imagined in the period we are studying. Yet learned journals based on countries tend to cover all periods, producing a certain homogenising effect, especially in cases such as Germany and Italy where unification is rather recent. The unified nation state is often taken as a norm, and hence the goal towards which earlier processes were moving. This kind of teleology is unhelpful and encourages anachronism.

The big plus of area-based history is that it encourages researchers to think about diverse historical phenomena in relation to one another.[30] We have already discussed holistic history, and it seems that, despite the existence of work such as Braudel's, area-based history works best when it takes entities smaller than countries. It is particularly effective for zones or topics where a nation state is not the most meaningful unit. The approach has been especially generative when cities are used as case studies. However, it would be over-specialised to define sub-fields in specifically local terms. Where local archives are particularly rich, historians may use them repeatedly, but with a variety of historical problems in mind. It would be these problems, rather than the location of the archives, that defined the kinds of history they were undertaking.[31]

28 An interesting example is the role of Francis Bacon as Chancellor during the reign of James I. Recent accounts stress the aggressive state-building they engaged in: J. Martin, *Francis Bacon, the State, and the Reform of Natural Philosophy*, Cambridge, 1992.

29 This issue is elegantly addressed by John Iliffe in *Africans: The History of a Continent*, Cambridge, 1995.

30 This is precisely what the recent wave of work in environmental history has been doing; see, for example, A. Crosby, *Ecological Imperialism. The Biological Expansion of Europe, 900–1900*, Cambridge, 1986; W. Beinart and P. Coates, *Environment and History. The Taming of Nature in the USA and South Africa*, London, 1995; D. Worster, *Rivers of Empire: Water, Aridity, and the Growth of the American West*, second edition, New York, 1992.

31 D. Sabean, *Power in the Blood: Popular Culture and Village Discourse in Early Modern Germany*, Cambridge, 1984, is based on 15 years of 'piecing together all of the material I could find on the village of Neckarhausen', p. ix, before broadening out to regional and state archives; cf. L. Roper, *The Holy Household: Women and Morals in Reformation Augsburg*, Oxford, 1989.

METHODS AND APPROACHES

The second form of division is by method or, more loosely, approach. Two contrasting examples will help to clarify the issues involved – quantitative history and oral history. While the use of quantitative techniques in historical analysis is not new – debates about the effects of the Industrial Revolution using statistical measures have been going on for ages – its significant growth has been since the Second World War with the hugely increased impact of the social sciences on the discipline of history. There are a number of arguments for the use of statistical methods in historical research.[32] They are exceptionally well suited to the study of groups, since it is possible to examine meaningfully aggregates that would otherwise be dealt with impressionistically. Collective phenomena, if I can put it that way, come into their own. A closely related argument is that a degree of precision is offered by quantitative techniques that would not otherwise be available. Demographic work on age at marriage or on illegitimacy rates exemplifies the point since it enables historians to think about the nature of sexual activity among the young in more than vague and anecdotal ways. When age at marriage is high, illegitimacy rates low, and reliable contraception unavailable, historians have to reflect upon mechanisms of social control and varied forms of sexual expression. They can also examine periods of social transition with these issues in mind. Hence, another argument for quantitative techniques is that they reveal trends over long periods of time. There are a number of reasons why long-term trends are important. They provide a perspective that affords precise insights into periods of stability and change, and they reveal just those slow, almost imperceptible shifts that historians otherwise find difficult to conceptualise. Thus they also open the way for comparing different types of historical change, which work at different paces, and historians hopefully become more careful when it comes to attributing causes to significant shifts. Furthermore, better understanding of long term trends highlights the frequent discrepancies between perceptions of change and change itself. For example, there were widespread anxieties about population decline in many countries during the eighteenth century. Demographic evidence reveals that no such decline took place, and in England, for example, there was unprecedented growth. This insight is useful, not so that we can chastise eighteenth-century commentators for being

---

32 R. Floud, *An Introduction to Quantitative Methods for Historians*, London, 1979, introduction, sets out a strong case. C. Tilly, *As Sociology Meets History*, New York, 1981, ch. 2.

ARNOLD

2.4 *Estimate of English population totals, taken from Wrigley and Schofield,* A Population History of England 1541–1871 *(1981)*
This relatively simple graph offers an immediate sense of population trends from cursory visual inspection. The table referred to as the source for the graph consists simply of lists of numbers, the interpretation of which demand quite different intellectual skills. Wrigley and Schofield's Population History of England 1541–1871 *presents a wealth of quantitative material in diverse formats and thereby illustrates the huge range of ways in which data can be gathered, used and interpreted.*

wrong, but so that we can pay attention to how attitudes take hold and are to be explained. Just invoking what is 'out there' clearly will not do.[33]

Building historical work around quantitative methods is not unproblematic, and it is particularly dependent upon the quality of information available.[34] Consistency is a particular problem here; for long-term trends to be meaningful, the data across time and place have to be strictly comparable and

---

33 Distinguished work on demography includes, L. Henry, *On the Measurement of Human Fertility*, Amsterdam, 1972, and *Population: Analysis and Models*, London, 1976; P. Laslett, *The World We Have Lost*, London, 1965; E. Wrigley and R. Schofield, *The Population History of England 1541–1871: A Reconstruction*, Cambridge, 1993 (revised edition).

34 One of the most contentious uses of quantitative techniques has been in relation to American slavery. A recent assessment is M. Smith, *Debating Slavery: Economy and Society in the Antebellum American South*, Cambridge, 1998. Cf. J. Walvin, *Questioning Slavery*, London, 1996.

changes in their nature (mode of gathering, criteria for inclusion and so on) can undermine general conclusions based upon them. How such information is interpreted and what it is thought to demonstrate are equally contentious issues. Roger Schofield explored precisely such an issue when he asked what can be inferred from maternal mortality data about how women felt about childbirth. It is a particular challenge to find evidence concerning the relationships between human beings' *subjective* sense of risk and *statistical* risk as painstakingly reconstructed by demographers.[35] Claims about changes in women's attitudes would have to be documented using different types of evidence. Any sense of risk is a complex cultural phenomenon, which cannot simply be read off from the known occurrence of a particular event. It is both useful and important to know that maternal mortality was considerably less frequent than is usually supposed, but the wider conclusions we draw from this are less obvious. One productive route is to use such information as a stimulus for general historical reflection, so that quantitative materials are interpreted in the light of and after comparison with diverse qualitative ones. The limitations of quantitative sources are sometimes insufficiently appreciated, perhaps because they appear 'scientific'; it is vital to analyse critically the manipulations to which they have been subject before they reach the printed page. It is unfortunate to isolate quantitative from qualitative work; they are best seen as complementary. However, specialisation, especially in the skills needed to do first-rate quantitative work, tends to work in the opposite direction.

While there are close links between quantitative methods and economic history, many historians who work on economic phenomena do not in fact use statistical methods and vice versa. Economic history is potentially an extremely broad field: 'the history of actual human practice with respect to the material basis of life'.[36] We could say that economic history concerns itself with production on the one hand and consumption on the other. In spite of the concern with such huge, all-pervasive issues, economic history remains too little integrated with other approaches. Whereas 'quantitative history' signals

---

35 R. Schofield, 'Did the Mothers Really Die? Three Centuries of Maternal Mortality in "The World We Have Lost"', in L. Bonfield et al., eds., *The World We Have Gained: Histories of Population and Social Structure*, Oxford, 1986, pp. 231–60.

36 W. Ashley, 'The Place of Economic History in University Studies', *The Economic History Review*, 1, 1927, 1–11, at 1. For a poignant assessment of the state of economic history, which, although it concerns Great Britain, raises broad historiographical issues, see D. Coleman, *History and the Economic Past. An Account of the Rise and Decline of Economic History in Britain*, Oxford, 1987.

that specific methods are involved, 'economic history' implies privileging one aspect of human life; it is therefore regrettable that this aspect is often presented as impersonal. I would see economic history as more an approach than a method, although there are phenomena most historians would happily agree to call 'economic' and by that token the field possesses distinctive content. Yet economic history can draw on the powerful and highly theorised discipline of economics; indeed some economic historians practise in departments of economics. The use of economic theories, which tend to emphasise the rational choices of individuals, within the discipline of history raises a number of difficult issues, since they depend on models of human nature the implications of which are rarely explored sufficiently deeply. Invoking economic theory does not solve the question of what sustains conventional definitions of economic history. As we observed in the case of political history, the defence of economic history must rest on 'economic' being analytically distinguishable and useful for historical explanation. It may well be that, as with quantitative techniques, the skills are sufficiently specialised that designated groups of historians, who are looking less at individuals in the past as economic actors and more at trends, aggregates and so on, are required. Nonetheless some clear idea of the work done by the concept 'economic' is vital. We might say that methods and approaches such as these examine certain *levels* of historical phenomena most effectively, but this notion in turn requires careful scrutiny.

The notion of levels of historical phenomena could also be applied to oral history – a clear example of a method-based division in the discipline. Oral history is based on the idea that powerful insights can be derived from people talking about their experiences. It therefore gives a certain status to memory, no matter how complex or uncertain this mental faculty may be. It also assumes that everyone's memory is valuable and of potential historical interest. Although it is possible to do elite oral history, the voice of the past, to use Paul Thompson's phrase, is that of the humble, of working men and women, who did not have power as this has usually been defined, but who did have rich experiences of social change, family, work, politics and so on, that offer a distinct historical perspective.[37] So 'experience' is a key word for oral history, but it is experience evoked retrospectively by speaking about the past.

37 P. Thompson, *The Voice of the Past*, Oxford, 1988, first published 1978. See also *Oral History* (1972). L. Passerini, ed., *Memory and Totalitarianism*, Oxford, 1992, contains work by scholars from many countries; it was the first *International Yearbook of Oral History and Life Stories*. L. Passerini, *Fascism in Popular Memory. The Cultural Experience of the Turin Working Class*, Cambridge, 1987.

Arguments in favour of this method would include the point that it offers access to phenomena that are otherwise close to invisible. The complexities of household management would be a case in point, and many health and reproductive matters were experienced in private and were inaccessible to historians until women especially were interviewed. The *quality* of human relationships in the past can be effectively brought to life by oral history techniques, which do not depend on literal accuracy, but on getting inside people's heads. Where accuracy is an issue, oral evidence should always be cross-checked with other sources. Although potentially a highly sophisticated technique, oral history can nonetheless be widely practised, and is, in a number of senses, a democratising approach to history.

One potential danger associated with oral history, however, is that of over-identification with those being interviewed, a point that links in with issues in other historical fields – the cult of authenticity and romanticisation. Neither of these is confined to the practice of history, although they are especially important issues for historians whose professional training and surrounding culture encourage them to seek truths and authentic evidence, which become all the more precious if they have been garnered with much effort. A person speaking to a historian of their own experience generates an especially direct kind of evidence, which is all the more valued if it comes from those who were not previously considered significant historical actors. And if such testimony contains, as it so often does, accounts of suffering and deprivation, of heroism and stoicism, then our romantic sensibilities are readily engaged. This does not necessarily involve seeing the past as *better* than it was – a shallow interpretation of 'romantic' – but it may create an emotional aura that affects the resulting scholarship. Such emotional investments have their generative side, but they can also reinforce simple moral polarities, which are necessarily, given what we know of the human condition, strategic fictions.

THEMATIC HISTORY

The tenor of my remarks about method-based history implies that it is a somewhat artificial way of organising historical research. There is a point of view according to which the most satisfying accounts of the past involve a wide range of materials and of methods, and that, in any given piece of research, the two should be brought into harmony with one another. One possibility is to take a theme as the organising principle – for example, an idea that has been important and influential and that has many facets. The clearest early examples of such work came out of the history of ideas, although it must be admitted that they privileged written texts of a somewhat elite kind.[38] Arthur Lovejoy's classic book *The Great Chain of Being*, first published in 1936, took a pervasive model of creation and traced its history from classical times through to its demise with the development of evolutionary theory at the very end of the eighteenth century. Here, as in his other writings, Lovejoy used a wide range of written, although not archival sources.[39] The emphasis in the history of ideas has tended towards 'high' culture, although there are many themes that bring together more diverse aspects of societies. Perhaps it is significant that *The Past is a Foreign Country* was written by an American geographer. David Lowenthal's wide-ranging book looks at evidence from buildings, railway stations and museums as well as from more expected sources, in order to examine the ways in which the past is imagined and represented, in fiction and in poetry as much as in historical writings. It would be hard to know exactly what kind of history this is, although there is now a growing literature on what could be called 'heritage issues', an area in which historians have only recently become active.[40] A somewhat different kind of thematic history has been undertaken by Keith Thomas, for example, in his *Man and the Natural World* (1983). The theme – how human beings have treated nature over several centuries – is evidently huge, and it is the occasion for bringing together disparate topics, sources and issues. Thomas constructs a sort of bricolage, assembling huge numbers of examples, quotations and anecdotes in the service of his theme. Such thematic history is bound to be less easy to control and to organise in a linear fashion than more conventional types of history. It is best seen as a supplement to other forms rather than a substitute for them. Since it can cut the cake in strikingly fresh ways, it can be used heuristically, in generating ideas and reappraisals, as *Man and the Natural World* certainly did. Current interest in the history of animals, for instance, while it owes something to 'animal liberation' movements, is productive because it offers an unusual vantage point made possible by attending to themes and preoccupations of the past that do not fit into tidy packages.[41]

38 See, for instance, the *Journal of the History of Ideas* (1940) and *History of European Ideas* (1985).

39 Cf. A. Lovejoy, *Essays in the History of Ideas*, New York, 1960, which contains a complete list of Lovejoy's publications; *The Great Chain of Being: A Study in the History of an Idea*, Cambridge, Mass., 1936.

40 D. Lowenthal, *The Past is a Foreign Country*, Cambridge, 1985, and *The Heritage Crusade and the Spoils of History*, London, 1997.

41 See, for example, H. Ritvo, *The Animal Estate: The English and Other Creatures in the Victorian Age*, Cambridge, Mass., 1987, and *The Platypus and the Mermaid and Other Fragments of the Classifying Imagination*, Cambridge, Mass., 1998.

A wonderful example is Mark Jenner's study of seventeenth-century attitudes to dogs, who were often slaughtered in times of plague, which is designed to open up responses to the disease from a fresh perspective.[42]

THEORY-BASED HISTORY

Fresh perspectives have many points of origination, sometimes in theories. Most people see history as a relatively untheorised discipline, although whether this is good or bad depends on your point of view. It also depends on the country in which you received your training. Historiography in the English-speaking world, in contrast to the more overtly theoretical French, Italian and German traditions, tends to emphasise the empirical dimensions of history. Although (some) historians work closely with theoretical perspectives, this does not tend to take the form of producing theories of history, at least, it has not done so in the twentieth century.[43] The major theorists of society have not been historians. Whatever tradition they are trained in, historians are more accustomed to searching for particularities, to spotting what is unique or special about a situation, than to noting its kinship with other cases. The latter is precisely what comparative history as a method sets out to do, but there is hardly *a* theory of comparative history.[44] Until about 20 years ago, most people would have come up with Marxism if asked to name a theory important to the practice of history. Now there appear to be few attempts to develop Marxian historiography further. We could interpret this shift in a number of ways. It could indicate disenchantment with the worldview that Marxism represented. It could suggest that its key elements have already been incorporated where they are useful. Perhaps just fragments of Marxism remain alive. It is possible that, because of cultural shifts, historians have lost interest in the leading themes of Marxism, such as class struggle and the nature of production, because they ceased to be apt for the world we now inhabit. Intellectual

---

42 M. Jenner, 'The Great Dog Massacre', in W. G. Naphy and P. Roberts, eds., *Fear in Early Modern Society*, Manchester, 1997, pp. 44–61.

43 Of course there are exceptions, Arnold Toynbee being one, but in most countries his work is all but ignored.

44 See *Comparative Studies in Society and History* (1958). A particularly thoughtful and lucid discussion of comparative history may be found in G. M. Frederickson, *The Comparative Imagination: On the History of Racism, Nationalism, and Social Movements*, Berkeley, 1997. See also the Forum: Comparative Historiography: Problems and Perspectives, in *History and Theory*, 38, no. 1, 1999.

fashions do change, as a result of which theories fall out of favour, less because of explicit criticisms than because they are no longer vital and relevant.

Over the same period there has been a dramatic growth of interest in psychoanalysis. Although still regarded with suspicion in some quarters, it has become an accepted part of the historian's theoretical armoury, especially in the United States, where many large history departments include a psychohistorian on the staff and where special training courses are available to scholars who want to use psychoanalysis in their research but have no wish to develop clinical skills.[45] Yet most people, and scholars are no exception, think psychoanalytically without being particularly aware of doing so. Many of the explanations we give of behaviour in everyday life owe much to what are now commonplace assumptions about how the unconscious works. Since a significant proportion of historical explanation rests on such assumptions, psychoanalysis has found its way into historical practice. However, many historians still have little direct knowledge of psychoanalytic thinking or of the significant differences between its principal traditions: Freudian, Jungian, Kleinian and Lacanian. There have been attacks on psychoanalysis in history, as there have on psychoanalysis in general. Readers may find it helpful to remember that the use of psychoanalysis does not have to be doctrinaire, but can be quite flexible, where the starting point is the historical problem. I would advocate that historians adopt the more flexible posture, and employ assumptions about psychology and behaviour knowingly wherever possible.[46] The implication of my position is that the creation of separate sub-fields can generate rigid and artificial divisions – much better for historians to be open to a range of theoretical perspectives so long as they develop a critical purchase upon them.

45 It is vital to distinguish between the diverse and pragmatic uses of psychoanalytic theories, which are somewhat more acceptable to the majority of historians, and psychohistory, a formalised field, practitioners of which are committed to psychoanalysis as their principal explanatory device. Even within psychohistory there are huge variations in approach. See, for example, E. Erikson, *Young Man Luther. A Study in Psychoanalysis and History*, London, 1959, and *Gandhi's Truth. On the Origins of Militant Nonviolence*, London 1970; P. Lowenberg, *Fantasy and Reality in History*, New York, 1995, and *Decoding the Past: The Psychohistorical Approach*, New York, 1983.

46 D. Stannard, *Shrinking History: On Freud and the Failure of Psychohistory*, New York, 1980; *The Psychohistory Review. Studies of Motivation in History and Culture* (1972) and *The Journal of Psychohistory. A Publication of the Institute for Psychohistory* (1976), which was founded in 1973 as the *History of Childhood Quarterly*; for an exceptionally creative use of psychoanalytic ideas in history see L. Roper, *Oedipus and the Devil: Witchcraft, Sexuality and Religion in Early Modern Europe*, London, 1994. W. Runyan, ed., *Psychology and Historical Interpretation*, New York, 1988.

Historians need to be able not just to recognise and name specific theoretical perspectives, but to have some idea of the properties of theories in general. Theories work at a meta-level, that is, they are more general and abstract than empirical detail. They offer frameworks designed to explain a wide range of phenomena. It follows then that theories tend to have a certain predictive quality – in the case of psychoanalysis, it can be claimed that specific types of psychological damage will have particular effects. In practice, clinicians and historians work back from the effects to the putative causes. Psychohistory tends to emphasise childhood experience and its effects on later life without paying sufficient attention to the specific historical context, and for some historians this is reductive.[47] We might say, however, that psychoanalysis broadly defined takes the complexities of the mind seriously and in this way helps historians to develop more satisfying ways of understanding human actions and experience. It is also one possible way of exploring the significance of metaphors and symbols, which often attain their power precisely because of their ability to tap into the unconscious.[48]

There are two commonly voiced objections to the use of psychoanalysis in history. The first is that it is an individualistic method, which may possibly work in relation to individuals about whom a great deal is known, but that it fails when it comes to group phenomena. In fact many analysts, building on earlier psychological work, have thought about collective psychology and psychohistorians have addressed precisely this issue in studying how totalitarian leaders can command support, for example. The second objection is that it is wrong, if not downright impossible, to psychoanalyse the dead, and that the method is especially inappropriate when it is applied to societies that were themselves innocent of psychoanalytic ideas. The latter point always seems to me to be particularly obtuse – theories are designed to be general, to be applied to a wide range of cases, and if they are productive theories they do not just apply to the period in which they were formulated. The *unconscious* did not come into being in the late nineteenth century, it has existed for as long as there have been human beings.[49]

---

47 F. Manuel's biographical study of Sir Isaac Newton prompted particular fury: *A Portrait of Isaac Newton*, Cambridge, Mass., 1968; the preface and introduction discuss methodological issues.

48 *History Workshop Journal* has been notably receptive to psychoanalysis: for example, the special issues 26 in 1988 and 45 in 1998.

49 The best discussion of these points remains, P. Gay, *Freud for Historians*, New York, 1985. Psychohistorical accounts that engage with leadership include, C. B. Strozier and D. Offer, eds., *The Leader. Psychohistorical Essays*, New York, 1985; B. Mazlish, *The Leader, the Led and the Psyche. Essays in Psychohistory*, Hanover, 1990; and the books by Peter Lowenberg cited in footnote 45.

BRIDGE

'History' is not a defined body of knowledge but an abstract idea with many meanings. Thus, when we think about it as an academic discipline, it can easily seem overwhelming – it just includes so much that it is difficult to imagine where its coherence lies. I have argued in this chapter that there are a number of ways in which we can examine what is going on in the discipline (what could be called its content) in order to have if only a sketch map of it. Some of these involve thinking about the raw materials and how they are used. Others involve thinking about the method or theory applied to those materials. Yet others involve trying to understand how the discipline has been divided up and what these divisions mean for our understanding of the past. Partly they make research practicable, but they are also vehicles for powerful emotions and investments, for claims about how the past is best approached. In these respects history has much in common with other disciplines, upon which it has at times been extremely reliant. We may imagine cognate fields as resources for historians, or indeed as threats, since the study of the past is by no means the exclusive domain of history. In the following chapter I examine the complex and sometimes fraught relationships between history and its near neighbours.

History and Other Disciplines

DISCIPLINES IN HISTORY

History has not always been a discipline – a term that implies elaborate institutional, professional and communications structures. Before it became a separate field of study, history was a form of writing, in fact it was many forms. At its most simple, 'history' means description, as in 'natural history' accounts of the natural world. It is worth remembering that Pliny's great *Natural History* was not just about animals, plants and minerals, but also about history, biography, art history and so on.[1] For the Greeks histories were narratives of significant human doings, especially of wars. For the literate of medieval times, history was composed of chronicles, which described kinship relations, the distribution of property, the successes and travails of Christianity, conflicts between lords and the fate of kings. Lives of saints and martyrs (hagiographies) were also important. In the centuries that followed much historical scholarship was undertaken, but not by professionals called 'historians', since these did not exist. Rather it was produced by men (largely) who had other interests, concerns, professions and jobs; they were travellers, men of the church, doctors and lawyers. History was perceived as integral to theology, the gathering and study of antiquities, the practice of medicine and the law, the formation of collections, and the preservation of the material past.[2]

Histories that we can easily recognise as representing endeavours close to our own were produced in the eighteenth century, but their authors rarely taught history or saw their identity as that of 'historian': David Hume, Edward Gibbon, Voltaire, David Ramsay, and Giambattista Vico.[3]

1 Pliny the Elder lived between *c*. AD 23 and 79; he studied grammar, philosophy and rhetoric as well as nature.
2 On the writing of history see M. Bentley, ed., *Companion to Historiography*, London, 1997. Cf. M. Finley, *Ancient History. Evidence and Models*, London, 1985.
3 With the exception of David Ramsay, the historian of the American Revolution, all these figures are mentioned in J. Black and R. Porter, eds., *The Penguin Dictionary of Eighteenth-Century History*, London, 1994. On Ramsay, see A. Shaffer, *To Be an American. David Ramsay and the Making of the American Consciousness*, Columbia S.C., 1991.

Such works were widely read and admired, in part because they spoke with conviction to contemporary concerns. However, they were not the products of 'research' as we understand it, which involves intensive use of primary sources, generally including manuscripts, and protocols covering footnotes and bibliography together with consequent claims to scholarly originality. Over the nineteenth century history was widely institutionalised, in the sense of there being not only university posts but organised archives available to scholars. Only in the twentieth century has history been a staple of the higher-education curriculum with all the paraphernalia of a discipline.

One effect of discipline-formation is to isolate scholars within their own subject-based communities. Although it is always possible to read the books and articles produced by disciplines other than one's own, this is a different kind of activity from direct collaboration between people who have been trained in different disciplines. Encountering a discipline through reading its publications is a somewhat abstract, disembodied enterprise – it is difficult to sense its habits of mind, the distinctive qualities of its intellectual practices, and where the tensions and excitements lie. Furthermore, such reading tends to be highly selective, giving a rather distorted view of the other field. A relatively small number of authors become known outside their own areas and the reason why one rather than another gets widely taken up often remains obscure. Hence whenever we speak of 'inter-disciplinary' work and of history's relations with other subjects, the distinction between these two forms of cross-disciplinary encounter should be borne in mind.

In the light of these points it is somewhat ironic that history has been a separate discipline for only a relatively short period of time. Indeed the very notion of a discipline is rather recent. In earlier times there were recognised fields of knowledge, such as the medieval quadrivium of theology, logic, rhetoric and music, with university posts and special publications, but these were not disciplines in the modern sense, as is clear when we consider rhetoric, which was more akin to a method than to a discipline, and recall that theology was hailed as the queen of the sciences. In most European languages, 'science' implied 'systematic knowledge' until the eighteenth century; there was more interest in kinds of learning than in dividing knowledge up according to its subject matter. Intense intellectual specialisation is a feature of twentieth-century societies. For most of recorded history, the scholarly study of the past has been integral to a wide range of activities, hence its separation goes against the grain. Furthermore it is worth remembering how much of what is today widely read as history is written by those outside the university system – authors such as Marina Warner, Antonia Fraser, Michael

Holroyd, Elizabeth Longford and Barbara Tuchman, spring to mind.[4] The importance of recording, cherishing and using the past goes back a very long way indeed – it is therefore surprising that many historians have an impoverished sense of history's history. The sense of a past is central to many human endeavours – in institutions, professions and families, for example – and it is produced out of deep engagement with earlier times, which have never been the private property of 'historians'.

THEORY

This chapter, however, focuses on relations between modern academic disciplines, and, given the space I am devoting to history's interactions with other fields, the implication is that they are extensive, complex and vital for understanding the discipline as a whole. What do we mean when we talk about relations between disciplines? We could mean a historical appreciation of how areas of study have developed, which would show how disciplinary definitions are constructed and change, and the shifting purposes for which the past is studied. As academic life has evolved, especially since the Second World War, understanding relationships between disciplines involves considerably more than this. It includes: the transfer of information and insights between distinct fields; the movements of theories and concepts from one area to another; the inspiration that can come from venturing outside one's own immediate subject, when a different approach or mindset offers creative possibilities.

At first glance, the previous sentence does not contain any unusual or difficult words, yet it mentions matters which are widely misunderstood, or treated carelessly. Take, for example, 'theory' – relations between disciplines and the role of theory are closely related questions.[5] It is often said that historians are uncomfortable with theory, that they are 'mindlessly empiricist' in their tendency to search for 'facts' without possessing adequate interpretative frameworks. Hence the claim that when historians need theoretical insights they look outside their own domain, to economics or political theory, for example. The use of modernisation theory or of Habermas's ideas on the

---

4 M. Warner, *Alone of All Her Sex: The Myth and Cult of the Virgin Mary*, London, 1976, and *Joan of Arc: The Image of Female Heroism*, Harmondsworth, 1983; A. Fraser, *King Arthur and the Knights of the Round Table*, London, 1970; M. Holroyd, *Augustus John*, London, 1996; B. Tuchman, *A Distant Mirror: The Calamitous 14th Century*, London, 1979.
5 Cf. *History and Theory: Studies in the Philosophy of History* (1961). Also relevant is B. Fay et al., eds., *History and Theory: Contemporary Readings*, Malden, Mass., 1998.

public sphere are cases in point.[6] This is an issue of major importance since it bears on the nature and status of historical knowledge and on ideas about historical method. It is therefore vital to be perfectly explicit about what we mean by 'theory'. In doing so we need to signal an issue to which we shall return in the following chapter, namely, the widespread use of the natural sciences as *the* model for reliable knowledge. Scientific procedures are still seen by some commentators as exemplifying a rationality that should be emulated by historians. This is the burden of David Stannard's critique of psychohistory, for example. The point is relevant to theory in two ways: first, the sciences, especially the physical ones, are perceived to possess intellectually powerful theories, which provide high-quality explanations, and second, a separation between theories and facts is taken to be self-evident. In both cases misleading extrapolations are made for the practice of history. We should note how the very vocabulary we use – 'factual' and 'empirical', 'theoretical' and 'conceptual' – affirms a separation between 'raw' data and what is done with them, although the reality is altogether more complex.

I take theories to have four main characteristics. First, 'theory' implies a general account of something, which explains more than one instance of it – case studies bear on theories, but the latter are more general and abstract than the former. Second, it implies that phenomena can be explained by reference to it, with the result that these phenomena are better understood at the end than at the beginning of any enquiry. Third, it implies that new cases will be illuminated by it – in history this is not the same as prediction, since history cannot be said to predict the future. But a theory of revolution might be developed, for example, in relation to the French and Russian revolutions, and then be found to be extremely useful in relation to, say, the Mexican Revolution.[7] Fourth, it implies the existence of a coherent perspective, embodied in the theory, which is able to bring together and render meaningful diverse phenomena. This is a corollary of its status as an abstract, general framework. Putting all these points together, it is apparent that 'theory' carries an aura of intellectual power.

It should now be clear why history, as it has generally been practised in the twentieth century, has not been a particularly theoretical subject. There has

---

6   C. E. Black, *The Dynamics of Modernization. A Study in Comparative History*, New York, 1966; B. Dmystryshyn, ed., *Modernization of Russia under Peter I and Catherine II*, New York, 1974; C. Calhoun, ed., *Habermas and the Public Sphere*, Cambridge, Mass. and London, 1992.

7   On comparative approaches to revolution see T. Skocpol, *States and Social Revolutions: A Comparative Analysis of France, Russia and China*, Cambridge, 1979; and on the Mexican case, A. Knight, *The Mexican Revolution*, 2 vols., Cambridge, 1986.

been a strong emphasis on providing, instance by instance, accurate and convincing accounts of what happened in the past. Much of the best history has proceeded by a kind of immersion in the sources, taking its explanatory devices out of those sources, which suggests that too crisp a separation between theories and sources is misleading and unhelpful. No empirical activity is possible without a theory, or at least elaborate presuppositions, behind it, even if these remain implicit, perhaps unconscious. All historians have ideas already in their minds when they study primary materials – models of human behaviour, established chronologies, assumptions about responsibility, notions of identity and so on. Of course, some are convinced that they are merely gathering facts, looking at sources with a totally open mind and only recording what is there, yet they are simply wrong to believe this. Since it is rather easy to show how full historians' minds already are when they do research, the persistence of contrary beliefs requires explanation. One possible explanation is that, as professionally based worldviews, disciplines generate accounts of themselves which practitioners are strongly encouraged to buy into, and that these accounts serve specific interests. The idea that history is primarily an empirical subject can be used to suggest that it taps directly into the historical record and simply gives a straightforward account of it. In this way, the truthfulness of history, its status as a discipline, and its special kind of authority, are all affirmed. Furthermore, stories about what makes disciplines special help to create boundaries between related areas of activity; distinct identities are important for cognate fields because otherwise the professional lives of practitioners and the integrity of their products would be under (perceived) threat. Once there is an infrastructure that supports disciplines, lines of demarcation between forms of intellectual authority have to be actively maintained. Frontiers between disciplines are artefacts; they are human productions doing particular jobs, even if those who create and sustain them are not fully aware of it.

We can rephrase these points in the language of ownership. Disciplines mark out territories that are 'theirs', and the resulting division of labour is designed to produce different sorts of knowledge and to prevent boundary disputes. When a scholar wants to take information or ideas from another field, it can be seen as borrowing, and, if conducted correctly, with due acknowledgement, a productive transaction has taken place. From the perspective of the other, donor field, a gift has been given. The same story can, however, be told differently with history as a kind of victim, under threat from other disciplines, which are taking it over, invading it, or simply behaving as if it did not exist. Whether transfers of intellectual property are seen as gifts, theft or pillage depends on your vantage point. It would be useful if the whole

3.1 Map of the world, using a traditional projection
This is probably the picture of the world that most people who read this book will have been brought up with. It is now more widely appreciated that it is based on conventions, which have become so familiar that the total image is both natural and authoritative. Maps are always laden not only with cartographic conventions but with value systems.

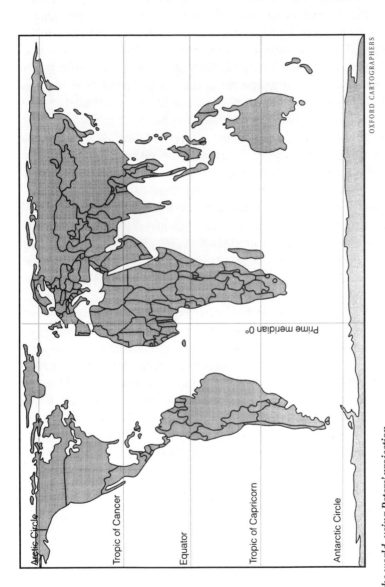

3.2 Map of the world, using Peters' projection

Here is a deliberate provocation to received pictures of the world based on a new projection system, which reflects more accurately the size of landmasses. Their distribution on the page remains conventional, however. Why should Australia and New Zealand be on the right rather than the left?

OXFORD CARTOGRAPHERS

idiom of knowledge as property, however appealing, could be critically scrutinised.

An alternative account eschews the property idiom and draws support from the facts that disciplines in general and history in particular are recent phenomena, and that history has been practised for centuries as integral to other endeavours. The sources that scholars draw on are not labelled with the name of a particular field of study: literature, history, sociology and so on. Within this framework, disciplines are recognised as constructs, the history of which is important; they are endowed, not with intrinsic, but with contingent properties. Many disciplines use materials from the past – so is there anything inherent in the materials that historians use that make them apt for history but not for sociology, for instance? If the answer is 'no', do historians have particular things they do with their materials? In so far as the question is answered in terms of specialised skills, we must defer our discussion until the last chapter. But if these particular things are understood in terms of approaches or theories, they are central to our concerns here. Unfortunately there are no clear-cut answers to these questions. The most productive way forward is to turn to four specific examples. I have chosen these fields – sociology, anthropology, philosophy and literary studies – because they have had a particularly significant impact upon the discipline of history since the Second World War. These examples inevitably reflect my particular concerns and interests. Different parts of the discipline of history have their own views and customs when it comes to affinities between fields. Many ancient historians and medievalists would put archaeology at the top of their list of cognate disciplines, and indeed the relationships between history and archaeology have been exceptionally intricate: at some points they simply merge.[8] For those concerned with the history of the environment, geography, especially new trends in historical geography have been important. In fact geographical approaches are becoming increasing central for studies of colonial and post-colonial situations.[9]

8   See the splendid chapter by Guy Halsall in M. Bentley, ed., *Companion to Historiography*, pp. 805–27. Note that this section of the book is called 'Hinterlands', a term dense with assumptions about the relationships between history and other disciplines. Also, D. P. Dymond, *Archaeology and History: A Plea for Reconciliation*, London, 1974; S. Tarlow and S. West, eds., *The Familiar Past? Archaeologies of Later Historical Britain*, London, 1999; P. Courbin, *What is Archaeology? An Essay on the Nature of Archaeological Research*, Chicago, 1988, esp. ch. 11; and, for a standard textbook, C. Renfrew and P. Bahn, *Archaeology, Theory, Methods and Practice*, second edition, London, 1996.

9   R. Butlin, *Historical Geography. Through the Gates of Space and Time*, London, 1993; L. Guelke, *Historical Understanding in Geography. An Idealist Approach*, Cambridge, 1982; M. Bell *et al.*, eds., *Geography and Imperialism 1820–1920*, Manchester, 1995.

In what follows I shall be stressing the uses historians have made of these four domains, but we should remember that such relationships are reciprocal. Other disciplines have undergone a 'historical turn'. They have their own historical concerns; after all, they were born in eras when the study of the past was not the exclusive property of one group and they continue to draw upon their own pasts for the purposes of identity construction and legitimation.

HISTORY AND SOCIOLOGY[10]

We must start with sociology as the first discipline after 1945 to have a major impact upon the study of history. Inevitably, sociology is no easier to define than is history.[11] By the mid nineteenth century, a considerable body of work existed that examined society as a distinct type of phenomenon. To look at organised aggregates of people was to undertake a particular kind of analysis, and was already recognised as such in the eighteenth century. By the end of the nineteenth century, sociology as a discipline could be said to exist and to have a number of different theoretical perspectives, which are most easily recognised by the names of the 'great men' with whom they are associated, above all Karl Marx, Herbert Spencer, Emile Durkheim and Max Weber. All of them were deeply interested in history. Thus these perspectives as they developed over the twentieth century were available to historians, and explicitly used by some of them. Social theory developed into a number of new avenues in the twentieth century, yet the self-conscious and explicit turn to it by groups of historians was particularly evident in the 1960s. After the war there was a marked interest, particularly in the United States, in modernisation theory, that is, in general accounts of how societies develop from an agricultural base in which there is relatively little division of labour into complex, modern industrial nation states.[12] This theory is inseparable from the context in which

10 See Peter Burke's volume, which, when first published in 1980, was called *Sociology and History* (London), becoming *History and Social Theory* (Ithaca, N.Y.) in 1993. In the preface to the latter he explains his thinking about 'sociology', 'social sciences' and 'social theory', pp. vii–ix. Also, C. Tilly, *As Sociology Meets History*, New York, 1981.
11 The history of sociology may be helpful here: see, for example, G. Hawthorn, *Enlightenment and Despair: A History of Sociology*, Cambridge, 1976. Cf. S. Bruce, *Sociology: A Very Short Introduction*, Oxford, 1999. See also *American Journal of Sociology* (1894), *British Journal of Sociology* (1950) and, for a journal that examines these issues from a critical perspective, *History of the Human Sciences* (1988). See also *Social Science History: The Official Journal of the Social Science History Association* (1976).
12 See A. Smith, *The Concept of Social Change: A Critique of the Functionalist Theory of Social Change*, London, 1973.

it was developed, namely the economic activities of the 'first world' in putting funds into so-called under-developed countries in order to fashion them in their own image. Thus, modernisation theory combined economic, social and political concerns. Although its teleological approach, which assumes the modern west as the goal of all historical change, has been widely criticised, aspects of modernisation theory remain deeply entrenched in historical practice, in taken-for-granted terms, such as 'tradition' and 'modernity', construed as radically different social states, in 'development' itself and in 'isation' words, such as secularisation. We should note that models of social change frequently draw upon biological accounts in general and evolutionary theories in particular, as Herbert Spencer did explicitly, and they usually assume that the bottom line of a society is its economic relations.[13] This is because material existence, catering to basic needs, is the common ground for biological as for economic survival. The continuing appeal of economic determinism is a significant point. Many comments have been made about the recent demise of Marxism, with which economic determinism is often associated, as a paradigm for historians. For those who use Marxian ideas, the claim that relations of production determine other features of a society remains central, even if it requires considerable unpacking. While it may be that the whole package we call Marxism is now wholeheartedly espoused by very few historians, many practitioners who never saw themselves in this camp, are, nonetheless, economic determinists at heart.

If we associate the enthusiasm for sociology in the 1960s with anything it is with the concept of 'class'. When we say 'class', we are in fact referring to a whole panoply of issues that are highly charged politically.[14] Historians find it difficult to agree on definitions of class; it involves a type of social difference that combines social status, income, and cultural factors, including an awareness of the dynamics between classes and of one's own class identity. In the 1960s labour relations became a central topic for sociologically informed history, together with popular protest and forms of social difference that appeared cognate to but not identical with class, above all race and gender. The term gender was not widely used then, but only became common currency among historians in the 1980s. In France the term is still resisted as an Anglo-American imposition. But women's history underwent tremendous

---

13 It is significant that an outstanding intellectual biography of Spencer was written by a practising sociologist: J. Peel, *Herbert Spencer: The Evolution of a Sociologist*, London, 1971.

14 P. Corfield, ed., *Language, History and Class*, Oxford, 1991; R. Williams, *Keywords*, pp. 60–9; and P. Joyce, ed., *Class*, Oxford, 1995.

growth in the period, some of it prompted by an interest in showing the significance of female labour to match the attention being paid to male workers. It became crucial for feminist historians to consider whether oppressive relations between men and women were basically a form of class struggle, and to assess the adequacy of theories of class to explain the history of gender relations. These concerns are 'sociological' in that they derive from the theories and methods developed by sociologists. The discipline of sociology was never homogeneous; it contained sophisticated discussions about the use and interpretation of social variables, the analysis of social structure, and the social construction of identity upon which historians drew. These discussions contained both general and specific levels of analysis, and they were frequently comparative and historical, thereby constituting a rich resource for historians working on class and on social inequalities generally. It was at this time that Eugene Genovese wrote a highly controversial Marxian account of slavery.[15] Thus a Marxian approach to society contained a number of ideas, theories and concepts that could be applied to a wide range of historical cases, as indeed Marx himself applied them.[16] In particular, the analysis of modes of production and their implications, class oppression, revolution, ideology and imperialism were taken up by historians.

The example of Marxism raises a vexed question for historians, which arises whenever they employ an already articulated theory. In sociology such a theory would be applied to a number of cases, but a sociologist would be less likely to start with the case study and then apply a mixture of theoretical devices to it, which is precisely what many historians do. Eclecticism was less prevalent in the 1960s, but nonetheless historians tend to begin with particular instances in all their complexities and then seek frameworks to help make sense of their material. When an elaborate theory is adopted in its entirety, there is a danger that it will not fit well with sources that are often patchy and uneven. The result can be a mechanistic approach to history in which two levels of analysis – theory and case study – are not adequately integrated. The lack of fit can derive from a mismatch between the language of the theory and that of the case study: for example, if the former uses class, but the latter concerns a society that deployed quite other terms of social distinction such as caste. Looked at from a sociologist's perspective, there are also problems. They

---

15 E. Genovese, *The Political Economy of Slavery*, New York, 1965; Genovese has written many other important works on slavery: for a brief assessment see Smith, *Debating Slavery*, esp. pp.16–23. See also M. Finley, *Ancient Slavery and Modern Ideology*, expanded edition, Princeton N.J., 1998.
16 See Rigby's essay on 'Marxist Historiography' in Bentley, ed., *Companion to Historiography*, pp. 889–928.

are more likely to look for the rigorous application of a theory, and to find eclecticism sloppy and intellectually unacceptable. The perception that applying social theory to historical work produces an overly rigid approach was one of the reasons for historians turning away, not just from sociology, but from a number of overtly theoretical orientations, and towards what is known in sociology as grounded theory. This is in fact what many historians do even if they do not describe it in this way. Grounded theory seeks to develop an apt framework out of the materials themselves and hence it is necessarily more pragmatic and flexible than adherence to a pre-existing theory. The dissatisfaction with a mechanistic use of theory also helps to explain the love affair between anthropology and history, to which we shall turn shortly. In order to understand this shift better, we can return to class and note changing attitudes to the concept among historians, which have taken them from a primarily economic understanding of class to a more cultural one. What historians have found especially appealing in anthropology is precisely its close attention to culture.[17]

In the Marxian tradition, class relations arise out of the modes of production and the social relationships they produce. While Marx himself thought about these relationships in highly sophisticated terms, it is fair to say that for much of the twentieth century, class has been understood as deriving from economic structures. Because of the oppositional quality of Marxian history and of the sub-fields such as labour history where it found enthusiastic expression, economic inequalities and the nature of class oppression were construed as the primary phenomena for historians to explain. Marx and some of his followers, such as the literary critics Georg Lukács and Raymond Williams, were interested in the nature of class consciousness, but many historians' reading of Marx persuaded them that this was a mere product of economic forces. However, by the 1970s, it was becoming increasingly clear to historians that class consciousness was an elaborate and messy phenomenon in its own right. The more social historians dug into the subject, the more its connections with material conditions seemed intricate, even obscure. Furthermore, there was evidence, for example from eighteenth-century England, that class consciousness preceded shifts in the labour process that had hitherto been seen

---

17   On history and anthropology see chapter 31 by J. Goodman in Bentley, ed., *Companion to Historiography*. Cf. D. Gaunt, *Memoir on History and Anthropology*, Stockholm, 1982, which surveys the relationships between history and anthropology in many countries. It should be stressed that anthropology has a number of branches, not all of which are concerned with culture. Historians have been most responsive to social and cultural anthropology.

as primary.[18] In other words, what people in the past believed about their social relationships, the metaphors through which they were expressed, and the emotional aura that surrounded them became significant historical phenomena in their own right, demanding appropriate analysis, i.e. what is styled a cultural approach. The so-called subjective elements of class identity were given increasing attention, supposedly objective indicators less.

The notion of *reducing* one historical phenomenon to another is pertinent here – it is often invoked when theories are applied to historical materials. The charge is over-simplification, that is, offering too limited a form of historical explanation. Briefly, the charge of reductionism involves recasting the type and level of phenomena from one that is complex to another that is less so: by implication, one too basic to be satisfying. Psychological explanations, especially psychoanalytic ones, are magnets for such criticism. They are often dismissed as simplistic, reductionist. In the shift from relations of production as determining social relations to class consciousness as a special phenomenon, *not* reducible to economics, the growing interest in culture was manifest, and cultural analysis has been strongly associated with anthropology. In fairness to Marxian traditions, we should record that throughout the twentieth century culturalist approaches were being developed, for instance by Antonio Gramsci, who has been important precisely for those historians on the left, such as E. P. Thompson, who explored the complexities of social identity and practice.[19] Other forms of cultural Marxism have come into the field through writers, such as Raymond Williams, who came from literary backgrounds.

ANTHROPOLOGY AND CULTURE

In fact, we can discern the shift towards cultural analysis in another problem associated with class as a concept, namely the tendency to reify it, rather than to see it as always held in relationships. When we reify something we treat it, inappropriately, as an object. The whole thrust of E. P. Thompson's famous and deeply influential Preface to *The Making of the English Working Class*, first published in 1963, was to affirm 'that class is a relationship, and not a thing'.[20]

---

18 For example, the classic article by E. P. Thompson, 'Eighteenth-Century English Society: Class Struggle without Class?', *Social History*, 3, 1978, 133–65.

19 For example, E. P. Thompson, *Customs in Common*, London, 1993, pp. 10–11. Cf. R. Williams, *Marxism and Literature*, Oxford, 1977.

20 E. P. Thompson, *The Making of the English Working Class*, Harmondsworth, 1968, p. 11. Cf. P. Joyce, ed., *Class*, Oxford, 1995.

Yet the habit of assigning individuals to classes, as we would assign animals and plants to taxonomic pigeonholes, is deeply entrenched; it is indebted to certain styles of sociology, which examine social variables and social roles, and which can generate a rather static model of human society. For this reason too, a cultural approach, which pays more attention to the complexities of human relationships, is appealing.

Like sociology, anthropology began to take shape in the nineteenth century. The serious study of other, exotic cultures had begun centuries earlier, and was given impulse by the waves of European exploration of other parts of the world, such as the 'discovery' of America, then of the South Seas, Australia and so on. The experience of co-existing with another culture was common enough, and often led to detailed accounts that could be called ethnographic. Anthropology was also pursued by scholars of the Bible, by men of the church who worked outside their own cultures, by antiquarians who collected remnants of classical and medieval cultures, by lawyers mapping diverse human arrangements and so on. Thus, in a sense what we call anthropology is a very old intellectual concern that has long been allied with history. It draws its energy from human beings' curiosity about other, different human beings, and from the scientific impulse to map human nature, which took particularly clear shape during the Enlightenment.[21] Subsequently anthropology developed in a number of directions: it has become usual to distinguish between physical, social and cultural anthropology – the last two have closer affinities with the discipline of history than does the first. Nonetheless archaeology and physical anthropology sometimes make common cause, and by that route the latter impinges upon the practice of history.[22]

Over the nineteenth century, anthropology became a self-conscious discipline, possessing strong links with both sociology and the biological sciences. In so far as it mapped exotic cultures, often figured as 'primitive', while historians were examining their own societies, the two fields diverged. The conditions for them coming back together were, from the historian's point of view, the recognition that there were significant similarities between superficially different societies and that the methods anthropologists had developed might be useful to them. The kinship between these two disciplines can be

21 R. Smith, *Fontana History of the Human Sciences*, London, 1997; C. Fox et al., eds., *Inventing Human Science: Eighteenth-Century Domains*, Berkeley, 1995. See also, G. Stocking, *The Ethnographer's Magic and Other Essays in the History of Anthropology*, Madison, Wis., 1992.
22 For example, P. Garnsey, *Food and Society in Classical Antiquity*, Cambridge, 1999.

understood as having three dimensions: the shared content of history and anthropology, common methods, and overlapping accounts of practice.

The transfer in terms of content is easy to understand: both fields analyse social phenomena. Initially the kinds of societies were seen as rather different – 'primitive' and 'civilised' – but then their similarities were increasingly recognised. Anthropologists developed a number of ideas and concepts that can be used by historians. Ritual, fetish, kinship, magic, possession, symbol, shaman and the gift relationship, would all be obvious examples where, even if the concept was not exclusive to anthropology, that field endowed them with a rich significance upon which historians could draw. Sometimes, a familiar historical pattern looks different, appears freshly clarified, when it is described in a new vocabulary. To see (some) popular protest in the early modern period as akin to ritual practised in, say, Africa, throws into sharp relief the purpose and significance of such behaviour. From having been seen as conflictual and disorderly, such forms of behaviour now appear to follow patterns, widely understood by contemporaries, and producing positive effects for all concerned.[23] This is to recast historical phenomena so that they can be viewed afresh, since if we see forms of protest as disordered and disruptive, then a quite different set of explanations will be given to those deemed appropriate for a structured and familiar ritual. Similarly, the recognition that magic is an elaborate belief system performing a wide range of social functions, rather than unfounded ideas now known to be simply wrong, enables witchcraft, astrology and alchemy, for example, to be examined more sympathetically. There is no longer any need to stress their inherent irrationality, which becomes not just irrelevant but a mistaken and anachronistic value judgement.[24]

Anthropological approaches to gifts have been particularly important for historians. To trace gift relationships in historical cases points up the reciprocity in social relationships rather than taking the notion of 'gift' in its obvious, common-sense meaning of something freely given without expectation of exchange.[25] The anthropological cast of the term encourages historians to think about where exchanges occur and how they operate within

---

23 One of the best-known historical pieces in which the influence of anthropology is visible is N. Davis, 'Women on Top' in her *Society and Culture in Early Modern France*, Stanford, 1975, pp. 124–51. Cf. L. Hunt, ed., *The New Cultural History*, Berkeley, 1989, ch. 2.

24 Keith Thomas's *Religion and the Decline of Magic: Studies in Popular Beliefs in Sixteenth- and Seventeenth-Century England*, Harmondsworth, 1973, is often taken as exemplary of this trend – it was first published in 1971.

25 Marcel Mauss's *The Gift*, London 1990, is an anthropological classic. First published in 1925, it continues to offer inspiration to historians.

wider networks of social relationships, whereas a non-anthropological definition takes gifts at face value. There are many further examples of historians taking terms and phrases from anthropological accounts and applying them to their own work, largely on non-exotic settings. Such transfers are possible because the two fields are concerned with similar phenomena. Yet this has been only one facet of the relationship between history and anthropology, and it does not really make sense without the anthropological mindset that many historians have found deeply inspiring. Integral to this mindset are methods that we think of as 'anthropological', and ways of imagining our own intellectual practices.

Before we turn to these matters more explicitly, we need to tackle the tricky issue of exoticism, a notion which carries considerable moral opprobrium. It arises because anthropology as a discipline was built on the study of 'exotic' cultures. The fear is that both anthropologists and historians draw upon and are implicated by unjustifiable relationships between imperialists and those they colonised. Finding something exotic can be understood as covering its exploitation with a veneer of glamour. Exoticism is a difficult topic, not just because it is inherently complex, but also because it has got caught up in matters of political correctness and become highly charged emotionally. The allure of what is palpably different is a widespread phenomenon; it does not seem to me that it is automatically wrong, it is simply a persistent feature of human relationships. However, there is no doubt that this allure takes on a particular significance when there are dramatic disparities in the power of the knowers and the known, whether these are nations, classes, races, sexes, ages, other kinds of groups, or, indeed, individuals. We suspect that the dominant side constructs the weaker party as an exotic other, which can then be colonised, exploited and trivialised: exoticisation is thinly-veiled domination. While there may be some truth to this, it is only a partial one, and historians need to be able to admit that they are frequently drawn to their field of study precisely because it is exotic, containing just such an allure for them. In other words, what is different and enticing is also to be studied, revered and idealised. Exoticising is one way of managing the highly troubling and disruptive reactions that cross-cultural encounters provoke – reactions which are typically both positive and negative, and much more besides.

The issue of exoticism is important because it bears on both the methods and the frame of mind adopted by those who study cultures very different to their own. No one approaches such a situation with an empty mind; there is bound to be some baggage. One of the keystones of anthropological fieldwork is the simultaneous sympathetic identification and critical distance of practitioners in relation to those they are studying. The existence of baggage is not denied, and, if possible, it is put to productive use. Anthropologists are trained to be as non-judgemental as is feasible; they should painstakingly reconstruct how and why things are done and respect logics other than their own. At the same time they need to be analytical, putting pieces together so that their account makes overall sense and will be convincing to other anthropologists. In other words they act as mediators between different worlds, seeking to do justice to the other world while speaking to their own, much as historians do. An anthropological approach, which privileges different belief and value systems from those of the observers, has enormous appeal, but it is distinctly possible that historians would not have been drawn to it without the thrill of reading about 'exotic' situations.[26] Part of the power of nuanced ethnographies is precisely the curiosity they elicit about how human beings can be so very 'other'. Such curiosity can be prurient, but it can also mobilise awe and prompt serious comparative analysis. Imagining oneself an anthropologist or a Martian can be a compelling device for viewing what is familiar with fresh eyes.

Thus, however much we may be suspicious of exoticism, it is an unavoidable feature of many disciplines, including both history and anthropology, and can be a spur to serious reflection, often of a comparative nature. Anthropology is based on such comparisons in that the payoff of long fieldwork in specific areas is a fund of insights that are compared with the findings of other practitioners. The point about comparisons is that they point up the similarities *and* the differences between societies. There have to be some likenesses for the dissimilarities to stand out and have significance. How a historian, or indeed an anthropologist, makes such comparative judgements is a complex matter, but they always require an abstract analytical framework in order to do so. For instance, a scholar already committed to the existence of shared fundamental patterns across all human societies, that is to a biological approach, will be able to find common ground far more readily than one who believes in the diversity of human behaviour, in the powerful effects of local circumstances, that is, in the primacy of culture. What is like and unlike between cultures is not a given, but is negotiated by scholars, according, among other things, to their own concerns and agendas.

26 A splendid example of these points is Clifford Geertz's famous article on Balinese cock-fights, which appeared in his *The Interpretation of Cultures*, New York, 1973, and which has wielded extraordinary influence over historians. Geertz is particularly associated with the notion of 'thick description' – detailed accounts of behaviour that serve as a starting point for deeper understanding. What we could call historians' infatuation with Geertz illustrates the influence of anthropological method and of its general mindset. See also Hunt, ed., *The New Cultural History*, ch. 3.

Earlier I suggested that anthropology, in emphasising meaning rather than social description, appealed to historians because of the importance it gave to culture. This has been implicit in everything I have said about anthropology, but it is time to be more explicit. While it would be totally misleading to imply that all anthropologists are interested in culture, it would be fair to say that, as a discipline, anthropology has paid careful attention to what goes on in people's heads. This may seem a rather bizarre definition of culture, a notoriously elusive term, but it is not a bad place to start. Culture gives priority to the ways in which our worlds are endowed with meaning.[27] This involves taking extremely seriously what people believe and why – their belief systems, worldviews, cognitive frameworks. Many generations of historians had found this relatively uninteresting, preferring to examine events and actions, to describe past phenomena and to seek causal explanations. It further involves looking carefully at the outward manifestations of cultural activity – objects and images, dance, myths, buildings and so on. These had not been much studied by traditional historians for reasons to do with pre-conceptions about 'high' and 'low' culture. A number of areas of *high* culture, such as art, architecture, poetry and music, had long been hived off as separate, specialised areas of study, and they largely remain unintegrated into general history. These fields are respected, but not understood as central to the political, economic and social processes at the heart of mainstream history. Other areas of culture, such as glassware, jewellery, pottery, tools, clothing and body decoration, were not thought appropriate for historical study; they were not 'high' culture, and were best left to archaeologists, curators, collectors and so on. Such areas commanded less respect and were seen as less intellectually demanding; they were associated with everyday life not significant achievements, and designated 'applied' rather than 'pure' arts, in a hierarchy that gave greater value to abstract and allegedly non-functional endeavours. 'Decorative' implies peripheral phenomena, which would be marginal for a field such as history that continued to emphasise political processes with big ramifications.[28]

The post-war desire to radicalise history involved taking seriously many phenomena that had previously been neglected and rejecting the frameworks that had trivialised them, which both broadened the scope of history and invited a sympathetic response to behaviour previously thought to be alien,

27 See, e.g., R. Williams, *Culture*, London, 1981; J. Bremmer and H. Roodenburg, eds., *A Cultural History of Gesture*, Cambridge, 1991; C. Ginzburg, *The Cheese and the Worms: the Cosmos of a Sixteenth-Century Miller*, Baltimore, 1980.

28 For a different approach see K. Scott, *The Rococo Interior: Decoration and Social Spaces in Early Eighteenth-Century Paris*, New Haven, 1995.

even threatening.[29] It was thus overdetermined that culture, now more broadly defined, would become a pressing concern and that historians would turn to a field – anthropology – that seemed both more all-embracing and more respectful of its objects of study than their own. At the same time, anxieties were expressed that anthropology was complicit with imperialism and colonialism. Thus 'culture' seems to do more justice to the full range of human experience, and only when given the inflection of *high* culture does it become narrow and exclusive. It emphasises what people make of the world, that is to say the construction of meaning, rather than the world itself. It was unavoidable that studies of cultural phenomena were suffused by worries about value judgements, their appropriateness and their political implications.

This discussion has indicated some of the tricky paths that anthropologists and historians travel when they make common cause, precisely because there is so much political heat generated by debates about how societies can and should know each other, and the purposes to which the resulting knowledge should be put. Sometimes anthropology inspires far more sympathetic and open engagements with the past, but at others it appears, somewhat ironically, to underwrite passing retrospective judgements on forebears and contemporaries for the quality of their relationships with other cultures. A related issue is orientalism – now used as a term of abuse, in that it implies fierce criticism of the ways in which eastern societies were studied by western ones. Unfortunately, this tends to foreclose discussion, rather than inviting deft analysis.[30]

HISTORY AND PHILOSOPHY

Anthropology is hardly the only discipline concerned with what goes on inside the head. Historians have turned to a number of fields and intellectual frame-

---

29   This can be seen in terms of the growing interest in a history of everyday life, which was already more valued in countries with a tradition of studying the history of folklore. Two examples that suggest the impact of anthropology on history are clothing and popular healing: D. Roche, *The Culture of Clothing: Dress and Fashion in the 'Ancien Régime'*, Cambridge, 1994; D. Gentilcore, *Healers and Healing in Early Modern Italy*, Manchester,1998.

30   The term orientalism is primarily associated with the literary critic Edward Said, whose book of that name appeared in 1978. Although hugely feted, the work is not without its critics: J. MacKenzie, *Orientalism: History, Theory and the Arts*, Manchester, 1995; B. Turner, *Orientalism, Postmodernism and Globalism*, London, 1994; E. Sivan, *Interpretations of Islam: Past and Present*, Princeton, 1985, ch. 5.

works to help them make sense of the human condition. So far we have noted a number of relevant terms – ideology, consciousness, belief system, culture and so on. Some major historical traditions have focused more strictly on the *intellectual* component of mental activity – the history of ideas, of political thought, and of science, to name the most obvious cases. The subject matter of all these sub-fields is inherently difficult, and sometimes requires considerable specialist knowledge. They deal with abstract thought and by virtue of that are linked with philosophy – the humanities domain most closely concerned with the nature of human cognition. Philosophy is also an academic discipline, although its reach is at once so extensive and so intellectually precise that it seems quite distinct from, say, geography or literature. The kinds of questions philosophers ask, such as 'what exists ?', 'what can we know about the world?', have been posed over many centuries, not by a specialised professional cadre, but by a range of thinking people. In this sense philosophy is a long-standing and integrated activity.

History is allied with philosophy in a number of ways. First, history studies phenomena best called philosophical: for example, when it examines the scientific revolution of the seventeenth century or contract theories of society.[31] Second, since philosophy explicates thought processes, it has a great deal to say about how historians fashion arguments, the sorts of explanations they offer, their assumptions about how the past can be known, their models of causality and so on. Indeed many historians have been deeply involved in the philosophical aspects of their field.[32] There is a third way in which history and philosophy are currently allied. Like sociology and anthropology, philosophy offers general accounts of human existence. Hegel, the early nineteenth-century German philosopher, influenced many generations of historians who conceptualised history in a Hegelian manner and searched for the development of the world-spirit.[33] In this case, an entire system of thought was constructed in which human history and its study played a major role. Integral to such a system was an account of the human mind, a model of humanity that could serve as the basis and guide for historical enquiry.

All historians without exception employ such models, although they often do so unthinkingly. There are times, however, when they actively embrace a specific model, system, or theory of human nature and apply it to their work,

31 S. Shapin, *The Scientific Revolution*, Chicago, 1996; M. Lessnoff, ed., *Social Contract Theory*, Oxford, 1990.
32 The journals *History and Theory* and *Rethinking History* (1997) bear testimony to this.
33 On Hegel, see M. A. Gillespie, *Hegel, Heidegger and the Ground of History*, Chicago, 1984.

and generally it has come from outside history. I invoke the notion of philosophy here to draw attention to the processes whereby historians turn not so much to a defined discipline, as to general accounts of humanity. Putting it this way is necessary because when historians deploy structuralism, post-structuralism, post-modernism, terms such as 'the self' and 'identity', or the ideas of authors such as Michel Foucault, Roland Barthes, and Pierre Bourdieu, they are working at a level of abstraction that is best summed up by the word 'philosophy'.[34]

Let us take the case of the hugely influential French writer, the late Michel Foucault.[35] Sometimes he is described as a historian, which is seriously misleading. Foucault did detailed historical research – evident in *I, Pierre Rivière* (1973) – but he usually suppressed much of the historical detail when he published. He had a strong interest in psychology, psychiatry and mental health issues, partly as a result of his own experiences, but that does not make him a psychologist. Nor can he properly be described as either a sociologist or a literary critic, although he wrote both on social matters and on texts. Describing him as a philosopher draws attention to his interest in human thought, in working at a highly abstract level and in encompassing diverse phenomena in his writings. Foucault's impact upon the practice of history has been phenomenal, and it can serve as an example of the influences of 'philosophy', especially in the 1980s and 1990s.

Foucault's effects upon the practice of history have taken three main forms. First, his early book *Madness and Civilization*, first published in 1961, was written at a time of unprecedented criticism of medicalisation especially in relation to mental illness. It outlined the ways in which categories of 'deviant' people had been separated out from their communities and enclosed in state-run institutions – for example, in seventeenth-century France. Foucault's work, by analysing the knowledge/power nexus, contributed to a widespread interest in medicalisation. More specifically, he drew historians' attention to the importance of psychiatry as a subject and provided a plausible overview of shifts in the naming and treatment of those designated mad over considerable periods

---

34 Foucault will be discussed below. On Barthes see S. Sontag, ed., *Barthes: Selected Writings*, London, 1982, and on Bourdieu, R. Jenkins, *Pierre Bourdieu*, London, 1992.

35 A good introduction to Foucault's writings is P. Rabinow, ed., *The Foucault Reader*, New York, 1984, although it contains nothing from *The Birth of the Clinic*, London, 1973, which has been particularly influential in the history of medicine. For commentary on Foucault, see J. Goldstein, ed., *Foucault and the Writing of History*, Cambridge, Mass., 1994; G. Gutting, ed., *The Cambridge Companion to Foucault*, Cambridge, 1994; and D. C. Hoy, ed., *Foucault: A Critical Reader*, Oxford, 1986.

of time. Many of the details of his account have been challenged by historians specialising in medicine, but it continues to hold an appeal which is not easily amenable to empirical refutation.[36]

Second, Foucault addressed the nature of human knowledge and how it has changed. In several books he charted significant shifts in science, medicine and philosophy, not in terms of great thinkers – an approach he was dismissive of, challenging the very concept of an 'author' – but in terms of 'epistemes', which are whole ways of knowing. These determine what it is possible and permissible for people to think and investigate at any given time. Epistemes are the cognitive conditions of existence under which we live. Epistemes change, although Foucault does not explain exactly how this occurs. In some brilliant analyses of events, texts and images, he showed how they embodied fundamental assumptions, and thereby appeared to offer ways into western societies that had a critical, politically radical edge. For him, what was on the surface was often not just misleading but precisely the opposite of the truth.[37]

The third area in which Foucault made an impact illustrates the point perfectly. This is the history of sexuality, which was already becoming a fashionable subject when Foucault published the first volume of his trilogy, which appeared in English in 1979. In it he argued that discourses of sexuality, from the eighteenth century onwards, recast the relationships between individuals, families, the state and related institutions, and 'experts'. This had a number of consequences: for example, 'deviant' types, such as the homosexual, were invented in what were repressive rather than permissive moves. Thus when in the nineteenth century there was a growth of interest in sex and increasing numbers of people wrote about it and discussed it, this was not a sign of permissiveness but rather of how discourses serve to manage, shape and control experience. Furthermore, 'Victorian' disapproval of discussions of sexual phenomena and anxiety about 'deviance' signalled a compulsion to attend to the nature of sexuality. In the process new subjectivities, that is fresh forms of identity, were created. Later volumes drew extensively on classical sources, and have been particularly controversial.[38]

---

36 P. Burke, ed., *Critical Essays on Michel Foucault*, Aldershot, 1992, is a convenient collection of reviews and commentaries.

37 See especially *The Archaeology of Knowledge*, London, 1972 and *The Order of Things*, London, 1970.

38 Volume 2 was entitled *The Use of Pleasure*: English edition, New York, 1985; volume 3, *The Care of the Self*, New York, 1986. A compelling critique is, J. Davidson, *Courtesans and Fishcakes. The Consuming Passions of Classical Athens*, London 1997.

What does Foucault mean by discourse? This is not an easy term to define, but we can pinpoint two significant features of it. First, it refers to cultural products not to material conditions, so that texts become the principal sources. I use the term 'text' advisedly. The notion of discourse and work that deploys it rely heavily on the study of language. Although it is sometimes claimed that anything can be treated as a text – a political demonstration, a room, a professional association – the whole approach has been shaped by a conviction of the power of the written word and of the intellectual effectiveness of theories of language to open up its capacity to structure all human experience.[39] Second, discourse implies that there is a more or less coherent worldview behind the texts, and that the ideas they express have palpable effects. The example of naming the homosexual as a permanent human type demonstrates the point, since this then became the category through which men who are erotically drawn to other men came to experience themselves and their world. According to such a classification, there are fundamentally different kinds of human beings; sexuality is not fluid but is rather an orientation over a lifetime, and homosexuality is clearly marked out as different from the norm. Hence, delineating sexual types is not an innocent scientific exercise but the exercise of power through discourse.[40] Defining otherness in contrast to oneself is precisely a form of power.

To undertake discourse analysis is to investigate the power of ideas and of the language through which they exist and in which they are expressed. Power formations are thus to be understood not in terms of elites, governments, forms of taxation and so on *per se*, but in terms of the discourses that make them possible. At first sight 'discourse' shares some features with 'ideology', which although widely used now by historians, came originally out of Marxian intellectual traditions.[41] Yet ideology presupposes the existence of opposing interests at any given historical moment; classes, or groups akin to classes, promote their specific interests through ideologies in which those interests are veiled. Ideologies are instruments of class or group domination; they are sites of conflict grounded in everyday experience. In contrast, Foucault's approach involves neither classes nor conflict and it certainly does not posit specific,

---

39 I stand by this claim despite Foucault's famous discussion of Velasquez's *Las Meninas* in *The Order of Things*, pp. 3–16.
40 As critiques of a supposedly scientific taxonomy of sexuality were formulated, new oppositional vocabularies arose, such as 'gay' and 'queer' which then entered historical practice.
41 On 'ideology', see R. Williams, *Keywords*, pp.153–7; J. Larrain, *The Concept of Ideology*, London, 1979; and F. Lentricchia and T. McLaughlin, eds., *Critical Terms for Literary Study*, second edition, Chicago, 1995, ch. 22.

socially rooted interests. Ideologies are best understood in terms of the material conditions in which they are forged, even if they bear exceedingly complex relationships to them. The study of discourses is not a first step, which
leads the historian on to consider material life; instead the primacy, the determining quality of discourses is asserted. Interest groups are not slogging it out,
by a variety of means, for power. Rather, discourses are insinuating, and individuals and groups cannot simply adopt another position, since the structures
of thought are too deeply entrenched.

Clearly both ideology and discourse are useful concepts for historians and
both have their limitations. They also have their moments in history. Scholars
turn to an idea or approach when it seems apt for that time: history's relationships with other fields and their most influential authors display just such
timely turns. This is all too clear in relation to Foucault. He began publishing
in the late 1950s, many of his most influential books were published in the
1960s and early 1970s, and most were quickly translated into English. Yet for
most of the 1970s, it was mainly historians and philosophers of science who
read them in the English-speaking world. It was not until the 1980s that a ver-
itable explosion of worldwide interest in his work occurred, led particularly by
literary critics. In the late 1990s the enthusiasm is beginning to subside. It is
extremely difficult to explain how trends get started, take hold and die away.
Nonetheless they have a great deal to do with politics in its broadest sense. It
is crucial to recognise that historiographical shifts in general, and the ones
with which this chapter is concerned in particular, are political phenomena
in two related senses. First, despite the general political conservatism of the
1980s, it was at that time that criticisms of medicine, science, technology and
imperialism really gained momentum and enjoyed wide interest not just
among specialists but in the general population. It is no coincidence, for
example, that environmental history, which touches on all these issues, developed at just this time, as environmental movements themselves were enjoying
wide support.[42] A critical analysis of dominant discourses, one which showed
their constitutive political dimensions, was appealing partly because it located
the politics in the ideas themselves, and in so doing invited a language-based
analysis. Scholars turn to intellectual resources from related disciplines, often
outside their own field, because they seem able to illuminate their immediate
preoccupations.

---

42   R. Nash, ed., *American Environmentalism. Readings in Conservation History*,
     third edition, New York, 1990, (first edition, 1968); W. Cronon, *Changes in the
     Land. Indians, Colonists, and the Ecology of New England*, New York, 1983; R.
     Grove, *Green Imperialism. Colonial Expansion, Tropical Island Edens and the
     Origins of Environmentalism 1600–1800*, Cambridge, 1995.

The second sense in which we may speak of the politics of inter-discipli-nary relationships is more narrowly professional. Given the organisation of academic life, new approaches are valued, especially if they claim to offer fresh insights, a radical slant and cutting-edge analysis. While traditional scholarship remains highly valued, there is always the burden of showing that it has not been done before. This accounts for many transfers between dis-ciplines, both in terms of content and approach, because the claims to nov-elty seem obvious and convincing. Thus, in turning to other disciplines, historians are often maximising their own power, status and prestige. The relationships between history and literature illustrate many of these complexities.

LITERATURE AND TEXTS

Let us begin by considering our terminology. I have mentioned literary *theory* and *literature*, but what about literary *history* and literary *criticism*?[43] Often we speak of these matters in terms of the country and language of the literature, thus 'French' becomes shorthand for French literature, but does not imme-diately specify any particular approach to texts. Of all these terms, 'literature' is evidently the most general; it applies to any country and leaves open which orientation to writings is adopted. Yet even such a broad and apparently neu-tral term raises important questions for the relationship between literature and history as disciplines – what counts as literature and hence as suitable for lit-erary treatment and what about aesthetic merit? Can anything written be 'lit-erature'? Assuming the concept is still relevant, how is artistic merit to be defined? It is possible to define literature in terms of its constituent genres: conventionally poetry, fiction and drama. Historians may use such sources, but rarely draw upon them as their main materials. Moreover, literary genres are always blurred around the edges, and the methods used by literary critics can easily be applied to letters, newspapers and periodicals, treatises, even government reports, in fact to any kind of writing. Perhaps, then, history should be seen as a sub-field of literary studies!

Historians of literature have long been interested in the *ideas* expressed there – the work of the American scholar, the late Marjorie Hope Nicolson,

---

43 Cf. Lentricchia and McLaughlin, eds., *Critical Terms for Literary Study*; M. H. Abrams, *A Glossary of Literary Terms*, sixth edition, Fort Worth, 1993; D. Lodge, ed., *20th Century Literary Criticism: A Reader*, London, 1972.

being an excellent example.[44] She drew on poetry to explore scientific ideas, and in *Mountain Gloom and Mountain Glory*, she charted the processes whereby mountains came to be aesthetically valued when previously they had been treated as uninteresting, even repellent excrescences. In effect she wrote literary *history* so that it was the history of ideas. In this case, the affinities between literature and history emerge through the use of (written) sources that speak to the concerns of both. Nicolson was a literary *historian* rather than a literary *critic* because she set texts firmly in context and although she analysed them, their formal properties were not her main concern, nor was their quality as literature.

Literary *criticism* implies close attention to texts and also a fine awareness of aesthetic issues. Literary *history* is a broad church: it does not have to put ideas at the forefront. Many works of literature have little to do with the history of ideas or shifts in mentalities. The lives of authors can be historically placed so that biographies of literary figures are 'history' and 'literature' at the same time.[45] Exceptionally well-written history is also, of course, a form of literature. It is easier to see this in the past: by any standards, Edward Gibbon and Jules Michelet were magnificent writers. These relationships between literature and history are of long standing, and in some forms can be traced back to classical literary and historical writings.

However, the relationships between literature and history have recently taken on quite different qualities.[46] For instance, literary critics have become increasingly interested in texts that were previously studied by historians. This is particularly evident in relation to science, medicine and the law.[47] Sources not previously thought of as within the purview of literature have now been taken under its remit. At the same time, familiar literary texts, such as novels, have been interpreted as the carriers of broad political and ideological shifts, which may therefore be traced in them. Literature is seen not as a (passive) reflection of historical change but as a significant (active) vehicle of it.[48] Indeed, literary approaches are profoundly shaping the contemporary practice of

44   M. Nicolson, *Mountain Gloom and Mountain Glory*, Ithaca, N.Y., 1959. I. Boal, 'Marjorie Nicolson and the Aesthetics of Nature', *Antipode*, 28, 1996, 304–15 is a discussion of her legacy.
45   For example, M. Holroyd, *Bernard Shaw*, 4 vols., London, 1988–92; N. Boyle, *Goethe: The Poet and the Age*, vol. 1, Oxford, 1991; H. Brogan, *The Life of Arthur Ransome*, London, 1984.
46   *New Literary History* (1969) and *Literature and History* (1975).
47   For example, M. Poovey, *Making a Social Body: British Cultural Formation, 1830–1864*, Chicago, 1995.
48   For example, N. Armstrong, *Desire and Domestic Fiction: A Political History of the Novel*, New York, 1987.

history. Some of the ways in which this has occurred have already been mentioned. One of the most far-reaching is the claim that anything can be treated as a text, hence critical methods are deemed to have exceptionally broad application. Texts are not transparent documents but elaborate creations, parts of discourses and hence implicated in the nature of power. Complex relationships between texts exist; this is known as inter-textuality. Cultural power resides not in authors but in their products, rendering it misleading to name and speak of authors, since they do not, cannot, determine or control how their products are read and used. These ideas can be a real stimulus for historians, who certainly have as much to learn from literary critics as they have from practitioners of other cognate disciplines. However, the issues raised by closer relationships between literary and historical practices remain contentious; they go right to the heart of historical practice, and, as a result, historians need to be willing and able to engage with them.

In practice many different approaches to texts are currently being adopted; historians are sometimes insufficiently attentive to the variety of approaches with which any given piece of writing may be analysed. Disciplines use each other highly selectively and in ways that are charged with significance – criticism of traditional scholarship and of political positions, claims to radicalism and so on. It was thus inevitable that what is often called 'the linguistic turn' provoked controversy. The word 'linguistic' was used because of an indebtedness to Ferdinand de Saussure, the early twentieth-century theorist of language, who insisted on the arbitrariness of the sign.[49] Words (signs) do not possess any inherent link with what they represent, hence 'table' (the word, a signifier) is an arbitrary term for the surfaces off which we eat and on which we write (the thing, the signified). This gives language a more independent existence than is generally assumed. It also means that languages, in the sense of grammars and vocabularies and of usage, are *the* embodiments of culture, offering privileged access to the past. We cannot make claims about protests, rebellions and revolutions, then, without first understanding the categories of thought through which protagonists experienced their lives, made criticisms, and sought alternatives – a point that should be well taken by practising historians. Fundamental categories are in language rather than in the physical world. However, it follows, just as inexorably, that what can be known about the past is limited.

Accordingly, texts do not offer access to what was, only to what was said about it. For example, scholars are having to recognise that there are severe limits to what we can really know about witchcraft. The sources tell us not

49   J. Culler, *Saussure*, London, 1976.

what happened but what witnesses and commentators *believed*.[50] The resulting conflicts between scholars are about the status of that 'it'. We shall return to this issue in Chapter 4, but for now we can crudely characterise the two sides of the debate: either texts are all we have and we can only do history on that basis, or there was a material world back then, to which we can get access, and claiming otherwise is a dangerous subversion of the discipline of history. Like all polarisations, this one contains distortions, and there are a number of more nuanced positions that can be adopted. Yet mentioning this simplified polarity is useful because it points up why feelings run so high on the subject. On the one hand, there is a perceived threat to the very core of the discipline of history from literary theory. On the other, historians are thought to be making epistemological claims that cannot actually be sustained. In the middle are a wide range of interpretative strategies that historians can use, many of them associated with other disciplines. I have used literary *theory* in this context deliberately. Most literary *historians* are not particularly preoccupied with theoretical issues, while a new, distinct group has grown up within literary studies that, as the saying goes, 'does theory'. This involves considering both the nature of texts in general and issues concerning their interpretation. Setting theory apart in this manner is hardly unproblematic since it is usually applied to and refined through specific cases, which are indispensable instruments of thought, as is the case in philosophy. It seems odd to detach theory from its lifeblood. What is called *literary* theory inevitably draws on other disciplines, above all philosophy in the broad sense defined above, and also more specialised domains such as linguistics and semiotics.

INTER-DISCIPLINARY HISTORY

I have suggested that, although we continue to recognise the existence of distinct disciplines – indeed we have no choice in the matter given the nature of academic institutions – many of the boundaries between them have been called into question through an array of processes that concern politics and fashion, certainly, as well as the generative transfer of materials, approaches and theories between fields. Yet such transfers, like the political imperatives that energise them, bring entailments, some of which I have mentioned in this

---

50 This does not mean that the documents are useless as evidence; rather the contrary, as distinguished recent work on witchcraft shows: for example, R. Briggs, *Witches and Neighbours: the Social and Cultural Context of European Witchcraft*, London, 1996; L. Roper, *Oedipus and the Devil: Witchcraft. Sexuality and Religion in Early Modern Europe*, London, 1994.

chapter. History is eclectic, hence the range of its debts, and the complexity of its relations with other disciplines. Sometimes these are to be understood in terms of the use of theories; indeed 'theory' can be a useful concept for clarifying relations between disciplines, yet this should not be taken to imply that in historical practice 'theory' is something special, set apart. In the business of doing history, 'theory' is a constant presence, whether acknowledged or not. And since we cannot escape it, it is better to understand, not only its role in current historical practices, but its origins, which lie in a pre-disciplinary past.

One final step we can take in thinking about history and other disciplines is to examine the notion of 'inter-disciplinary history'. There is a certain ambiguity surrounding what is meant by 'inter-disciplinary' – is it about exchanges between fields that remain distinct or a rather more intimate blending of domains with already blurred edges? The idea of inter-disciplinary *history* is sufficiently established to have its own journal, founded in 1970 and published in the United States. Its many thematic issues have helped define the parameters of these debates. The phrase 'inter-disciplinary history' implies continued allegiance to a discipline combined with openness to other perspectives. We can usefully turn to a specific example. In 1986, there was a special issue on history and art history, which appeared in book form two years later: *Art and History: Images and their Meaning*. The very title indicates something of the framework within which the book is working. For example, 'images' tends to imply two-dimensional representations, but what about three-dimensional objects? Many historians, following the inspirational work of Michael Baxandall and Svetlana Alpers, now use the term 'visual culture' to signal their interest in studying whatever a given culture throws up, rather than restricting themselves to 'Art', which implies aesthetic value judgements.[51] A further step would be to invoke 'material culture', which implies an inter-disciplinary approach to objects.[52] The 12 papers in *Art and History* largely con-

---

51 See for example, M. Baxandall, *Painting and Experience in Fifteenth-Century Italy*, revised edition, Oxford, 1988, and *The Limewood Sculptors of Renaissance Germany*, New Haven, 1980. The special issue of *Art History*, 21 no. 4, 1998, dedicated to Michael Baxandall, is illuminating. S. Alpers, *The Art of Describing*, Chicago, 1983 and *Rembrandt's Enterprise: The Studio and the Market*, Chicago, 1988. It should be emphasised that Baxandall and Alpers work on 'high' art, placing it in a rich historical context. For different approaches, see D. Donald, *The Age of Caricature: Satirical Prints in the Reign of George III*, New Haven, 1996 and M. Pointon, *Strategies for Showing: Women, Possession and Representation in English Visual Culture 1665–1800*, Oxford, 1997.

52 Cf. *Journal of Material Culture* (1996); S. Lubar and W. Kingery, eds., *History from Things: Essays on Material Culture*, Washington, 1993; S. Pierce, ed., *Experiencing Material Culture in the Western World*, London, 1997.

cern images, although several do examine architectural materials. None relates to the applied or decorative arts, or to sculpture. They are diverse case studies, mainly by scholars who are *either* historians *or* art historians. Although the brief introduction makes encouraging noises about the need to draw history and art history closer together, the book remains a set of disparate studies. Inter-disciplinarity in this case is a goal that remains to be fully conceptualised and brought to fulfilment.

In many countries the divisions between history and art history run deep. In the USA by contrast, where a significant number of the major universities have large and diverse history departments, scholars, admittedly in small numbers, are employed who are equally at home in both fields.[53] And yet even there the vast majority of those who use art-historical evidence remain concerned with major figures, that is with artists and architects who are within the canon. The notion of a canon, which defines who are the most important figures worthy of study and, by that token, lineages of cultural achievement, has been under attack in recent years. It was strenuously argued, for example, that in both literature and art, women were largely excluded from the canon. While this was certainly true, with a few honourable exceptions that served to confirm broad assumptions about gender differences, the result of such critiques was not an overturning of the very idea of a canon, but adjustments to its membership criteria. Inevitably the value of canons in and of themselves has also been equally strenuously affirmed, largely by conservative critics.[54] In history we do not really have canons, partly because creative individuals are not at the core of the subject and partly because aesthetic quality is not a major concern of the discipline. There is a rough equivalent in the range of topics that, by common consent, form the core of the field. Thus, even if in recent years we have seen the growth of the history of sport and the history of animals, most historians would see these as extras rather than as constitutive of the subject. In these examples the subject matter has not come from other disciplines. By contrast, we might say that, in the case of 'Art with a capital A', the subject matter is already 'owned' by another field, and that it possesses a sufficient measure of internal complexity to require specialist knowledge. The specific type of internal complexity possessed by art is part of its cultural prestige. For this, as well as other reasons, many general historians would never think of trespassing into the area and are actually rather

---

53   For example, Debra Silverman: see her *Art Nouveau in Fin-de-Siècle France: Politics, Psychology and Style*, Berkeley, 1989.

54   Cf. H. Bloom, *The Western Canon: The Books and School of the Ages*, London, 1994, on the western literary canon.

afraid of images – an alien category of evidence for those used to words, the primacy of which is constantly affirmed in academic life. Yet if we think in terms of 'visual culture' or 'material culture' instead of 'Art', the situation looks rather different, and the way is open for a more flexible blending of disciplines. Visual culture implies, for example, both that the variety of cultural forms around at a given moment should be considered and that traditional assessments of aesthetic quality need not be the primary consideration when selecting sources to study. Visual culture, like material culture, is a more *historical* category than 'Art'.

BRIDGE

In this chapter we have explored the relationships between the discipline of history and some of the fields with which it interacts. They reveal a great deal about historical practice. This is hardly surprising given, for instance, the fact that the past is not divided up rationally for scholarly convenience. We impose divisions upon it in a variety of ways, all of which are expressions of our own priorities and values. What is generally called 'history' is closely connected to other scholarly practices, although the details of these connections change markedly over time and according to the historical specialism in question.

Many of the richest sources for historians are studied by cognate fields. In looking at the history of popular culture, for example, there is possibly more visual material than anything else – a visual culture perspective sees this as integral to the historical situation and proposes that it should be acknowledged and fully analysed in resulting accounts.[55] Visual culture is inclusive, for example, by including items accessible to the non-literate. So we are not talking of 'Art' here. Historians can and should draw on diverse ways of approaching visual material, rather than simply on traditional art history. Their orientation to such material should not be connoisseurial, that is, preoccupied with attribution, value and artistic quality, but rather what we could call integrative. Nonetheless, there is always a danger of historians treating visual sources as transparent documents offering windows onto other times. We will need to examine the whole concept of the document in more detail in the next chapter. The point is that, just like other sources, images and objects possess many layers of meaning; they do not give direct access to the past, but contain their own logics, and hence require careful interpretation.

---

55 For example, R. Scribner, *For the Sake of Simple Folk: Popular Propaganda for the German Reformation*, Oxford, 1981.

Thus, one of the advantages of separate fields is the possibility of careful reflection upon the special sources and problems of each one. Primary materials come in many different forms, and the specialist ways that have been developed, sometimes over centuries, for their interpretation demand consideration by those in other disciplines. The boundaries around disciplines may be constructions, but that does not mean they are trivial or to be ignored. Historians can learn much from other disciplines, but in order to do so they have to know something of their *modus operandi*, and that in turn involves appreciating their history. They cannot afford to be ignorant of the issues and approaches of related areas; they need to appreciate the variety of possible relationships between disciplines. One payoff is a sharper appreciation of what is distinctive about their own.

HISTORY CHALLENGED

The whole basis upon which disciplines operate in institutions of higher education in the twentieth century lends intellectual authority to their products. What does this authority consist of? What underpins it? In what ways, if any, is historical knowledge special? One account goes something like this. Historians produce knowledge of the past, which draws its authority from a number of sources. These include the meticulous study of a wide range of primary materials, the evaluation of results by a range of experts, the provision of transparent scholarly apparatus so that claims can be checked by other scholars, specialised training in approaches and techniques, and the careful scrutiny of references and qualifications when university appointments are made. When it comes to publication, refereeing guarantees quality. The evidence historians use indicates what happened, and thus historical knowledge offers a kind of objectivity and in this respect is unlike, say, literary criticism where a significant element of subjectivity is involved. While historians cannot predict the future, they can explain the past, which involves showing why things happened. Some areas of history, such as cliometrics, are more 'scientific' than others, and the goal of the discipline as a whole is recounting what really happened.

Over the last 20 years virtually every aspect of this account has been energetically challenged, and like most forms of knowledge, history has been subject to critical scrutiny. Earlier chapters mentioned some of the trends that have brought increased scepticism about knowledge claims in general. The critique of *historical* knowledge is especially significant for a number of reasons. It constitutes a major element of collective identity, for example, for nations, occupations, organisations and classes. It is the base upon which the policies of governments and institutions are constructed. The past is frequently appealed to in support of current decisions, most obviously by governments, leaders and political parties, so to take away the certainties promised by history has broad ramifications. Historical knowledge is a prop for individuals as for groups. Yet, despite the fierce attacks on historians' claims to really know the past, the manipulative use of historical arguments in public life goes largely unchallenged. Unsubstantiated claims, which need to be distinguished from 'historical knowledge' are widely bandied about. In academic circles, attacks upon the status of historical knowledge have come largely from other humanities disciplines, which insist on the interested nature of all knowledge. Since historians set store by the quality of their knowledge, such attacks appear especially threatening. It is neither responsible nor right for historians to shrug and accept that it is all just a matter of opinion – if they did, what would set history apart from other fields, from journalism, from casual claims about the past? The discipline of history *is* important, precisely for the reasons I have listed, so it matters what accounts are given of the past, and there is a need to feel confident about their reliability.   Mistaken claims need to be challenged.[1]

STANDARDS AND QUALITY

In this chapter I examine some of the ways in which it is possible to think about the quality of historical knowledge and the arguments that are available concerning its assessment. It will be necessary to consider the concepts – truth, objectivity, knowledge, evidence and so on – that are an indispensable part of such reflections. But first, an observation. When assessments are made of the quality of knowledge, where do the standards for making such a judgement come from? There are two possibilities. Either the standard comes from *outside* history, from types of knowledge that are regarded as particularly secure, or it is specific to the discipline of history itself, which offers knowledge distinctive enough to generate its own standards. In the first case historians will be looking, generally nervously, at highly authoritative knowledge forms, that is, at the natural sciences. This is not a new issue: ever since producers of natural knowledge started to claim in a vigorous and coordinated fashion in the seventeenth century that they were setting new standards of

1   I have in mind especially scares about rising crime and child abuse, which are rarely based on the meticulous evaluation of historical evidence. This would involve, for instance, assessing changes in record-keeping and analysing the intricate relationships between occurrence, prosecutions and convictions.
2   For two very different approaches to truth, see S. Shapin, *A Social History of Truth: Civility and Science in Seventeenth-Century England*, Chicago, 1994, and F. Fernandez-Armesto, *Truth: A History*, London, 1997. O. Handlin, *Truth in History*, Cambridge, Mass., 1979, is less about the concept 'truth' than about historical practice in the USA over the previous 50 years.

reliability and truth, others have felt compelled to emulate them.[2] It is only relatively recently that more historians have claimed that the natural sciences fail
to provide suitable criteria for their field.[3] There are considerable advantages
to being able to assert that, in its way, history is as safe, epistemologically
speaking, as science. It certainly assists in claims to prestige and to the disinterested nature of the subject, since knowledge of such high quality is
deemed the very opposite of both ideology and opinion. The sciences themselves have been subjected to strong critiques, according to which their claims
to authority and objectivity are flawed. Nonetheless, especially in the popular
imagination, the relationship between science and truth is felt to be close, and
this spills over into the general assumptions made about models of reliable
knowledge. In academic circles, where many people naturally enough respect
the truth claims made by scientists, there is widespread confidence in science
as a paradigm of knowledge. The alternative, and one I shall argue for in this
chapter, is to set standards of reliability from *within* the discipline to take
account of its distinctive qualities – we do not study nature experimentally, but
past human societies, over which we have no control.

TRUTH AND RELIABILITY

Even in the remarks I have just made, I have shifted the grounds of the argument somewhat from an emphasis on truth to one on reliability. We must now
turn to the concept of truth and consider its relevance for the practice of history. What do we mean by truth?[4] One aspect of any answer must be the
highest possible levels of accuracy and precision. Dictionary definitions of
'true' stress fact, reality, exactitude and faithfulness. There are historical phenomena, such as military manoeuvres and government procedures, where it
is possible to give accounts that would satisfy most commentators in terms
of their precision and accuracy. We will come to the complexities of sources
as evidence shortly, but it is not particularly contentious to claim that, with
careful research, narratives can be produced, of some aspects of the past, the
adequacy of which can be satisfactorily judged. In this sense they may be
deemed 'true'. Yet truth also carries connotations of completeness, of an

---

3 There have long been some historians who were sceptical of the suitability of
   the natural sciences to provide epistemological paradigms for their field, e.g.
   R. Collingwood, *The Idea of History*, Oxford, 1946.
4 Fernandez-Armesto distinguishes between four ways in which truth has been
   understood: 'the truth you feel', 'the truth you are told', 'the truth of reason',
   and 'the truth you perceive through your senses'.

account that is, by any standards, *absolutely* satisfactory. It is hard to imagine how historical, or indeed any other type of writing, could fulfil such stringent criteria, which imply a distant, all-encompassing overview and tests capable of verifying its privileged status. At one level, this is simply unrealistic – how is it possible for historical work to achieve so much? At another level, it appears misguided because hubristic, aspiring to a quasi-divine omniscience that is simply not available to mortals. It is healthy to acknowledge the provisional nature of our knowledge. However, it does not then follow that the quality of historical knowledge is unimportant, only that the concept 'truth' does not seem terribly productive.

Similar arguments can be mounted in relation to objectivity. The very term implies impartial, disinterested perspectives, which we know to be chimeras, simply not attainable, especially in a subject where evaluation and interpretation are central skills. One problem with the term 'objectivity' is that it is too cut and dried, and hence unhelpful because it implies the existence of vantage points that are absolutely without bias. Although we now recognise such vantage points to be unattainable, the commitment to weighing up and considering carefully a wide range of evidence is nonetheless a valuable one, in fact, it is central to the practice of history. The opposite of objective is subjective, which can carry pejorative connotations.[5] It implies not just one person's views, tinged with emotion, but a partial, insubstantial perspective that is not to be trusted. The common polarisation of objectivity and subjectivity is unfortunate, giving too much trust to the former and too little to the latter. It could just as well be argued that objectivity is faulty because it is cold and detached, whereas subjectivity is more warmly, honestly human. The historian's path lies somewhere in between: it combines open recognition that we are interested parties in our studies with a clear sense of how to make the resulting knowledge as judicious as possible. My stress on reliable rather than on objective, truthful knowledge is thus intended to be realistic and honest. Historians should not promise what they cannot deliver. We therefore need to be clear about what they *can* deliver.

WAYS OF KNOWING

Perhaps part of the problem concerns 'knowledge' itself. The use of a single term in relation to a wide range of disciplines does rather suggest that

---

5   See Williams, *Keywords*, pp. 308–12 for the tortuous history of 'subjective' in English.

comparability between them exists. Instead of ranging fields on a single scale according to the quality of the knowledge they produce, it might be better to think of each one as possessing a different combination of ways of knowing. In other words, perhaps we need to think about knowledge*s*. After all, it is immediately apparent that 'knowledge' has a variety of meanings, including awareness, information, understanding, insight, explanation and wisdom, and that these involve distinct relationships between knowers and known. There is a world of difference between 'information', which makes us think of data and facts, and 'understanding', which implies a deep grasp of processes and events in the past. The latter term thus implies the capacity for abstract analysis, which the former does not. Furthermore, 'insight', 'wisdom' and 'understanding' also suggest an ability to empathise with historical actors and to build up a sense of what motivated them. It is inevitable that there should be no consensus on the desirable balance between these forms of knowledge within historical practice. Strong identification with people in the past is regarded by some as suspect, because it implies an emotional commitment that clouds the ability to make judgements, while for others it is a political necessity because it allows previously neglected viewpoints to be heard sympathetically.

It is commonplace to recognise that we know things with varying degrees of certainty. (I am not speaking here of ranking entire fields on a scale, but of pieces of information.) When it comes to human behaviour, the difficulty of achieving high levels of certainty is hardly a secret. Take the obvious example of lying. People lie rather frequently; sometimes they are aware of it, at others not. It is quite difficult to prove that someone has lied – legal processes would be considerably easier if lying were amenable to clear demonstration. All scrupulous historians realise that evidence may be deceptive and endeavour to incorporate appropriate forms of awareness into their practices. The strength of historical arguments will depend on the available evidence – its nature, quality and quantity – and hence, in thinking about the status of historical knowledge, the complexities of sources and their interpretation is a central question. I am suggesting that there is nothing particularly arcane about these points, hence my emphasis on common sense as a guide. Of course people can and must be trained to think critically, but this is to refine techniques that are actually part of everyday life. The point is perfectly obvious if we consider for a moment the ideas of reliability and trust. How do you decide whether someone or something, is reliable? Consistency is clearly vital; if a person makes ten claims all of which turn out to be corroborated by other evidence, this is a high level of consistency and reliability. Let us suppose another person has a much lower success rate and that it is necessary to choose between conflicting accounts given by these two individuals, the former will seem a much better bet. There is, of course, no guarantee that this time they are still being reliable, but it seems an inherently more plausible assumption. The more independent witnesses corroborate that account, the more reliable it will be deemed. This is why one of the central parts of the historian's craft is searching for and then evaluating a variety of accounts and diverse types of evidence.

I could have expressed this argument in terms of truth, but precisely because the term suggests a final, complete account, it is somewhat misleading, unless 'true' is always in inverted commas, which is rather irritating for readers. The significant issue is, rather, trust, which can be established in a variety of ways. In the end, however, the decision whether to trust an individual, an institution, a source or a historical account depends on weighing up a number of factors and making a final judgement based on previous experience, political preferences and so on. Such judgements, by their very nature, have an emotional component. Hence, competing accounts of the French Revolution cannot simply be evaluated according to purely rational criteria. The historian's assessment of them will necessarily depend on such issues as whether they are predisposed to be critical of the *ancien régime* or sympathetic to the difficulties of the French monarchy, to see class as at the root of the political turmoil, to consider the revolution a progressive process, the harbinger of the modern order, or an eruption of unnecessary brutality. These are competing views with a strong moral component; nonetheless each can be argued for more or less convincingly, with evidence that is more or less impressive. In making a final judgement on a historical account, the degree of trust it elicits in us is crucial.

I have just referred to evidence and also to sources as if the two were more or less the same thing, but these words do carry distinct connotations. Sources are simply 'raw' materials of whatever kind. They have the *potential* to bear on a historical problem, but it is always necessary to show precisely how they do so. To call something evidence implies that the case for its relevance has been made – evidence bears witness to an issue. In a sense evidence is a philosophical concept – if I ask for evidence of something, I have a set of logical problems in mind, to which this thing we call 'evidence' will speak. The use of evidence in legal settings may be a useful analogy. In an adversarial system each side has to provide the evidence it finds most compelling to the case in question, and the jury has to weight it all up, just as historians do. The fact that a significant proportion of criminal convictions are found to be 'unsafe' vividly illustrates how extremely complex the whole process is. As a concept, 'evidence' draws attention to the need to demonstrate points in a manner that will be convincing to the relevant community of belief. A discipline is indeed a community of belief – assumptions about adequate knowledge are negotiated socially, and, as a result, criteria of judgement emerge that vary with time, place and circumstance; accordingly, the nature and status of historical knowledge cannot be constants.

There is a further concept we can consider in relation to the reliability of history – the document. Some historians are very fond of stressing the centrality of documents in making any case about the past. What is meant by document, the noun? It means a special kind of primary source with a direct relationship to what is being studied. Certificates of birth, marriage or death, passports and visas, transcriptions of legal proceedings, letters, telegrams would all be examples. I have chosen them precisely because they seem strongly factual, especially reliable, uncontentious in their documentary status. To document means to make a record of and, by implication, to generate an authoritative, authentic account. Hence one sense of 'documentary', when used of films, television programmes and photographs. In fact, such records are hardly unmediated; they necessarily pass through human agents, who select, alter and make mistakes, that is, they transform and translate. They may also deceive. Inevitably some documents are more reliable, less overtly mediated than others, but all, by their very nature, are, nonetheless, mediations. Yet despite our *intellectual* understanding of their limitations, we continue to place special trust in some categories of documents, to have faith in sources that appear authentic. It may be that habits of wanting, even needing to believe in the possibility of true historical stories run exceedingly deep. It may also be that a pervasive scepticism about the nature of all sources goes against the grain, that it is destabilising to recognise just how little from the past can be recovered. A more critical view of what it is possible for historians to know has generated anxieties among many practitioners, and these should be viewed sympathetically. Criticism does unsettle. On the other hand, fears prompted by a critical vantage point should not be allowed to spiral into claims that the entire discipline is being threatened by sceptical approaches to knowledge. It is preferable to recognise, and calmly engage with, the complexities and tensions that much thinking about the nature of history has thrown up in the last ten years, and then to see where the genuine strengths of the discipline lie.

The epistemological complexities of history can be more sharply focused if we return to the notions 'document' and 'documentary'. I mentioned that one meaning of these words stressed reliable, solid records. But there is another, equally revealing, meaning – personal testimony. Within documentary film movements, for example, there has been an emphasis on providing an accurate record, but this is not incompatible with an equally notable point – their commitment to expressing the individual perspectives of both subjects and film makers.[6] Indeed much documentary work sought to give voice to those, generally outside established elites, who were able to speak to the nature of daily life in a particularly compelling manner. There is a concept that joins these two apparently divergent meanings – authenticity. The two meanings of 'documentary' are simply two facets of what is meant by 'authentic' – genuine and personal. Authenticity is a highly problematic category in historical practice and it is right that we offer a critique of it, noting how, even in apparently politically sophisticated work, it is not only present, but traded upon, sometimes in quite emotionally manipulative ways. Authenticity can imply truth claims that are rooted in the emotions, especially those connected with suffering, and not fully amenable to reasoned argument or critical evaluation. This was often a feature of women's history, and in oral history it is also evident. The use of slave narratives would be a further example, where we feel that an especially vibrant source has been tapped into, offering a fresh, previously marginal and emotionally powerful set of voices.[7] Similar issues arise in relation to the Holocaust.[8] I share those emotional responses even as I am aware that we need to subject them to scrutiny. Claims to authenticity are problematic because they grant privileges on emotional grounds. The first-hand testimonies of the marginal, for instance, may indeed be inspiring and fresh, but memory is a notoriously treacherous faculty. Hence it is vital to be clear about what such accounts can and cannot reveal and to avoid unthinking sentimentality.

Let us consider a specific example. During the inter-war period in the United States, there was a huge growth of interest in documentary techniques, much of it sponsored and funded by the government. The activities of the Farm Security Administration in commissioning photographs of the conditions of poor white southern farmers is a case in point.[9] Indeed these poignant

6   See, for example, W. Stott, *Documentary Expression and Thirties America*, New York, 1973.

7   P. Curtin, ed., *Africa Remembered: Narratives by West Africans from the Era of the Slave Trade*, Madison, 1967, is an interesting collection. The interest in the subjectivities of slavery has been greatly encouraged by literary works, e.g. Toni Morrison, *Beloved*, London, 1987.

8   For me, by far the most compelling account of the trickiness of memories and records of the Holocaust is Bernard Schlink's novel *The Reader* , London, 1997, first published in Zurich in 1995 as *Der Vorleser*. See also, C. Browning, 'German Memory, Judicial Interrogation, and Historical Reconstruction: Writing Perpetrator History from Postwar Testimony', in S. Friedländer, ed., *Probing the Limits of Representation: Nazism and the 'Final Solution'*, Cambridge, Mass., 1992, pp. 22–36.

9   On the Farm Security Administration see S. Baldwin, *Poverty and Politics: The Rise and Decline of the Farm Security Administration*, Chapel Hill, N.C., 1968.

photographs, like John Steinbeck's novel *The Grapes of Wrath* (1939, and the widely acclaimed film, 1940), have become emblematic of the time and are frequently used by historians as 'documents'. Although not funded by the FSA, the controversial book by James Agee and Walker Evans, *Let Us Now Praise Famous Men* (1941), was part of this trend and Walker Evans' extraordinary

PHOTO: LIBRARY OF CONGRESS

4.1 *Bud Fields and his family at home, Alabama, 1936, by Walker Evans*
This poignant image neatly illustrates the pleasures and pitfalls of documentary photography. It is visually compelling partly because we recognise the family group from many pictures we have seen previously. The textures of materials and the facial expressions are gripping. But Walker Evans's photograph is also shocking in the grinding poverty it depicts and in the child's nudity. It certainly can be treated as a document, as just about anything can be, if and only if it is carefully interpreted using as wide a range as possible of related materials. It emphatically does not speak for itself – nothing does.

pictures have been widely used by historians. Evans' photographs are amazing because, like Agee, he identified so strongly with the poor whites with whom they lived for several months. Furthermore, unlike some contemporary documentary photographers, Evans (he claims) did not pose his subjects, but encouraged them to pose themselves. The results are intensely moving because they seem to give, simultaneously, a noble and a bleak view of their subjects' lives. Nonetheless, we should be sceptical about what we can 'know' as a result of such documentary activities. Photographs, for instance, can be printed in many different ways, clipped, altered in size, given various titles or none, all of which affect their emotional impact. Moreover, given that they are intensely personal, what generalised insights can be derived from them is unclear. And yet, they *do* convey something extremely significant at an emotional level, so much so that 'the depression' and some kinds of documentary photography have become virtually synonymous.[10]

I am suggesting that there are many ways of knowing; sometimes they become so entangled that it is difficult to be clear about the epistemological claims involved. I have evoked these diverse ways by referring to notions, such as information, insight, explanation, understanding and wisdom, that are all linked to knowledge in some way. Whereas gathering information implies collecting and organising data, wisdom implies the accumulation of human experience and the ability to discern and comprehend its main patterns. Disciplines vary in the value they give to these different forms of knowing. What makes the status of historical knowledge a particularly complex matter is that it is a subtle blend of all these ways. Hence, we should always be suspicious of simple formulae and blanket definitions, and accept that taste plays a part in the history we think is 'good' and 'bad'. However, just because there is an element of taste does not mean that no general criteria of judgement exist.

EVALUATING HISTORICAL WRITINGS: SOURCES

Criteria for judging the adequacy of historical writings relate to three aspects of the discipline: the use and interpretation of sources; the aptness and

10 On Walker Evans, see J. Thompson, *Walker Evans at Work*, New York, 1982; on the depression, A. Badger, *The New Deal: the Depression Years, 1933–40*, Basingstoke, 1989 and R. McElvaine, *The Great Depression: America, 1929–1941*, New York, 1984. See also J. Tagg, *The Burden of Representation*, Basingstoke, 1988; G. Clarke, *The Photograph*, Oxford, 1997, ch. 8. *Robert Capa: Photographs*, New York, 1996, is useful for thinking about documentary photography and received understandings of historical events.

effectiveness of conceptual frameworks; the quality of the writing itself. In the first case we should always run a checklist in order to assess the ways in which sources have been used, although we need to bear in mind that 'sources' is an inherently heterogeneous category, hence the checklist has to be flexible. The most basic sub-division is between primary and secondary sources, which, although it appears simple, can be quite blurred, as we have already noted. To recap briefly, 'primary' source covers all original documents produced at the time one is studying, and the implication is that these bear direct witness to the events, people, processes and so on of that moment. Furthermore, 'primary' implies that it has not gone through the head and hands of another historian. A crude definition of secondary sources would be that they are the writings of other scholars, not necessarily historians, but anyone who has commented upon a historical situation, possibly using primary sources, without being a participant in it. However, a moment's reflection reveals that such definitions are treacherous. What is a primary source for one project might be a secondary one for another, and vice versa. Journalism is a good example of the point – as commentary it could be considered a secondary source; it would become a primary source for those studying the history of the media. Two implications follow: the status of sources changes according to the research project in question, and the primary/secondary distinction is less important than an overall assessment of the source's relevance to a given project and of how well it is used. In both cases the mode of production of any given sources requires scrutiny. In other words, we should not fetishise 'primary' sources, but seek whatever is helpful. Having located the sources that are particularly valuable for a given project and acquired a clear sense of why, historians then find that using a variety of sources will generate more powerful insights than using only one type.

The writing of biographies neatly illustrates these points. In writing a *general* biography, if the subject published extensively, it would be essential to look at their unpublished work too, and especially at intimate records, such as letters and diaries, as well as at comments by a variety of friends, acquaintances, colleagues, relations and so on. Yet, for a study of an individual's *public image*, their reputation, journalism and other representations of them would become privileged sources; what people said and did in private would be less relevant except in so far as it shaped public perceptions of them. An *intellectual* biography would place more emphasis on education, institutions, networks and achievements, thereby drawing upon distinctive sets of sources. A *popular* biography would be judged rather differently, and would draw on sources that recounted stories in the individual's life that made for good reading and historical 'colour'.

Judging which sources are relevant to a specific piece of research is quite an art, and often outstanding work derives from an imaginative use of sources that are at first sight oblique. So, of any piece of historical writing we need to ask, what sources have been used, how have they been selected, have they been used in their entirety or only in part, have they been interpreted in a plausible manner, is the result derivative or original? Have the limitations and specificities of sources been taken account of? These questions immediately suggest the need for a context in which to evaluate any piece of history. How is it possible to answer these questions unless we have other pieces for comparison? Hence the use of secondary sources is as vital as primary ones. Is the author aware of relevant work by other historians? Deciding what is 'relevant' is never straightforward. Have authors taken account of recent ideas and do they acknowledge their debts both responsibly and in sufficient detail? Many of these questions are answered through the careful scrutiny of footnotes, which should be seen as just as dense and interesting as the main text.[11] Usually they indicate not just sources of information but the author's approach, theoretical debts and intellectual lineage.

THE CHIMERA OF COMPREHENSIVENESS

It may be helpful at this point to make explicit an issue that is always lurking around the question of the use and selection of sources. There is a widespread fantasy among historians and their readers concerning comprehensiveness. Thus, if writing on an individual, the author is expected to read 'everything' about them. It is best to be blunt and state that in some, even many cases, this is just impossible. And if we take more wide-ranging subjects, the point is even clearer. And yet, the thought of having missed something generates an anxiety commonly experienced by professional historians. We want, indeed are expected, to exhibit a kind of mastery of our fields and of our chosen topics. We constantly worry about missing something. Such fears need to be probed. The goal of completeness is simply impractical, especially since, as the world of scholarship expands, there is more and more to read. Distinctions need to be made between new information and new interpretations, and between writings that are likely to change a research project and those that are not. With the development of the internet the problem has got far worse, and this is not just because of the volume of materials made available, but because it is increasingly difficult, especially for students, to evaluate their *quality*.

11   Cf. A. Grafton, *The Footnote: A Curious History*, Cambridge, Mass., 1997.

The only ways forward are through careful selection, through being thoughtful and open about the criteria of selection, and through traditional forms of evaluation. By 'traditional' I mean those techniques associated with the practices of scholarly footnotes, which embody quality controls that are indispensable in academic life. Unfortunately even this is only a partial solution, since the growth in the amount published means that scholars are likely to find works in footnotes with which they are unfamiliar and it is simply not practical to check every item in every footnote one reads. In any case the languages historians have at their command are always a limiting factor. Nonetheless the principles hold good. They rest on making one's sources and procedures open to the scrutiny of others, and on drawing upon other work of proven quality. The goal of reading and working comprehensively is, in one sense, worthy; it implies a seriousness of purpose that helps to raise the quality of historical knowledge. But because comprehensiveness can be so hard, if not impossible, to attain, it can also become a crippling ideal. There are what could be called 'last word' books – books so comprehensive and thorough that they command special respect.[12] To produce such a volume requires a huge investment of time, which even dedicated scholars may be unable or unwilling to give. It follows that the quality of historical knowledge cannot be judged by absolute criteria, but must be evaluated in terms of the goals, selections and so on operative in any given piece of writing. Critics are naturally entitled to debate the wider value of these goals and of the forms of selection they dictate.

ASSESSING FRAMEWORKS

To turn to the second set of criteria for judging the adequacy of historical writings, it should be apparent that the questions around conceptual frameworks and those around sources are intertwined. Generally, the conceptual framework chosen exercises a large measure of influence over the sources used and vice versa. A harmonious fit between framework and materials is crucial. Have the key concepts in the framework been adequately explained and their use justified? It is helpful if authors explain why they have chosen one framework rather than other, and what the strengths and shortcomings of competing

12 This is not to say such works are uncontroversial. See, for example, C. Webster, *The Great Instauration: Science, Medicine and Reform 1626–1660*, London, 1975; J. Gage, *Colour and Culture: Practice and Meaning from Antiquity to Abstraction*, London, 1993; I. Kershaw, *Hitler 1889–1936: Hubris*, London, 1998.

frameworks are. To a degree, the framework will depend on the historical genre involved, since we evaluate various types of academic writing rather differently. For instance, in the standard journal article, where there are severe constraints on length and the expectation of original research, it is necessary to launch straight in by setting up the historical problem to be addressed swiftly and deftly. Clarity of focus is paramount. The audiences for journals differ from those for books; imagined readerships shape all academic writing. Thus, the status of a piece of historical knowledge is bound up with the type of writing through which it is expressed, that is, with both genre and implied audience. If a framework is particularly distinctive and up front, then the status of the piece in which it is used will usually be linked to the esteem in which the framework itself is held. Hence a 'straight' Marxian article would now be viewed with considerably more scepticism than it would have been 20 years ago, because the framework itself is thought to be, if not exactly obsolete, at least blunted in its critical capacities. The evaluation of historical work is all too frequently coloured by reactions to what are essentially intellectual fashions. By contrast with Marxism, psychoanalysis has enjoyed a huge increase in its intellectual status over the last two decades. To be sure there are a number of forms of psychoanalytic theory as well as highly diverse ways of applying it to the past, which should not all be lumped together, and its whole basis has been passionately criticised; nonetheless, it is widely valued. Thus, once again it is clear that historical knowledge can only be evaluated in context.

JUDGING WRITING

The third way of judging a historical account is as writing. This may surprise readers since history students are rarely taught how to write or shown the effects of literary style on responses to academic texts. But there is absolutely no doubt that, just as dull writing turns people off, so compelling writing enhances readers' reactions. In fact it is an integral part of the knowledge. Two examples of these points spring to mind. The first is the capacity to generate large-scale narratives, not just to tell a complex story but to integrate large amounts of disparate evidence to make an overall account that is plausible and compelling. This is an extremely challenging undertaking, and, as a form of writing, the so-called 'grand narrative' has lost favour with many historians; indeed is thought by many to be ideologically suspect. Big stories tend to appeal more to historians who are not narrowly academic. The late Barbara Tuchman is a good example – she twice won the prestigious Pulitzer Prize and wrote on an extraordinary range of issues. *The March of Folly. From Troy to Vietnam* (1984) explores a theme – 'the pursuit by governments of policies contrary to their own interests' – over many centuries.[13] Excellent writing and a generous canvas are a potent combination. In such writing, the literary quality, the insights it contains and the overall approach taken are closely bound together.

The second example is the ability to evoke vivid images in readers' minds, which is usually achieved through a combination of description and anecdote. Fine historical writing uses detail to further understanding. Perhaps 'description' is misleading because it implies low-grade intellectual activity: simply recounting what is there. In fact, description is exceptionally telling because it selects pertinent details and thus, when done well, moves effortlessly into analysis. A brief yet vivid story or description can be an extremely effective distillation of a broader historical point. It makes what is past lively, immediate and interesting, and helps readers to build up mental pictures.

There is a range of devices, including non-literary ones, for making the past alive for readers, but their status as devices needs to be kept in the foreground. Thus, on the one hand, we have living history movements, where people dress up and re-enact behaviour characteristic of other times and, on the other, we have lively writing that both jolts readers into fresh insights and helps them to build up a more systematic understanding of historical processes. Two completely different notions of historical knowledge are involved. These two devices tend to be aimed at different audiences, which should immediately prompt us to think, once again, about the *varied* types of historical knowledge in existence. The former is aimed more at children, whose interest in and ability to grasp abstract analysis is bound to be limited. Nonetheless there is a more general point to be made here about the status of historical knowledge. We communicate accounts of the past largely through the written word, and it is by these means that 'history' is judged. Yet seeing something directly is accorded special status; that is the premise of living history and of most illustrations in historical publications. Elaborate reconstructions in fiction films or TV dramas are treated similarly. Such a status is recognised (rationally) as deceptive by scholars, although the (emotional) appeal of pictures and reconstructions remains undimmed, and it is popularly assumed they afford their audiences some kind of 'knowledge'.[14] Historical knowledge, in the sense I am

13 B. Tuchman, *The March of Folly*, London, 1997, p. 2.
14 M. Baxandall, *Painting and Experience in Fifteenth-Century Italy*, revised edition, Oxford, 1988, p.152, is particularly eloquent on historians' sloppy use of pictures. Television is becoming an increasingly important source of such historical 'knowledge', with serialisations of novels and costume dramas easily blurred in viewers' minds with documentaries, themselves works of art.

using it here, is *always* built up painstakingly by a number of means. Evaluating its quality involves being aware of how these processes work. So we need to recognise that while the use of rhetorical devices is integral to all communication, it is essential to discriminate between them and to critically assess each one in order to evaluate their intellectual power.

At a professional level, the quality of historical writing is absolutely central to its persuasiveness. I have already suggested that this rests in part on an ability to describe and to use well-chosen examples that evoke other worlds. For example, in a whole range of her writings, Olwen Hufton has examined the poor in early modern Europe, and the lives of women of all kinds, especially in relation to their religious and charitable activities.[15] Using her vast experience of archival materials, she draws out the most telling, pointed, poignant examples, and the quality of her writing suggests a strong ability to give a historical account from the point of view of the less privileged. These reactions are necessarily personal; just as there can be no consensus on who are the 'best' fiction writers, so there can never be complete agreement on the quality of historical writings. My hunch would be that female readers respond particularly warmly to Hufton, because her writing taps into themes with which many women identify.[16] Furthermore, and this is true of all effective historical writing, Hufton displays a strong understanding of how human beings work, which is evident in the frameworks and sources chosen as well as in the writing itself. A historical account that makes simplistic assumptions about motivation, for example, could be technically well informed and so on, but unable to command widespread support because it is not, on a human level, believable. There is no consensus on these matters either, and it remains a sad fact about the discipline that crudely reductive assumptions about the primacy of self-interest, in human nature and in historical explanation, continue to be produced. The contrast with a historian such as Natalie Zemon Davis could not be more marked. In her discussions of the Martin Guerre story, for example, she continually stresses the complexities of early modern imposture and of contemporary forms of identity that lay behind it. Motivation is, she acknowledges, uncertain and changeable; sometimes it must be speculated about if it is to be discussed at all. Yet, and this is a crucial point, she does not as a result throw up her hands in despair, or draw back from the challenge of

15 O. Hufton, *The Poor of Eighteenth-Century France 1750–1789*, Oxford, 1974, and *The Prospect Before Her. A History of Women in Western Europe, vol. 1: 1500–1800*, London, 1995.
16 For example, her moving piece, 'Women in Revolution 1789–1796', *Past and Present*, no. 53, 1971, 90–108.

doing what can be done, that is, what the sources, our historical imaginations, and the accumulated insights of the discipline permit.[17]

EXPLANATION

I fear that some professional historians may be quite impatient with the ways in which I have tackled issues about the status of historical knowledge. It might be thought, for example, that a book of this kind should produce unequivocal statements on the subject. I have argued that this is not possible. Furthermore, so far I have laid no special stress on explanation as the goal of history.[18] This is partly because I have pointed up the inevitable lack of consensus on what constitutes an adequate explanation. I want now to probe a little what is generally meant by 'explanation'. Dictionary definitions suggest that it involves making phenomena intelligible, making them known and accounting for them. Historians certainly perform all these operations. They elucidate what has happened in such a way that questions asked about the past are given plausible answers and that its meaning becomes clearer. In other words, explanation is a form of interpretation. Throughout *History in Practice* I am suggesting that historical interpretation is a subtle blend of diverse elements, such as the sources selected, the manner of their use, the context in which the historian works, their training, commitments and prejudices. The problem with the term 'explanation' is that it implies a more rigorous and logically exacting process than does interpretation. Explanation is after all a philosophical term, and philosophers who analyse forms of knowledge are interested not just in how particular disciplines explain their phenomena but in comparing the quality and types of explanation that they offer. While these are important exercises for the philosophy of history, I am not sure that they help those new to the field. Furthermore, such discussions tend to play down two significant

17 N. Zemon Davis, *The Return of Martin Guerre*, Cambridge, Mass., 1983, and 'Remaking Imposters: from Martin Guerre to Sommerby', Hayes Robinson Lecture Series no. 1, London, 1997; see also her *Fiction in the Archives: Pardon Tales and their Tellers in Sixteenth-Century France*, Cambridge, 1988, and the French film, *The Return of Martin Guerre*, 1982.
18 M. Stanford, *An Introduction to the Philosophy of History*, Oxford, 1998, chs. 3 and 4, and C. Lloyd, *Explanation in Social History*, Oxford, 1986. His definition of key terms at the beginning is useful. See also, R. Atkinson, *Knowledge and Explanation in History. An Introduction to the Philosophy of History*, London, 1978, esp. ch. 4. Such works can be rather 'technical' in that they presuppose an aquaintance with philosophical matters and their applicability to historical practice can be unclear.

issues. First, there is no agreement on what constitutes a *satisfying* explanation. This is because they are different views on where the resting point in any explanation should be. The differences derive from theoretical commitments, aesthetic preferences, ideologies, beliefs and so on. Second, the degree to which an explanation is adequate depends not just on how the original questions were framed but on the audiences at which the answer is directed. These differences are particularly clear if we compare history books aimed at each stage of the educational process or the presentation of historical arguments in monographs with those given in museums.

Traditionally, historians have sought to explain the origins of major patterns of change and to offer causal explanations of them.[19] (Hence the popularity of exam questions which ask students to evaluate two different explanations of an event as if these were mutually exclusive.) The job of the historian, we could say, is to show *why* the Renaissance, the Chinese revolution, the collapse of the Roman empire and so on occurred. I have not started with these questions because I wanted first to build up a sense of how historical accounts can be evaluated, and specifically to suggest that evaluation always happens in a context. Major elements of this context include available sources, other historical accounts, prevailing assumptions about human nature, and historiographical fashion. Historiographical fashion covers a great deal, including philosophical preferences concerning evidence and explanation.

One pertinent historiographical fashion is the loss of confidence in causal explanations, in our ability to give clear answers to 'why' questions, which has taken place over the last 30 years. A number of trends account for this shift. The range of types of history undertaken has expanded hugely, which has muddied the waters when it comes to deciding where the main changes in the past occurred, that is, where to look for the most significant causes. We no longer imagine that causes were *either* political *or* economic *or* social, but rather see all of these at work, and find them all dependent upon, or at the very least bound up with, cultural shifts, with changes in ways of understanding and feeling about the world. In other words, conventional hierarchies of explanations no longer seem as plausible as they once did. Nor do we like the idea of invoking single causes or one type of cause, preferring to chart a wide range of factors. Hence questions like 'was the French Revolution caused more by economic than by political factors?' have come to seem rather

---

19 E.g. Atkinson, *Knowledge and Explanation in History*, ch. 5; Stanford, *An Introduction*, ch. 3; and P. McClelland, *Causal Explanation and Model Building in History, Economics, and the New Economic History*, Ithaca, N.Y., 1975. Note the large number of books with 'the causes of' in their titles.

artificial. And, as I have already hinted, we are increasingly intrigued by the mental changes that go along with political and economic ones. These are, by their very nature, harder to pin down, and hence confidence in causal explanation, according to which one thing happens first and produces a clear effect that can be linked to it, has been undermined. It seems too neat and one-dimensional. There are three inter-related issues here; the difficulty in tracing clear sequences of cause and effect, especially when 'culture' is taken into account, the undermining of confidence in monocausal explanations, and the sense that different facets of a society, such as 'politics' or 'economics', are inextricably linked to one another.[20]

I would suggest that two further issues may be linked with the change in climate concerning causality and history. The first concerns reductionism, a matter broached in earlier chapters. Once historians dwell on multi-factorial explanations, an emphasis on single causes appears reductionistic. It would be easy to parody historians' ever-growing desire to insist on the complexity of the past, but the phenomenon is nonetheless real. It must also be seen in a broad intellectual context. The dramatic growth of interest in academic circles and amongst the general public in psychoanalysis, for example, has heightened awareness of the sheer range of human responses. As a result, the significance of the unconscious cannot be dismissed, and psychological matters can be discussed in a less judgemental fashion. Furthermore, psychoanalysis itself is a 'historical' discipline. The dramatic growth of interest in the nature of memory and in commemoration among historians owes a great deal to the historical dimensions of psychoanalysis. Like many of its key thinkers, Freud was profoundly interested in historical study. Psychoanalysis as a field is historical in that it examines the nature and content of memory, legacies of past events, historically persistent symbols, and cultural products as evidence for the structure of the unconscious.[21] Furthermore, we should mention that one impact of post-modernism, post-structuralism and critical theory has been to insist not just on the complexity and diversity of human minds, but on their capacity to play. The point is that play is unpredictable, a force for subversion, inversion and pleasure.[22] The result is a much less tidy view of

---

20 These historiographical shifts are evident in writings that blend culture and
    economics, such as P. Curtin, *Cross-Cultural Trade in World History*,
    Cambridge, 1984 and J. Goodman, *Tobacco in History: The Cultures of
    Dependence*, London, 1993.
21 See, for example, the special feature on 'Psychoanalysis and History' in
    History Workshop Journal, 26, 1988.
22 See, for example, M. Bakhtin, *Rabelais and his World*, Bloomington, Ind.,
    1984, and P. Stallabrass and A. White, *The Politics and Poetics of
    Transgression*, London, 1986.

human existence, which spills over into what are considered appropriate and satisfying historical explanations.

The second issue concerning causality and history leads in precisely the same direction. I have noted several times that sources can be misleading, deceptive. The more the complexities of the 'raw' materials are acknowledged, the harder it is to generate unselfconscious confidence in crisp causal explanations. For some historians, the intricate, tricky nature of all sources is an irritation, which simply needs to be taken account of before getting on with business as usual. In their frame of mind, there *is* an accurate account to be had, but the obstacles have to be removed first. But for others, this trickiness is the result of how the human mind works. Human existence is not straightforward, hence any account – primary or secondary – is bound to be selective, and, if you like, 'biased', even when the author was unaware of any falsification. Accordingly, the status of historical knowledge is a far more complex matter than it seems, and certainty is an elusive quality.

In fact there are some much broader themes here, such as fraud. We may usefully distinguish a number of different aspects of fraud in relation to the practice of history. First, sources can be fabricated or adjusted in some way at the time, whether intentionally or not. This is relatively straightforward, but it should always be borne in mind. Second, sources can be produced fraudulently after the event. Probably the best-known recent example of this is the Hitler diaries, which were proved to be fraudulent after they had been 'authenticated' by a well-known historian.[23] The intention behind such a deceit is, presumably, making money. Third, processes of historical interpretation can be so extremely contentious that we reach for a word like fraud, such as duplicity. Recent debates about the 'reality' of the Holocaust exemplify the point.[24] A radical right-wing revisionist position, which casts doubt on established claims about the numbers of Jews killed, has to account for existing supporting evidence, and thereby to engage in debates about interpretation and deception. Fourth, historians have become increasingly interested in fraudulent behaviour in the past, and Natalie Davis in particular has argued that forms of

23   On the Hitler diaries, see, R. Harris, *The Media Trilogy*, London, 1994, which includes *Selling Hitler: The Story of the Hitler Diaries*, first published in 1986. We should note the persistent claims that Anne Frank's diary was a fake, and that special tests were undertaken to disprove the allegations: see the Foreword to Barnouw and van der Stroom, eds., *The Diary of Anne Frank. The Critical Edition.*

24   Friedländer, ed., *Probing the Limits of Representation: Nazism and the 'Final Solution', History of the Human Sciences*, special issue, vol. 9, no. 4, 1996; I. Gutman, ed., *Encyclopedia of the Holocaust*, 4 vols., New York, 1990, see vol. 4, pp. 1797–1802 on 'Estimated Jewish Losses in the Holocaust'.

imposture are historically specific and hence exceptionally rich in the historical insights they afford. But the interest goes deeper than this. Such cases involve complex legal procedures and by studying them we can reconstruct notions of evidence in *other* societies, think about *their* standards of proof, and consider *their* notions of an adequate explanation. In this way historical research can be a means of reflecting, albeit indirectly, upon the practice of history. It can achieve this by keeping in the foreground of historians' minds the uncertainties of both evidence and interpretation.

SPECULATION AND BELIEF

It would be possible to recast a great deal of what I am saying by noting that historians seem to feel more comfortable now with the idea that history has a speculative dimension, which, far from being a weakness on the part of particular practitioners, is built into the subject itself. It follows that it is quite acceptable for historians to use both hypotheses and heuristic devices, that is, suppositions to think with. And perhaps this is what has made the recent interest in counterfactuals possible. This involves, as the term suggests, setting aside known outcomes, and asking about alternative scenarios – 'what if' history. What if William the Conqueror had been defeated at the Battle of Hastings in 1066? What if Constantinople had not 'fallen' to the Turks in 1453? What if Australia had been 'discovered' at another time and by different people? What if the South had won the American Civil War? It is a game, and one that has long been played for its entertainment value. Recently, and in the hands of professional historians, it has been used as a device to sharpen historical analysis, although this enterprise is hardly ideologically innocent. It tends, for example, to affirm traditional modes of history by privileging the actions of great men and high politics.[25]

It is often easiest to be precise about a concept by considering its opposites. The key concept in this chapter has been 'historical knowledge', so it may be worth considering what is *not* taken to be historical knowledge. Three terms are relevant here: opinion, ideology and myth. 'Opinion' is used when we want to draw attention to what a particular person thinks, without any particularly strong evidentiary base to back it up. Hence to call any bit of historical knowledge an opinion implies that it is not well grounded, a merely personal view.

25 N. Ferguson, ed., *Virtual History: Alternatives and Counterfactuals*, London, 1997, and Stanford, *An Introduction*, pp. 89–93.

To call it 'ideology' is to make a somewhat different point, namely that it was driven by some prior commitment, such as a strongly held belief best understood as political, although here too a claim is being made about evidence. In the case of ideology, the evidence may well be there, but the charge is that it is being distorted or ignored because of the historian's deepest assumptions. The notion of myth is altogether more complex. 'Myth' suggests an invented story, a narrative devised to achieve certain ends that are usually assumed to have a strong emotional component. Sometimes, we use the word myth to imply that an account has been made up, that it lacks any basis however appealing it may appear. Once again, evidence is an issue – myths do not need evidence to generate compelling stories. Yet we also use myth in relation to history in another way. When we talk about historical myths, we are not so much contesting what happened, as drawing attention to the intense affect that surrounds certain views of the past, so intense that they resist debate and modification.[26] Myths are simplified and exceptionally highly condensed accounts. In other words, historical myths are thought to be less knowledge than *belief.*

Discussing terms that might be taken as opposed to historical knowledge raises a difficulty that has been lurking in this entire chapter. I have argued that *everyone* has beliefs, ideologies and emotional investments, and that to charge a historian with doing so should hardly be seen as a damning criticism. Yet in ordinary usage, *knowledge* is rightly seen as something apart from opinion and so on, in being grounded in the rigorous use of evidence. Is there a tension here? Indeed, is there a tension between being a professional historian who, as rationally as possible, sifts evidence, and produces knowledge claims, and being a person who holds and respects profound beliefs? Put starkly and in some situations, a tension would seem to be undeniable. In practice, historians try to strike a balance, to be aware of any possible problems, to raise their own consciousnesses. Striking a balance and being judicious does not sound exciting, but they are the key to producing something that will count as historical knowledge without, on the one hand, making claims to certainty it cannot deliver, and, on the other, making no claims for it at all.

26 S. Wilson, 'The Myth of Motherhood a Myth: The Historical View of
    European Child-rearing', *Social History*, 9, 1984, 181–98; I. Kershaw, *The
    'Hitler Myth': Image and Reality in the Third Reich*, Oxford, 1987; and N.
    Henshall, *The Myth of Absolutism: Change and Continuity in Early Modern
    European Monarchy*, London, 1992.

BRIDGE

It is not possible to make sensible statements about the status of historical knowledge, without having a good understanding of how historians work, and of how the discipline and its products are shaped by their contexts. It is the purpose of this book to address, in general terms, both these issues. I argue that the practice of history is a complex and messy business and that historians are necessarily eclectic and pragmatic in their methods. Hence I have not tackled the status of historical knowledge in what could be called a philosophical manner. Indeed, I have suggested that 'truth' and 'objectivity' may not be the most helpful concepts for our purposes, and that reliability and judiciousness are more relevant. In this vein, we need to take account of the limitations both of sources and of the accounts we generate using them. One way of taking this further is to assess the distinctive array of skills that historians deploy in their practice, and this will be the subject of the final chapter. But first I shall examine an issue – periodisation – that is absolutely fundamental to the practice of history, yet rarely drawn out for critical inspection. Periodisation may be defined as the carving of past times into named chunks, which are then used to organise historical ideas. Without it, historical knowledge would scarcely be possible. It demands careful analysis and in probing this theme we will observe that the manner in which periodisation is undertaken depends precisely on historians' contexts.

5 Periodisation

HISTORY AND TIME

History is the systematic study of the past, and at its heart is time. Time is a complex concept, which is most rigorously analysed by philosophers, physicists and astronomers. Historians display a more practical concern with the idea since they are interested in the effects of the passage of time on human societies. Inevitably these are extraordinarily diverse; there are no predictable patterns and the pace of change depends not only on particular circumstances, such as wars and revolutions, but on which aspect of the social formation is in question. Politics and the practice of government, for example, sometimes change extremely fast, in days or weeks, while attitudes, styles of child-rearing, and religious belief generally take far longer to alter their character. Measuring time and giving names to discrete periods are tasks basic to the discipline of history. Thus one of the most fundamental operations historians undertake is periodisation, a term we can use as a convenient shorthand for a number of time-related tasks that are rich with implicit historiographic assumptions.

The basic measures of time – hours, days, weeks, months and years – were not invented by historians. But they use them as fundamental, taken-for-granted tools, and they give them meaning by assigning additional tags to them, as Daniel Defoe did when he wrote *Journal of the Plague Year*, an account of the Great Plague of 1665 by an invented eyewitness. The practice of history is inextricably linked to ideas of time, to calendrical systems, and above all to the metaphors through which we think about periods. Precisely because all of these are part of our mental furniture, it is difficult to bring them up for conscious inspection. Here is an occasion when imagining oneself to be a Martian, or an anthropologist, can be particularly helpful. Cultivating an outsider's eye, we can ask, with deliberate naivety, what is implied by notions like 'the age of uncertainty', 'the golden age of capitalism', or, a particular favourite of mine, 'the grand century of the lady'?[1] There are *always* historical interpretations present in such phrases.

1 J. K. Galbraith, *The Age of Uncertainty*, London, 1977, P. Guiral, *La vie quotidienne en France à l'age d'or du capitalisme 1852–1857*, Paris, 1976; A. Calder-Marshall, *The Grand Century of the Lady: Regency and Georgian Elegance in the Age of Romance and Revolution*, London, 1976.

Ideas about periods, and the terms in which they are expressed, are largely inherited from earlier generations and these shape the most fundamental assumptions we have, not just about how the past is to be divided up, but about its interpretation. This inheritance is unfortunate because conventionalised period terms seem to hamper fresh thinking; through periodisation particular views of history are naturalised, so that it is difficult to bring them up for critical scrutiny. Novelty is possible, however, and it stems from fresh metaphors and from new historical interpretations. Inevitably period terms have their own complex histories, having been put in place at a variety of times and for diverse purposes, some openly partisan. Tracing and understanding this baggage are important parts of historical practice and should be accorded more priority than they currently are. However, historians are not the only group that participates in the process of shaping the past. Politicians, writers, artists and film makers, as well as institutions such as museums, are also significant players. Nonetheless, historians both reinforce and help to change the shapes of history, and they have to do so in a way that makes sense to others; otherwise names for periods, and the assumptions behind them, would not take hold.[2] I have noted how these names carry implicit historical approaches, and they also carry subjective responses to other times. A brief example illustrates these points. To call the era between the death of Charles I in 1649 and the restoration of Charles II in 1660 'the interregnum' presents it as an interruption between two monarchs and implies both that monarchy was the normal state of affairs and that the continuity of the monarchy was, and continues to be, an important feature of British society. For most of that period Oliver Cromwell was 'reigning', even if he was not called the king. By contrast, to stress the 'Commonwealth' – England was a republic between 1649 and 1654 – draws attention to the experiments with a radically different social and political order. Making choices about period terms is not just an intellectual operation, it involves emotional commitments and aesthetic preferences. At stake here is how the historian's imagination works. It is simply wrong to neglect the imagination, and to prise it apart from the other mental operations scholars perform.

The recording of significant dates and the development of calendars are exceedingly old activities, without which neither the practice of history nor periodisation would be possible.[3] Time-keeping activities contain two facets

2 Cf. G. Kubler, *The Shape of Time: Remarks on the History of Things*, New Haven, 1962.
3 D. Ewing Duncan, *The Calendar: The 5000-Year Struggle to Align the Clock and Heavens – And What Happened to the Missing Ten Days*, London, 1998; S. Burnaby, *Elements of the Jewish and Muhammadan Calendars*, London, 1901; R. Sewell and S. Dîkshit, *The Indian Calendar*, London, 1896.

that are in tension with one another. They have been highly interested enterprises, serving the needs of church, state, legal and administrative systems. At the same time, they claim, and have been accorded, a kind of objectivity, for example, by basing time on astronomical principles, and they purport to record events dispassionately and as accurately as possible. Dates, chronology and forms of periodisation still seem to offer value-free information, but this is deceptive. Assumptions are built into the very recording processes themselves, historical actors introduce distinctive spins upon even quite basic chronological information – we should never forget the inventiveness of human memory – then historians and others add layer upon layer of meaning to events and eras. Historians should be sceptical about the accuracy of chronological information, aware of how units of time shape historical interpretation, often in quite arbitrary ways, and alive to the manner in which we project patterns onto the past, in order to make them meaningful. All of these factors affect the types of research done; for instance, by drawing scholars towards some periods and away from others, they allow some eras to appear exciting and alluring, others dull, uneventful and unappealing. This occurs because those who study the past identify with their objects of study in complex ways. The manner in which periods are thought about and represented is a central part of these processes of identification precisely because they work at a variety of emotional and intellectual levels.

DIVIDING UP THE PAST

There are a number of criteria according to which the past can be divided up, not just to produce manageable chunks but to organise our thoughts about it, to offer readings and accounts of it. In effect we are talking about a range of taxonomic systems, which overlap, and can be used in a variety of ways. We are quite familiar with such situations, readily accepting that dogs are classified differently according to context: for zoological, breeding, showing, feeding and other practical purposes – those that bite or bark and those that do not, for example. Each criterion places the emphasis in a different place, and has a different use, the value of which is context-dependent. Nonetheless we can combine these taxonomies flexibly and pragmatically when choosing a pet. The stakes in classifying the past are somewhat grander, since implicit evaluations – political, aesthetic, ideological – of whole societies are involved. Common divisions are according to rulers or dynasties, around key events or individuals, descriptively by epoch, century, decade or millennium, in terms of the type of government, and according to perceived cultural styles, moods and patterns.

Rulers and dynasties are among the most obvious and commonly used forms of division, reflecting long traditions of scholarship that place leadership in government as a key phenomenon and accord primacy to the political order. Obvious examples include, Tudor, Georgian, and Victorian (England); Bourbon and Napoleonic (France); Carolingian (Holy Roman Empire); Wilhelmine (Germany). Thus a ruler or a family of rulers can embody a period; it is as if the one who heads the state holds together disparate historical phenomena in an extension of that role. Sometimes the implications are even stronger: Mao's China, Stalin's Russia, Mussolini's Italy, Franco's Spain and Pinochet's Chile are at first sight descriptions of a particular era of a particular nation, but in fact they convey the dominance, not just of a regime, but of a highly powerful individual, over the entire society. Can it be coincidence that such a formulation seems especially apt for authoritarian regimes? It is striking, then, that the use of rulers and dynasties confers a large measure of unity on a period, a unity that may exist largely at a symbolic level in the body or bodies of rulers. Not just Hitler, but small fragments associated with his person – the moustache, the salute – can evoke the entire regime in our imaginations.[4] Absolutism, and its embodiment in Louis XIV, the 'Sun King', also demonstrates the point.[5] Related notions, such as 'Saxon' or 'Norman' when applied to periods carry similar connotations, and, in addition, by virtue of their association with areas such as architecture, convey the idea that a whole culture is involved since, in one of their meanings, they describe a political dominance rooted in ethnicity. It is not just rulers and dominant groups, but elected leaders who can function in this way. In the case of eighteenth-century England, we might remember a succession of powerful prime ministers who made it plausible to speak of an age of Walpole or an age of Pitt. Much later Winston Churchill, and, in the United States, President Franklin D. Roosevelt functioned in this way. Indeed the identification between Roosevelt, the depression and the New Deal has been remarkably strong. I suspect this form of periodisation is particularly compelling when the country in question has undergone a profound transformation or crisis under someone's leadership. It reinforces a sense of the agency of special individuals.

In mentioning these examples I do not mean to imply that they have been treated uncritically by professional historians. Nor do I want to suggest that the associations between epochs and political leaders are without foundation.

4　This has become possible largely through the power of film, which has conveyed, in both documentary and fictional form, an exceptionally vivid sense of what we mean by 'Hitler': less an individual than an ensemble of historical phenomena and emotional reactions.

5　P. Burke, *The Fabrication of Louis XIV*, New Haven, 1992.

I am merely offering examples of one type of periodisation, and drawing out what is implicit within it. Furthermore, we should note how many of the related adjectives (Anglo-Saxon, Louis Quinze, Napoleonic, Victorian) are also terms of style. This is especially obvious in relation to houses, furniture, jewellery and clothing. While we associate 'style' with art, music, fashion and other cultural products, it is in fact an important, if largely unrecognised, part of historical practice. Style can mean what is characteristic of a given artist, that is of an individual, but it is also used, and has been since the eighteenth century, to sum up a period and to differentiate between periods – rococo and neo-classical, for example.[6] Style and periodisation are closely related, jointly shaping the historical imagination. A particularly telling instance is 'Victorian', which is now applied beyond the boundaries of Britain or its empire to suggest visual styles of the second half of the nineteenth century. Furthermore, as is evident in the phrase 'Victorian values', it suggests a style of thinking and responding to the world.[7] Indeed, the very phrase implies a response to that style, or rather it implies two polarised responses: either approval for strong traditional moral stances, or criticism of their inappropriate use in a later period. In using a word like style there may be a danger that we trivialise the effect of period terms by implying that these are merely matters of personal preference or taste. This is not my intention. On the contrary, period and style terms shape the way in which whole eras can be imagined and thought about, as the phrase 'Victorian values' reveals.

EVENTS AND PERIODS

A second important criterion for diving up the past is key events, such as assassinations, battles, revolutions and wars. One of the most significant

6 J. Mordaunt Crook, *The Dilemma of Style: Architectural Ideas from the Picturesque to the Post-Modern*, London, 1987, 1989; B. Allsop, *Style in the Visual Arts*, Newcastle, 1968; M. Finch, *Style in Art History: An Introduction to Theories of Style and Sequence*, Metuchen, N.J., 1974. Rococo is primarily associated with French art of the first half of the eighteenth century: 'in France it fell out of fashion in the 1740s to be decisively superseded by the earnest ideals and Republican Roman virtue of Neoclassicism': P. and L. Murray, *Dictionary of Art and Artists*, Harmondsworth, 1960, p. 277. Scholars debate the definition and usefulness of such terms, but for our purposes the point is that they become loaded with other associations, which shape the sense of a period. For example, rococo suggests femininity, *ancien régime* decadence, neo-classicism austere masculinity.
7 R. Samuel, 'Mrs Thatcher and Victorian Values' in *Island Stories: Unravelling Britain* (volume 2 of *Theatres of Memory*), London, 1998, pp. 330–48 (first published 1992).

examples of this approach, however, is none of these – the birth of Christ. There could be no more eloquent example of how a single historical event can be made into a structuring principle and of the cultural baggage it necessarily brings with it. Since one counts backwards for eras BC and forwards for those AD, the importance of the turning point is made manifest, and every time the dating system is used, the global significance of the birth of Christ is unthinkingly asserted. There is now a certain distaste for using BC and AD, and while this is understandable, since Christianity is only one of many world religions, I am not sure that BCE and CE (variously, before the common or Christian era) really solves the problem; it simply repackages the same idea. This example raises the vexed question of whether standard, universal dating systems are really necessary or helpful. So long as conversions between systems are possible, it would seem to be most generative for historians to work within the forms of *dating* of the culture they study, although they will always be needing to rethink the forms of *periodisation* they are using since this underpins historical interpretation.

The relationships between key dates and periodisations are intricate and there can be no better example of the point than the French Revolution, although of course only the beginning of it constitutes a clear 'event' and even that is debatable. The fall of the Bastille on 14 July 1789, when a hated symbol of the *ancien régime* yielded, without much resistance, to the mob, has become a useful, emotionally apt convention for marking the inception of the 'French Revolution'. Hence we can say, metonymically, '1789', and conjure up a whole historical era. The French Revolution is important because it marks a fundamental shift in French society, recognised as such at the time. The abolition of feudalism and the transformation of subjects into citizens exemplify the point. The Revolution was also taken to be symptomatic of later changes that went far beyond the boundaries of France – the modernisation of administration and warfare, for example. The French were neither the first to behead a king in recent times nor the first to try to rethink a polity anew, yet the French Revolution has special status. Thus it was natural for many generations of historians to think of this as a decisive turning point, which would help them clarify their general interpretations of European, even world history.

Historians of many different orientations could join in acknowledging its significance. Hobsbawm's *The Age of Revolution: Europe, 1789–1848*, first published in 1962, is a case in point. His concern was with the relationships between political and economic change – the phrase 'age of revolution' embraces the industrial revolution too. Palmer's *The Age of the Democratic Revolution* (1959, 1964) put a rather different spin on the era, because it sought to interpret the French and American revolutions together, and to draw out the strong affinities between the two nations in this era. So, in the national consciousness of many states, as in historians' imaginations, '1789' is an emblem, even if what it is an emblem of varies dramatically. The vogue for celebrating centenaries makes the point particularly vividly – the mere fact of the celebration implies shared national and international values, while in practice events as controversial as the French Revolution cannot unite a people, still less the discipline of history.

Using a key event of this kind as a periodising device may be misleading. There are many phenomena that showed marked continuity across the revolutionary divide, despite its tumultuous nature. Although the prominence of health care for all citizens was high on the revolutionary agenda, medicine is arguably one example. In both science and medicine many 'bigwigs' worked throughout the period and remained more or less consistently prominent over a number of regimes.[8] Changes in institutional structures were more apparent than real. The invocation of Lavoisier, who was guillotined in 1793, in fact for his tax-collecting activities, as a *scientific* martyr fits one particular view of the Revolution as a rupture and a barbaric one at that.[9] Other accounts present significant continuities from the 1770s to the early decades of the nineteenth century. Prior commitments shape historians' claims about continuity and change. Ideally, careful forms of periodisation are made appropriate to the research task in hand. The choice of key events is value-laden, allowing very different stories to be told. It helps to know what lies behind their choice and how they are acting as symbols.

In thinking about dating and periodisation in relation to the French Revolution, three points should be made. First, although its dating is contentious and depends upon both the kind of crisis it is believed to be and the interpretation of its outcome, historians develop conventions for dealing with the difficulties. These should not cause problems so long as they are recognised as such and the rationales behind them explained. Second, the Revolution was understood at the time as a special event, which would forever change the course of European, possibly world history. It was a conscious process of collective self-fashioning and re-invention, which included, of course, the revolutionary calendar, along with metric systems of weights and measures and

8   D. Weiner, *The Citizen Patient in Revolutionary and Imperial Paris*, Baltimore, 1993; L. Brockliss and C. Jones, *The Medical World of Early Modern France*, Oxford, 1997, esp. the Conclusion.

9   On Lavoisier, see S. French, *Torch and Crucible: The Life and Death of Antoine Lavoisier*, Princeton, 1941; D. McKie, *Antoine Lavoisier, Scientist, Economist, Social Reformer*, London, 1952; and A. Donovan, *Antoine Lavoisier: Science, Administration and Revolution*, Oxford, 1993.

MUSÉE DE LA RÉVOLUTION FRANÇAISE, VIZILLE

5.1 Republican Calendar, by Philibert-Louis Debucourt (1794)
During the French Revolution there were innumerable attempts to construct a fresh
social, cultural and political order. The elaboration and use of new systems of
measurement is a particularly telling example. The metric calendar demonstrates
how far-reaching the search was for structures that carried none of the values of
the ancien régime. *To rename and reorganise time was a fundamental step indeed*
and it never took proper hold. Nonetheless the attempt reveals both how ingrained
and how symbolically charged the representation of time is.

the cult of the supreme being.[10] Historians need to pay careful attention to deliberate re-thinking about the naming and measurement of time. Third, the Revolution raises vast questions about periodisation, especially on a large scale – the conceptualisation of centuries and decades. These cannot be resolved empirically, since they involve models of change in general, of revolution as a process, and of the specific period. We can see this particularly clearly when we think about the use of 'modern'. For many commentators, the French Revolution was the beginning of the 'modern' era – but what does such a claim involve? We now recognise the complexities of 'modern' and 'modernity' and the manner in which our own era is implicated in their definition. One does not have to be a post-modernist to appreciate how intricate the manoeuvres around modernity are. It is vital to recognise that here we are not in the territory of research, of finding information that will clarify the matter, but of interrogating received ways of patterning, organising and imagining the past.

It should come as no surprise to discover that dramatic changes, used as historical markers, carry a certain magic. There is a mystique to them; perhaps they are the historical equivalent of a *rite de passage*. This was captured, for example, in *Reds* (1981), a Hollywood version of the Russian Revolution. Historians, like others, project humanoid features onto abstractions, and hence can easily imagine changes in past societies as resembling the major, symbolic transitions of an individual life course – birth, growth, maturity, death and so on. A good example of this is the ubiquity of falls – of the Roman empire, Troy, Constantinople. The naming, recognition and packaging of such transitions can be said to be unifying. By 'unifying' I do not mean that everyone holds the same opinion, but rather that there is a shared sense of the general significance of a particular event or process, and that it becomes an accessible point of reference, sometimes as it is happening and more often for later generations. As a result, these events act as organising principles within historical research.

To my mind one of the most striking instances of this phenomenon is the First World War of 1914–18, where we can see the processes I have just described occurring at four distinct levels. First, participants themselves took it to be an unprecedented phenomenon of huge significance, and I define as participants everyone who had to cope with its impact, not just people on the

10   On the revolutionary calendar see C. Jones, *The Longman Companion to the French Revolution*, Harlow, 1988, pp. 425–30 and F. Furet and M. Ozouf, eds., *A Critical Dictionary of the French Revolution*, Cambridge, Mass., 1989, pp. 538–47.

battlefields.[11] Those who treated shell-shock victims, for example, had to think anew about trauma, and therefore also had to think anew about the nature of the human mind. Second, the management of social issues was changed decisively by the war, so that leaders of post-war societies were conscious of a major transition taking place. The depression on the one hand and the widespread commitment to welfare policies on the other are examples of phenomena that brought fundamental changes to many geographical areas in the wake of the war. Third, historians have certainly recognised the First World War as basic to the construction of period categories, even if, inevitably, they differ on precisely what weight it should be given. Arno Mayer, for example, suggested that it was a major watershed, because it was only after the war that landed elites decisively lost their political power. This is only one example of how an event can be used to construct periodisations. Fourth, the war has been given significance as an organising event through its cultural representation, both at the time and subsequently. The current enthusiasm for books about that war, whether fictional or not, is indicative of the grip it holds on significant swathes of the population. Poetry and poets have played a crucial role in giving the First World War a potent cultural identity.[12]

As I shall argue in the next chapter, what is best called public history, which includes museums, the media and historical novels, has a massive impact upon the ways in which the past is imagined. The First World War is an excellent example of this very point, and I am mentioning it here to show how periodisation is involved. Our sense of 'natural' boundaries, of discrete periods, derives not so much from abstract analysis as from diffused understandings of where the turning points are. And these in turn come from a variety of sources, including poetry and art. Professional historians examine these supposedly natural boundaries from a critical standpoint, and may, as a result, want to develop arguments that run contrary to common ideas; that, indeed, is their job. But they too inhabit a wider world in which commitments to forms of periodisation are woven into the fabric of everyday life. Their proposed changes may well take hold, but it is, I believe, hard to go against the grain when it comes to major events as historical markers, since these are constantly

---

11 L. Woolf, *After the Deluge: A Study of Communal Psychology*, London, 1931 started with a discussion of the war as 'a catastrophe and a landmark in history'. Cf. A. Marwick, *The Deluge: British Society and the First World War*, second edition, Basingstoke, 1991.

12 A. Mayer, *The Persistence of the Old Regime: Europe to the Great War*, New York, 1981. On poetry see, J. Silkin, *Out of Battle: The Poetry of the Great War*, second edition, Basingstoke, 1998; D. Hibberd, ed., *Poetry of the First World War: A Casebook*, London, 1981; J. Silkin, ed., *The Penguin Book of First World War Poetry*, Harmondsworth, 1979.

affirmed in arenas over which historians have no control. The two world wars are indelibly etched on the national consciousness in most of the countries that took part and I very much doubt that a radical revisionism, which demoted their significance, could ever take hold, even assuming that there were strong intellectual arguments to back it up. I have spent some time on events as period organisers because they lend themselves to symbolisation. Because they can be presented as unitary, simple, discrete units, they easily get a grip on us, fit into larger patterns, and work their magic through all the means cultures afford them.

DESCRIPTION AND PERIODISATION

I shall turn now to a third form of periodisation, one that is less overtly emotionally charged, and more subtle in the ways it works. This is *descriptions* of a time period, which sounds simple, but, as is apparent from the examples 'modern' and 'early modern', they are rather slippery and contain hidden agendas. There are many different definitions of modern history, and we have already noted that 'modern' is a tricky term. 'Modern' has several meanings.[13] It is often helpful to think about the opposite of such terms, of what they may stand in contrast to. The most familiar pairing until the nineteenth century was ancient and modern.[14] This is instructive, since the contrast indicated, in the seventeenth century, for example, an anxiety about whether the moderns could ever live up to the high achievements of ancient civilisations, especially Greece and Rome. Gradually, over the eighteenth century, anxiety gave way to confidence, so that what was recent, new, up to date, was increasingly given value for these reasons alone. 'Modern' could then be associated with innovation, with what is palpably related to the present and to the future. Thus in advertising from the early twentieth century, 'modern' was synonymous with 'clean', 'hygienic', 'not using coal' and so on. Modern history usually carries the connotation of being closely related to the present and, as a result, it can be both Whiggish and teleological. It tends to be implicitly goal-directed in that it takes the present as that which is to be explained, as if this were the point towards which previous trends were leading, and it departs from the assumption that 'the winners'' standpoint is a kind of baseline.

13 Williams, *Keywords*, pp. 208–9.
14 R. Jones, *Ancients and Moderns: A Study of the Rise of the Scientific Movement in Seventeenth-Century Europe*, second edition, Berkeley, Ca., 1961.

'Modern' can also be given a rather different set of inflections. The ones I have just described are in fact relative, that is, modern is defined in relation to where one is standing now. The second way of thinking about modernity is absolute, since it seeks to specify a particular set of historical conditions that qualify as 'modern'. Needless to say, there is no consensus on what the defining characteristics of modernity are. Possibilities include: advanced capitalism, economic specialisation and high levels of the division of labour, the types of urbanisation found initially in the nineteenth century, the period since the French Revolution, the development of cultural avant-gardes, post-Newtonian science, the use of steam (then electric and nuclear) power in industrial production, mass production, the discovery of the unconscious, and the legacy of the Enlightenment.[15] It is not necessary to choose between such criteria, but many commentators put the interpretative weight in a particular zone – economic, cultural or intellectual. Smuggled in here are notions of progress, the value given to specific areas of human achievement, and causal priorities, that is, which changes are deemed to have the greatest capacity to alter human existence most profoundly.

There is an implied contrast between *early* modern and modern history. Earlier, the main distinction had been between the medieval period and modernity, where the former was construed as more static, with a slower pace of change than the latter, and also as lacking those institutions that make for modern life – printing, for example. In current historical usage, the early modern period sits between the two, its precise boundaries undefined. Early modern also implies a kind of teleology; 'society' is moving towards modernity but it is not quite there yet. The term suggests a dependence upon, a subordination to what is modern, as if it were a mere prelude, the overture to the main proceedings. When does 'medieval' end and 'early modern' begin? Is it perhaps with Columbus's encounter in 1492 with the continent now named

15 It is vital to distinguish between 'modern', 'modernism', 'modernity' and 'modernisation'. 'Modern', the adjective, is discussed in the text above. 'Modernism' generally refers to cultural movements, especially in art, architecture and literature, and when applied to other phenomena implies a cultish or celebratory approach to what is 'modern'. 'Modernity' concerns a general state or condition, and is what sociologists have focused upon. 'Modernisation' refers to broad processes of transformation, especially social and economic change. See M. Berman, *All That is Solid Melts into Air: The Experience of Modernity*, London, 1983; M. Abrams, *A Glossary of Literary Terms*, sixth edition, Fort Worth, Tex., 1993, pp.118–21; H. Ritter, *Dictionary of Concepts in History*, New York, 1986, pp. 273–7 , D. Peters Corbett, *The Modernity of English Art 1914–30*, Manchester, 1997, esp. the Introduction. Note that the *Journal of Modern History* (1929), accepts articles across a wide chronological span, including 'early modern'.

AKG, LONDON

5.2 Ptolemaic Map (1545)
Maps are effective ways of reminding ourselves that the world was experienced and
visualised in totally different ways at other times. Here there is no American Continent.

'America'? Or is it with Luther's act of attaching his 95 theses to the church
door in Wittenberg on 1 November 1517, the symbolic initiating move of the
Reformation? Could it be Copernicus's rejection of the ancient earth-centred
cosmology in favour of an 'infinite universe' recognisably like the one we
believe in today, published in 1543?[16] And when did the early modern period
end – with the French Revolution, the Enlightenment, Newton's path-breaking
work of the 1680s, the 'discovery' of Australia, the last major habitable land-
mass to be named, visited and charted by those who lived in Europe?[17] Again,

16   A. Koyré, *From the Closed World to the Infinite Universe*, Baltimore, 1957.
17   The Australian case is particularly interesting in relation to the broad
     implications of all forms of periodisation. It had been seen and visited by
     Europeans for some time before Cook's voyage of 1769–71. One history starts
     with the declaration, 'Australia was conceived officially ... on 22 January
     1787', which gives priority to its status as a British penal colony: F. Crowley,
     ed., *A New History of Australia*, Melbourne, 1974, p. 1. The whole approach
     to periodisation in the volume is striking. Cf. *Manning Clark's History of
     Australia*, Melbourne, 1993 (an abridgement by M. Cathcart) p. 3:
     'Civilization did not begin in Australia until the last quarter of the eighteenth
     century.' He also privileges 1787.

it is not a question of right and wrong answers, but of whose vantage point is privileged, of the power of symbolic markers, and of the weight given to distinct fields of human activity. For example, from the perspective of someone concerned with human rights, the Enlightenment and the French Revolution occupy a privileged position since they forged and disseminated a discourse of rights, which has been construed as a gift to the modern world.[18] Hence, the early modern period would end sometime around the Enlightenment, since those we associate with this movement of ideas articulated cogent critiques of existing systems of justice and the use of torture, and actively campaigned on these issues, as in Voltaire's defence of Calas, wrongly accused of murdering his son in a situation of confessional strife.[19] And we think of these concerns as 'modern'. For an economic historian, by contrast, such arguments would not cut much ice, whereas the advent of steam power, mass production, assembly lines and rationalistic time management certainly would. 'Early modern' would then loosely characterise a transitional era, of artisanal production within both workshops and families, increasingly sophisticated trading links, including internationally, and specialised markets.[20] Yet, by their very nature, these phenomena were subject to considerable local variation; hence it becomes extremely difficult to give overall names to periods with any degree of confidence. Despite Hobsbawm's influential *The Age of Capital*, which covers 1848–75, and many other works in similar vein, every history teacher tries to impress upon their students how difficult it is to say when capitalism began, and to assume such a statement could cover entire regions or countries.

Other innocent-sounding descriptions, such as 'contemporary' or 'medieval', raise similar problems. The former is now gaining currency, but how far back does contemporary history go?[21] Are we thinking about what is within living memory? In that case, contemporary history would include much

---

18 M. Freeman, 'Human Rights and the Corruption of Governments, 1789–1989', in P. Hulme and L. Jordanova, eds., *The Enlightenment and its Shadows*, London, 1990, pp. 163–83.

19 D. Bien, *The Calas Affair: Persecution, Toleration, and Heresy in Eighteenth-Century Toulouse*, Princeton. N.J.,1960; F. Venturi, *Utopia and Reform in the Enlightenment*, Cambridge, 1971; E. Peters, *Torture*, expanded edition, Philadelphia, 1996.

20 P. Hudson, *The Industrial Revolution*, London, 1992; P. Kriedke, H. Medick and J. Schlumbohm, *Industrialization before Industrialization: Rural Industry in the Genesis of Capitalism*, Cambridge, 1981.

21 Cf. H. S. Hughes, 'Is Contemporary History Real History?' in his *History as Art and as Science: Twin Vistas on the Past*, New York, 1964, pp. 89–107. A. Seldon, ed., *Contemporary History: Practice and Method*, Oxford, 1988. *Journal of Contemporary History* (1966).

of the twentieth century. Or is it to be taken more literally, to refer to now, our own times? But this remains ambiguous. In Britain, contemporary history is sometimes traced back to 1945, which affirms the end of the Second World War as a major turning point, but at other times it means simply the 'twentieth century'. While naming a century simply by giving it a number may sound equally innocent and descriptive, in fact centuries are often used in ways that are not simply literal. Invoking a whole century in this way is deceptive in any case, given the dramatic differences between the beginnings and ends of centuries. A phrase like 'the eighteenth century' offers only spurious coherence. In relation to British history, the phrase is sometimes taken to cover the period 1688–1815, that is, the 'long' eighteenth century, from the Glorious Revolution to the Battle of Waterloo.[22] This particular perspective is idiosyncratic and politically freighted; it is controversial even in a British context and makes no particular sense to students of other European countries. A historian of France might be inclined to have a 'short' eighteenth century, say between the death of Louis XIV in 1715 and 1789. From the perspective of the Thirteen Colonies/United States (often erroneously called simply 'America'), the shape of the eighteenth century also looks quite different, given the significance of the decisive break from the mother country in the 1770s. That is, to cast the point in more general terms, colonial periods and those of independence are *made* distinct, not just by historians but also by historical actors. For many countries the advent of 'independence' is certainly crucial, symbolising a process widely imagined as liberating. Yet in practice, given the continuing involvement of many imperial powers with their former colonies, a single *moment* of independence may not be a really useful marker for the organisation of historical work. An event that symbolises the change may be important emotionally, yet not particularly significant economically or legally.[23]

When considering period terms, it is vital to remember that historians necessarily make choices concerning them. In the case of the eighteenth century, for example, one alternative would be 'the Enlightenment', which is used both of a movement of ideas and of the time at which it occurred. 'The Enlightenment' carries quite specific connotations in that it suggests not only intellec-

---

22   W. Speck, 'The Eighteenth Century in Britain: Long or Short?' *The Historian*, Autumn 1996, 16–18, is a brief useful discussion of this idea. Cf. D. Blackbourn, *The Fontana History of Germany, 1815–1918: The Long Nineteenth Century*, London, 1997.
23   The on-going and extremely intricate relationships between Britain and the United States two centuries after independence would be a case in point: W. Louis and H. Bull, eds., *The 'Special Relationship': Anglo-American Relations Since 1945*, Oxford; 1986, J. Baylis; *Anglo–American Defence Relations 1939–1984: The Special Relationship*, second edition, London, 1984.

tual changes, but more specifically a move towards a more secular, rational-istic and democratic worldview. Specialists debate these matters, but the fact remains that associations, such as that between the Enlightenment and sec-ularisation, are entrenched. Like all words ending in '-isation', secularisation is problematic – a point we have already noted in relation to modernisation. Part of the problem is that they appear to refer to specific periods, while in fact being extremely vague and slippery. The eighteenth century was also an era of religious revival, a phenomenon that has rarely been studied by those who see themselves primarily as students of the Enlightenment. Definitions of the Enlightenment have varied quite dramatically. In the 1960s and early 1970s, the emphasis on a 'high' Enlightenment remained, that is, a concentration upon major thinkers, such as Diderot, Rousseau and Voltaire. It was also usual to privilege France as its epitome: civilised, urbane, sophisticated. By the late 1970s, work began to be published which challenged these views, and although the temporal boundaries of the Enlightenment will always remain contentious, there is now a much broader sense of what it encompassed, in terms of geographical areas, social groups and institutions. Low life and the Enlightenment can now be placed together with some plausibility, and we can envisage a plurality of Enlightenments that were loosely related to one another.[24] This example demonstrates how notions of periodisation are bound up with both historians' other tasks and their mental maps of the past. Inter-pretations of the Enlightenment – the very concept gives status to intellectual innovation – including the period it covers, contain wider implications, for the onset of modernity, for the boundaries between modern and early modern, and for the conceptualisation of different kinds of change, since it gives pri-ority to ideas while construing them as influential upon social practice – state-craft, local administration, justice, education and so on.

So far, I have discussed descriptions of periods in terms of large swathes of time, but we also have notions like the Roaring Twenties and Swinging Six-ties, which are considerably more focused. So why are some *decades* seen as worthy of naming as special, others less so? Why are some seen as definable periods (especially the last of a century) and others not? There are no straight-forward answers to these questions, which are designed to provoke ideas

24 A variety of perspectives on the Enlightenment can be gleaned from: N. Hampson, *The Enlightenment*, Harmondsworth, 1968; R. Darnton, *Mesmerism and the End of the Enlightenment in France*, Cambridge, 1968; P. Gay, *The Enlightenment*, 2 vols., New York, 1966 and 1969; R. Porter and M. Teich, eds., *The Enlightenment in National Context*, Cambridge, 1981; R. Porter, *The Enlightenment*, Basingstoke, 1990; D. Outram, *The Enlightenment*, Cambridge, 1995.

THE ESTATE OF LINDA McCARTNEY

5.3 *The Beatles, by Linda McCartney, 1967*
*The Beatles have become inseparable from the idea of the Sixties. Both 'the Beatles'
and 'the Sixties' possess dramatically diverse meanings.*

about the relationships between, to put it crudely, periods and identity. This
is clear in the case of the Sixties, which can carry either positive or negative
connotations; something about the speaker's identity is thereby revealed. The
Sixties is an organising idea and now we are beginning to see professional historians writing about it as an entity.[25] As anyone who lived through that decade
knows, 'the Sixties' is a myth, in that it is a strategically simplified fabrication,
but once in existence, we orientate ourselves with respect to it, and use it for
our own purposes. An equally telling example is the interest in the last decades
of centuries, that is, in the *fin de siècle* phenomenon.[26] Until recently *fin de*

25   E.g. A. Marwick, *The Sixties. Cultural Revolution in Britain, France, Italy and
the United States, c.1958–c.1974*, Oxford, 1998.
26   M. Teich and R. Porter, eds., *Fin de Siècle and its Legacy*, Cambridge, 1990; B.
Dijkstra, *Idols of Perversity: Fantasies of Feminine Evil in Fin-de-siècle
Culture*, New York, 1986; C. Schorske, *Fin-de-siècle Vienna: Politics and
Culture*, New York, 1979; A. Danchev, ed., *Fin de Siècle: The Meaning of the
Twentieth Century*, London, 1995; R. Pahl, *After Success: Fin-de-Siècle Anxiety
and Identity*, Cambridge, 1995.

siècle referred only to the 1890s, and more especially to a cultural formation presented in terms of decadence, ennui, sexual indulgence and the critique of bourgeois society. Then, in *our* '90s, historians began to explore what seemed to be a more general phenomenon. There was indeed something special about the end of centuries, they claimed. Now *fin de siècle* is used considerably more loosely, and not just by historians, to refer to the situation in which we find ourselves, a situation dominated by the idea of a new millennium, and by a strange mixture of fear and anticipation. It can be argued that this usage is sloppy and insufficiently historically precise, but it does illustrate how historians' identities are linked with periodisation, and how the terms of engagement with the past shift according to circumstance. In these cases it is pretty obvious that the observer's position affects their sense of periods, but the phenomenon is a general one, even if it usually occurs at rather subtle levels.

FURTHER PERIOD TERMS

A fourth way in which we can divide up the past is in terms of the type of government. I have already mentioned some examples of this mode – absolutism, the *ancien régime*. Another commonly used example would be Communist China or Communist Russia (actually, like 'America', 'Russia' is commonly misused). *Communist* 'Russia' differentiates it from *Tsarist* Russia. The type of regime, precisely because it has changed so radically, sums up an era, although these periods are of varying length. Epithets like 'Communist' and 'Tsarist' are relatively easy to use, but they generally carry, I suspect, some pejorative connotations. Would we say, for example, *democratic* Australia or *democratic* Canada, and if not, why not? It may well be that some forms of government are more clear-cut than others, making a label that denotes a distinctive political ideology especially attractive. Admittedly 'democracy' is a woolly concept, more an ideal than a state achieved, and there has been no single democracy party that is comparable in historical significance to the Communist Party. If it is reasonable to suggest that names go along with clearly identifiable types of government, which tend to be more authoritarian, then other types are being passed by in relative silence, perhaps taken as the norms against which 'communism', 'absolutism' and 'fascism' are judged. In the case of *ancien régime*, this process is perfectly clear: *ancien* is relative to what came later, which, it is implied, was clearly better. More specifically, *ancien régime* carries connotations of corruption, deceit and bankruptcy – financial, social and moral. Since it implies the existence of a subsequent, new and better political

order, *ancien régime* carries progressivist values.[27] Naming types of government, and organising historical periods around them, involves political judgements that are rendered less visible by being conventionalised.

A fifth way of discriminating between periods is in terms of cultural style,
which, naturally enough, appeals rather less to political and economic historians than it does to intellectual and cultural ones. Since these style terms are,
as we have already noted, powerful metaphors capable of further extension,
we may yet come to a time when we speak of governments as baroque or
rococo, and of factories as neo-classical![28] Baroque is a stylistic category, and
it is also used to describe an era of European history, although its boundaries,
are, not surprisingly, difficult to define. In all these forms of periodisation we
are thinking about ways of meaningfully evoking a period – the use of style
terms is just another case in point. 'Style' implies that there is a distinctive
flavour to a period, a flavour that suffuses its main products: music, art, literature, clothes, buildings, worship and so on. It lends a special kind of coherence to the past, not political or economic in nature, but aesthetic and
emotional. This is clear in terms that are not only stylistic, such as Georgian,
or Colonial, as used, for example, of the USA. I do not mean something narrow
and connoisseurial when I say 'aesthetic'; rather I want to suggest that matters of taste, of cultural preference, of intellectual and sensual response, are,
whether we like it or not, always at work when we organise our ideas of the
past.[29]

My argument is that in order to manage the past it has to be classified and
that one of the most important forms of classification is periodisation. Classification puts like things together in a coherent, systematic manner. Over the
centuries, historians (but not only historians) have developed comfortable,
conventionalised ways of doing this, so that we barely think about them. Their
function is precisely to lend to past times a sense of meaning, order and coherence. I am suggesting that although many historians would not use style terms

---

27 E. Williams, *The Ancien Régime in Europe: Government and Society in the
    Major States 1648–1789*, London, 1970; C. B. A. Behrens, *The Ancien Régime*,
    London, 1967; A. de Tocqueville, *L'Ancien Régime et la Revolution*, Paris,
    1856.

28 C. Friedrich, *The Age of the Baroque, 1610–60*, New York, 1952; W. Park, *The
    Idea of Rococo*, Newark, 1992; D. Irwin, *Neo-classicism*, Oxford, 1997.
    'Biedermeier' which is both a style term and a period term illustrates a
    number of my points: see M. Fulbrook, *A Concise History of Germany*,
    second edition, Cambridge, 1992, p. 122.

29 On taste see, for example, S. Bayley, *Taste, the Secret Meaning of Things*,
    London, 1991 and J. Curl, *Egyptomania: The Egyptian Revival, a Recurring
    Theme in the History of Taste*, Manchester, 1994.

and certainly few would think about those they do use as such, they exemplify the unifying function of period names. They enable us to see particularly clearly how a whole range of reactions to the past get mobilised when we shape it into discrete periods – reactions that are aesthetic, emotional, political and so on.

So far I have discussed five fairly obvious criteria according to which the past is divided up and mentioned some of the issues that lie behind them. But much has not been included in the types of period names already noted. What about terms such as Reformation, pre- and post-Reformation, counter-Reformation? These are similar to 'the Enlightenment', in that they refer to a movement and they suggest a set of themes and preoccupations as well as a specific historical period. In the case of the Reformation, there is no ambiguity at all about where the origins of change can be located. It implies a major transition, a process not an event, in the history of European Christianity. In effect the larger significance of Christianity for all aspects on human existence where it was the dominant religion is affirmed. And because these are matters of belief, where the pace of change can be slow, piecemeal and uneven, historians accordingly stress the local variations, the very different forms Christianity took, the complex interactions between reformers and those they wished to change. As a result, the location of chronological boundaries becomes even more difficult, since the phenomenon itself is protean.[30] When did the Reformation end? Might we, to take a provocative example, want to see English Methodism in the eighteenth century as part of a *longue durée* Reformation? The possibility immediately calls into question definitions of the Enlightenment, which has rarely been seen as including religious *revival*, yet the Wesley brothers, the reluctant founders of a separate Methodist church, can also be understood as responding to and expounding Enlightenment ideas.[31] Once we begin to reflect in this way, it becomes apparent why key events, with their seeming clarity, are so appealing as ways of organising the past. Yet the discussion should also reveal how misleading they can be – satisfying symbols, yes, secure historical indicators, no. Symbols are not 'bad', indeed they are central to human existence, but they function in ways that are not necessarily conducive to deeper historical understanding. Luther's actions

---

30 For a range of approaches to the Reformation, see R. Scribner, *The German Reformation*, Basingstoke, 1986; P. Chaunu, ed., *The Reformation*, London, 1989; J. Bossy, *Christianity in the West 1400–1700*, Oxford, 1985; E. Cameron, *The European Reformation*, Oxford, 1991.
31 J. Harrison, *The Second Coming: Popular Millenarianism, 1780–1850*, London, 1979; E. Gaustad, *The Great Awakening in New England*, Gloucester, Mass., 1965.

may indeed be significant, and they function well as a symbol, but they are somewhat arbitrary when used to mark the beginning of a historical movement or period such as 'the Reformation'. For example, many of Luther's theological ideas derived from earlier 'heretical' movements, and he himself was hardly an isolated individual.

Are books, which also act as symbols, more secure historical indicators? We might, for instance, want to take the publication of Descartes' *Discourse on Method* (1637) as not just a major turning point in European history, but as an apt symbol for the start of the Enlightenment, in that it was published in French not in Latin, it gives status to mathematical and scientific arguments, and it takes the individual as the centrepiece and starting point for philosophy. To do so would affect one's interpretation of the Enlightenment, as well as of the history of philosophy; it is not inherently less arbitrary than any other symbolic initiation. To any individual a given symbol will be more or less satisfying, yet all contain both implicit agendas and a measure of arbitrariness. They are indispensable, but not to be used uncritically, however seductive they appear at first sight.

METAPHORS AND THEMES

Another way of delineating periods, by themes, also warrants careful reflection. Examples include 'the age of anxiety', 'the age of equipoise', 'golden age' or the 'aristocratic century'.[32] The underlying principle is by now familiar: it is the desire to lend unity to a period, in this case via a combination of description and metaphor. Of course, all descriptions are metaphorically charged, but these themes work in different ways. 'The age of revolution' may be considered more descriptive in that, on seeing it, the reader's mind moves to *specific* revolutions, in France and the United States, and the industrial revolution. 'The age of uncertainty' is rather different; it is simply a metaphor. The reader forms a vivid image, but has nothing concrete to attach it to. It does imply that other ages were more certain, and we might be able to puzzle out that a claim is being made about a twentieth-century loss of various kinds of structures,

32 S. Dunant and R. Porter, eds., *The Age of Anxiety*, London, 1996; W. Burn, *The Age of Equipoise: A Study of the mid-Victorian Generation*, London, 1964; J. Cannon, *Aristocratic Century: The Peerage of Eighteenth-Century England*, Cambridge, 1984. The phrase 'golden age' appears in the title of hundreds of books, relating to many countries, such as Spain, Italy, the Netherlands, Brazil and Scotland, and to many periods: e.g. H. Kamen, *Golden Age Spain*, Basingstoke, 1988.

possibly psychic, economic, social or political, that gave shape to life in earlier times.[33]

Each theme works in a somewhat different way, but here I want to draw attention to one further example, because of its exceptional historiographical interest – the depression around the 1930s. There is something quite striking about the use of a term we have come to associate primarily with a mood to describe an era. Whatever the origins of the term, it is emotive, and it is so in a highly specific manner. It evokes the dependency of human well-being on large-scale economic trends, unexpected emiseration and the need for compassion on more than an individual or philanthropic basis. What is so extraordinary is the way these ideas mirror trends within the period itself, during which many governments and significant social groupings, especially of intellectuals, sought radical solutions to inequalities, to authoritarian regimes and to social deprivation in their own immediate surroundings.[34] Needless to say there is no consensus on the chronological boundaries around this particular depression.[35] And since many countries experienced an economic phenomenon that was close to being global, there were marked geographical variations. In this case, periods, images of periods, self-understanding and historians' accounts are closely interwoven; the underlying mechanisms are, however, quite common.[36] Many period terms derive in some way from the categories historical actors themselves used, or out of those forged by succeeding generations for their own purposes. They then become reified, and take on a life of their own. In the case of the depression, the desire to construct a record of social conditions and to develop a social critique of them, the broad concerns of the time and the enduring interest in the entire phenomenon, render the whole process more transparent than usual.

My aim is this chapter has been to demonstrate that forms of periodisation are theoretically dense. In particular I have argued that the manner of naming periods contains assumptions about where historical agency lies and

33 J. Galbraith, *The Age of Uncertainty*, London, 1977. His aim was to 'contrast the great certainties in economic thought in the last century with the great uncertainty with which problems are faced in our time', p. 7.

34 N. Branson and M Heinemann, *Britain in the Nineteen Thirties*, London, 1971; A. Badger, *The New Deal: The Depression Years, 1933–40*, Basingstoke, 1989; J. Garraty, *The Great Depression: An Inquiry into the Causes, Course and Consequences of the Worldwide Depression of the Nineteen-Thirties*, San Diego, 1986.

35 *The Great Depression: A Historical Bibliography*, Santa Barbara, 1984. Cf. S. B. Saul, *The Myth of the Great Depression, 1873–1896*, second edition, London, 1985.

36 The Italian Risorgimento would be another example: see L. Riall, *The Italian Risorgimento: State, Society and National Unification*, London, 1994.

about what the most formative aspects of a given society are. Historians, like most people, need a sense of coherence, and although in the case of scholars this is partly for practical reasons, to make research manageable, it also serves much deeper needs. The drive to find an epitome of a period, that acts to unify it, is strong, and to some degree it does not matter whether this is found in an individual, an event, a style of government or a theme. In all these cases the totality of the historian's imagination, which works through both metaphor and visual images, is engaged. Hence, it is significant what our mother tongue is, since this determines not only the precise terminology currently in use for describing periods, but their metaphorical resonances – the notions of the Enlightenment, *die Aufklärung* and *le siècle des lumières* are quite distinct. By the same token, dominant visual traditions also help to shape views of past times – the French, for example, have a more 'rococo' view of the eighteenth century than do the English!

HISTORIOGRAPHY AND PERIODISATION

Periodisation involves other historiographical issues as well, and in closing this chapter I shall mention just two of them, in order to reaffirm the importance of critical reflection upon the precise manner in which time is at the heart of historical practice. The first concerns the *amounts* of time any given piece of historical research or writing covers: what we could call its scale or compass. Deciding how long a period is to be covered is one of the historian's most important skills, and the chosen time-span should always fit with, be apt for, the kind of project envisaged. Let us take the example of *longue durée* history, now, sadly, little practised. The defence of taking long time-spans is perfectly clear and it relates to human rhythms, to the pace of some kinds of change, and to the distinctive qualities some eras possess. Thus there were specific preconditions for Braudel's three-volume study of *Civilization and Capitalism, 15th–18th Century*: he was primarily concerned with historical phenomena that change extremely slowly, or at least have done so at some periods. Furthermore, Braudel considered the relationships between different *levels* of change, hence a long time-span was necessary for these relationships to become clear. Braudel primarily wrote about the early modern period, and it is worth considering how well his approach would have worked for later periods.[37]

---

37 F. Braudel, *Civilization and Capitalism, 15th–18th Century*, 3 vols., London, 1981, 1982 and 1984; cf. his *On History*, London, 1980, esp. the essay on 'la longue durée'. See also the works cited below in the next footnote.

There are specific historical sub-fields, which, by their very nature, have to work across very long time-spans. The most obvious examples are demography and historical epidemiology, and some areas of economic history. Not only do the trends with which they are concerned take place slowly, but they need to be studied over long periods for their significance to become apparent. Shifts in morbidity and mortality, age of marriage, fertility and rates of illegitimacy would all be examples.[38] The nature and availability of relevant evidence tends to be patchy, and subject to marked local variations in terms of quality and of survival. Hence materials need to be aggregated if anything like national, or even regional trends are to be arrived at. Yet these are not merely practical matters, related to the accidents of record-keeping and preservation; they go right to the core of historical explanation. Judgements about how fast or how slowly things change depends upon accounts of how they change at all, upon historians' understanding of the detailed mechanisms through which human beings and their environments are transformed. Hence it is imperative to ask questions, such as precisely how do attitudes and behaviours change? At what pace do they do so? How are ideas and practices transmitted from group to group, person to person, region to region? How long does such transmission typically take? These are extraordinarily challenging issues, which are too often simply ignored. It is no coincidence, I think, that many early exponents of *longue durée* history worked on *mentalités*, that is, on aspects of human existence where the nature and pace of change is particularly difficult to reconstruct.[39] By contrast, in recent years, there has been a growth of interest in extremely fine-grained, small-scale historical studies. This is related to what is sometimes called micro-history, which can involve looking at a small community or geographical area over long periods of time. Case-study history is based on the idea that we can get at larger patterns by looking carefully at one or a small number of instances. While this trend in part reflects the professionalisation and specialisation of the discipline, the pressure to produce original research, constraints of time and so on, it also reflects the wider anxieties about historical explanation and more specifically about causal

38 E. Wrigley and R. Schofield, *The Population History of England 1541–1871*, London, 1981; K. Patterson, *Pandemic Influenza 1700–1900: A Study in Historical Epidemiology*, Totowa, N.J., 1986; D. Hackett Fisher, *The Great Wave. Price Revolutions and the Rhythm of History*, New York, 1996 (covers the medieval period to the present day).

39 A classic example would be the work of Philippe Ariès: for example, *Centuries of Childhood*, Harmondsworth, 1973 (first published in French in 1960) and *The Hour of Our Death*, Harmondsworth, 1983 (first published in French in 1977).

explanations to which I alluded in Chapter 4. Rather than focusing on big events and their origins, such history explores the intricate textures of a limited area, and a sense of scale can be introduced through taking a longer period of time.

Periodisation is about managing time, the ways we imagine and conceptualise it and the amounts of it that we study in any given project. Hence its centrality for the discipline of history. At the level of individuals, both historians and those they study, time is managed by memory. Thus the second historiographical issue concerns memory.[40] The writing of history is about the transmission of memories, although the extent to which this is explicit certainly varies from field to field. Historians rely on the memories of others when it comes to sources; they require others to have conserved and to want to remember the past for their professional existence. The practice of history is, after all, a highly specialised form of commemoration. Yet we need to problematise the very notion of memory.

We could do this, for instance, through critical reflection upon the relatively new field of oral history, which relies upon the existence of memory and upon its capacity to be recorded and interpreted in a meaningful manner. Oral history has been mentioned briefly in earlier chapters; for now, we can simply remind ourselves of some key points. As it has largely been practised, oral history involves talking to older people about aspects of life that would otherwise go unstudied. Accordingly it has laid particular emphasis on the voices of those who are marginal, neglected, forgotten. It is inevitably limited in the periods it can cover, and in the types of historical issue it can address. At first sight oral history is dependent upon what people remember accurately. However, memory is imperfect, producing 'recollections' that simply cannot be true. Hence oral historians stress the need to check material generated in this way by other means. This is a richly human field, where scholars are creating their own sources, where the personality of the interviewer, including their unconscious, is inevitably mobilised in a special form of interaction between historians and their subjects.[41] Interviews often pick up dimensions of the past, the ways in which people felt, which are not dependent on the literal exacti-

---

40 See, for example, J. Gillis, ed., *Commemoration: The Politics of National Identity*, Princeton, 1993; J. Winter, *Sites of Memory, Sites of Mourning: The Great War in European Cultural History*, Cambridge, 1995; B. Taithe, '*Monuments aux Morts?* Reading Nora's *Realms of Memory* and Samuel's *Theatres of Memory*', *History of the Human Sciences*, 12, 1999, 123–39.

41 K. Figlio, 'Oral History and the Unconscious', *History Workshop Journal*, no. 26, 1988, 120–32.

tude of their memories. The practice of oral history reveals some of the complexities of memory, of historians' use of it, and the way in which assumptions about the effect of the passage of time upon human consciousness shape the writing of history. The span of a human life is inevitably the privileged unit of time in this particular field.

BRIDGE

What is remembered and the forms in which it is given expression are important historical phenomena in their own right. Since these are highly selective, they are especially important, because the processes of selection and the forms in which memories are represented are supercharged with meaning. Thus there are more general trends at work in the coupling of *History and Memory*, to use the name of an Israeli journal founded in 1988. Historians of many kinds have become interested in the nature of memory. This is because giving them *tangible* form is such an important historical phenomenon in its own right and often a genuine spur to historical activity.

The Holocaust would seem to be a particularly compelling example of more general points about history and memory. There is now an unprecedented interest in that complex amalgam of processes we have named 'the Holocaust' – it is now at a *relatively* safe distance, while many of the participants are still alive. This is by definition a temporary state. It has given impetus to many forms of historical revisionism, which is occurring in a context where novels, memoirs, exhibitions and films on the subject proliferate as never before. Memory, commemoration, memorialising, reinterpretation are all involved, and each is subtly different. Historians are right inside this mêlée. It is a mêlée precisely because there are a number of conflicting perspectives, and the conflicts are not only about what did or did not happen, but about how such events should be written about, who has the right to do so, whether historians should assign blame and so on. These issues call into question the nature of historical evidence and its interpretation, the 'ownership' of the past, the validity of memory, the wider social role of the historian, especially in relation to judicial processes, and the propriety and desirability of retrospective punishment and blame. If we think that considering the effects of the passage of time is essential to the historian's work, then there can be no more tricky, important and challenging example than the myriad issues 'the Holocaust' – a reification if ever there was one – throws up. It does so precisely because historical phenomena and their representation are *not* the exclusive domain of the discipline of history. They are in the public domain, and the public is composed of numerous social, political and institutional constituencies, with conflicting interests. These are central matters for professional historians, and we can pursue them further by probing the idea of 'public history'.

6 Public History

WHAT IS PUBLIC HISTORY?

Many readers are likely to be unfamiliar with the phrase 'public history', which has been used in recent decades in the United States.[1] We should concede from the outset that 'public' is a difficult term; in this chapter I explore some of its principal aspects in relation to the practice of history. Whatever the complexities of 'public', public history is a useful phrase, in that it draws attention to phenomena relevant to the discipline of history, but too rarely discussed in undergraduate courses. This is not surprising. Universities are staffed by professional historians, and they teach what can be called 'academic' history. While the modern structures of higher education in general and the discipline of history in particular only came into being over the nineteenth century, they have become deeply entrenched. Professional, university-based history is a particular kind of history, although those who practise it tend to speak as if there were little else. Among other things, public history is *popular* history – it is seen or read by large numbers of people and has mostly been designed for a mass audience. For some historians, 'public history' is a central part of radical history movements, which are critical of elitist, over-professionalised history, and seek to promote politically self-conscious, community-based histories, open to all and usable in political struggles. It is true that much public history has been motivated by such concerns, but precisely because public history can be effective with wide audiences, it is equally a tool of establishments.[2]

---

1 E.g. B. Howe and E. Kemp, eds., *Public History: An Introduction*, Malabar, Fla., 1986.
2 A useful introduction to the issues is S. Benson, S. Brier, and R. Rosenzweig, eds., *Presenting the Past: Essays on History and the Public*, 1986, based on articles in the *Radical History Review*. In the introduction they distinguish between three types of public history: a slick form, found in the media and serving dominant interests; professional public history; and a radical people's history. In my view there is increasing overlap and interplay between these types. See also the special issue of *Gender and History*, vol. 6, no. 3, 1994, esp. the useful introduction by Barbara Melosh.

The issues around public history highlight some of the ambiguities of the term 'history' itself. Remnants of the past are everywhere, but they are not necessarily seen as 'history' or understood as elements in a structured account of the past. Public history involves 'history' in many senses: the academic discipline; the dissemination and display of its findings to wide audiences; the past itself in many different forms; and a diffused awareness of that past that varies from person to person, group to group, country to country. Museums and heritage sites are prime examples of the complexities of public history.[3] Indeed, when the phrase 'public history' is used, this is what many people have in mind. Heritage broadly defined is a growth industry, and many, if not most public displays involve an element of history. Yet there are relatively few museums that proclaim themselves as being about history in the more academic sense; they are generally associated with a place, a type of object, an activity or a person, and the history is an integral part of everything they do. Perhaps there is *least* explicit, academic history in the temples of high culture, such as museums and galleries of modern art, but even there it necessarily has a presence. Displays based on themes or events – war or particular wars, revolutions and political movements, technology, childhood – are concerned with the past without necessarily declaring themselves to be offering instruction in history. Naturally more overtly historical collections exist – the Museum of London, the Musée Historique de la Ville de Paris, the Risorgimento Museum in Bologna, for instance. Thus, although relatively few museums and kindred institutions are obviously connected with the (professional) discipline of history, most of them are, loosely speaking, historical and contribute to the views members of the general public hold about history.[4]

3 E.g., R. Samuel, *Theatres of Memory*, vol. 1: *Past and Present in Contemporary Culture*, London, 1994, esp. part 3 'Heritage', and particularly the brilliant essay 'Semantics', pp. 205–26. Cf. D. Lowenthal, 'Fabricating Heritage', *History and Memory*, 10, 1998, 5–24.

4 The connections are closest in archaeology, where the work of museums and that of academics are inseparable. Renfrew and Bahn, *Archaeology: Theories, Methods and Practice*, ch. 14 on 'Whose Past? Archaeology and the Public' is an excellent introduction to the issues of this chapter from the point of view of archaeology. For most historians there are few or no links with the museums/heritage world. For the general public it is difficult if not impossible to discern the academic history in what they see displayed. In this general area, see *International Journal of Heritage Studies* (1994); J. Arnold et. al., ed., *History and Heritage: Consuming the Past in Contemporary Culture*, Shaftesbury, 1998; T. Bennett, *The Birth of the Museum: History, Theory, Politics*, London, 1995; P. Vergo, ed., *The New Museology*, London, 1989; J. Elsner and R. Cardinal, eds , *The Cultures of Collecting*, London, 1994; D. Horne, *The Great Museum: The Re-presentation of History*, London, 1984.

The means by which publicly displayed collections have come into being are heterogeneous. Indeed collecting is now an important historical topic in its own right.[5] Since there are so many different kinds of museums and galleries that involve the display of history in one form or another, it is extremely helpful to have an understanding of how the objects were brought together, of the audiences who are being targeted and of the politics involved, including funding arrangements. There are great institutions, such as the Smithsonian in Washington, D.C., which are hugely significant for the practice of history by virtue of their size, influence, diverse holdings and resources. It is obvious that sites set up to attract large numbers of visitors, such as Colonial Williamsburg in Virginia or Longleat in Wiltshire, are relevant to the practice of history.[6] Also relevant are cathedrals and churches that attract visitors, apparently narrowly focused museums, such as those of regiments, as well as the hundreds of new museums being set up to cater to what seems to be every conceivable interest and enthusiasm.

As a result, museums are an increasingly important subject for those who want to understand attitudes to the past; they have ceased to be a specialised area for museum professionals, and have become major cultural forces in their own right. They bear upon the practice of history in such subtle, diverse and far-reaching ways that it behoves historians to give them careful consideration. Precisely because of the extensive political implications of what has been called 'the heritage industry', these are matters for intense public debate.[7] Yet museums work in insidious ways. The past they present is highly refined, in the manner of manufactured foods. This renders both the original materials and the means by which they have been processed relatively invisible. My claim may sound odd, given that museums make objects visible, and rely upon the sense of sight for their impact. Yet they display only selected objects, and these have indeed been processed – cleaned, mended, 'restored' and packaged – in a whole variety of ways. Furthermore, the elaborate ancillary materials and

5 See, for example, *Museums Journal* (1901), *Journal of the History of Collections* (1989), and items cited in footnote 4 above.
6 Williamsburg is an attempt to reconstruct life in colonial America in considerable detail. Longleat in Wiltshire, England, is a stately home that has long promoted other attractions, such as wildlife, in the search for commercial success.
7 In the USA, the *Radical History Review* has played an important part in bringing these issues to historians. The huge amounts of money available, for example, from the Disney Corporation for theme parks with historical dimensions, fuels public discussion. In Britain, a country intensely anxious about its historic past, this has focused on 'heritage' issues and on organisations, such as the National Trust and English Heritage, with interests in the area.

INSTITUT DE FRANCE – MUSÉE JACQUEMART ANDRÉ

OPPOSITE: ***6.1 Le Salon de Musique in the Musée Jacquemart André, Paris***
This magnificent nineteenth-century collection was built up by a
couple with a number of historical enthusiasms, including for
eighteenth-century elegance and luxury. Their house uses many forms
of display to create a feel for other periods. It is now a museum, which
is best seen as a display of a certain kind of nineteenth-century taste.
Yet it is so visually seductive that it is easy for visitors to forget that the
rooms are special kinds of inventions.

activities that are required for any item to be interpreted are not displayed alongside it. Museums have significant silences; their processes of selection, management and interpretation, are rarely accessible to the general public and remain unimagined by them.

The questions of silence and invisibility should serve to remind us of points raised in earlier chapters about the apparatus of scholarship and the goal of transparency, and of the importance of allowing readers access to the resources authors use. By their very nature museums cannot operate in this way and we should not expect them to; furthermore, there is no reason why the general public, which is not after all composed of scholars, would want the apparatus made visible. Nonetheless, it is important to be clear about the consequences of museums being major communicators to the public about the past, given their modes of display. While museums satisfy curiosity about the past, they also shape the forms such curiosity is permitted to take. They transmit ideas about that past through a variety of lenses, of which visitors are unlikely to be fully aware: they convey narratives and values as well as insights and information. Further, they often communicate a sense of the past and its meanings, about which professional historians feel profoundly uncomfortable. Two examples spring to mind. Many museums generalise about living conditions in the past, presumably in order to make it more accessible, including emotionally. This is particularly marked in relation to 'everyday life', where generalisations are particularly likely to stress the past as dirty or dangerous, or indeed as innocent and safer than today. Such claims are troubling because they are so value-laden – they touch points of vulnerability, such as fear of death, crime and disease. Museum displays also deploy more straightforward assumptions about causation than would be common among professional historians. Specifically, they allocate individual and collective responsibility more freely, given that they operate, more or less, within an idiom of heroes and villains. Displays for the public are likely to stress moral clarity and the agency of individuals. Even where named and well-known historical actors are not involved, the idioms of heroism and its flipside can, nonetheless, be deployed. These are significant matters, because there exists a widespread need to understand the past in precisely these terms, that is, in terms of achievement and blame. The desire for clear patterns of responsibility in relation to which we can position ourselves is powerful. It gives rise to the strong emotions evident, for example, in the feelings still elicited by anything to do with Japan among those touched in some way by their prisoner of war camps in the 1940s. So, we want to understand and respect the forms of public history found in museums, and acknowledge their influence, but equally we must be clear about their, admittedly diverse, effects on general historical consciousness, which operate at emotional levels that are hard to get a grip on. This point is all the more important because 'history' appears, in one form or another, in so many different kinds of museum.

While museums and heritage issues dominate many discussions of public history, I want to use the term more inclusively, because there are numerous forms of history that are directed at non-professional audiences and that can usefully be considered together, including documentaries, historical fiction and drama, non-specialist magazines, and memorials. The motives behind such ventures are truly diverse – public history is, for me, simply a convenient umbrella term. Inevitably it includes items, such as buildings and public spaces, which serve as forms of public history, but were not intended as such. The fact is that the past is everywhere; when we are in public our senses are constantly responding to stimuli that are gorged with history, whether we are aware of it or not. This is a kind of historical backdrop that exists in virtually all societies. In some cases however, it has become exceptionally prominent. This is the case in many western countries over recent years, where the celebration of anniversaries of significant events for the nation and/or for humanity seems to have reached excessive proportions. By virtue of the resulting media coverage and commercial exploitation, they exemplify the point that the past is everywhere. The past that is everywhere frequently springs into focus when it is under threat in some way – a building designated for destruction, a park about to be developed, a square altered in some way, a memorial moved. This too is the domain of public history, as David Lowenthal showed so eloquently in *The Past is a Foreign Country* (1985). The fact that this environmental public history is mostly *out* of focus, not demanding conscious attention as a form of history, does not make it unimportant. When change is proposed it becomes clear how fundamental such features are for local and national identity; hence they require historians' attention.

Public history is indeed diverse. Sometimes we are in the realm of entertainment, as is the case with much historical fiction, the Scarlet Pimpernel series of novels, written in the early twentieth century, being an excellent example. Set in the period of the French Revolution, and firmly on the side of the aristocracy, they have been frequently adapted for film and television.[8] Swashbuckling accounts of the past are pretty much knowing 'reconstructions' to provide their audience with a good time composed of thrills and spills plus good costumes and period effects. At other times we are in the more sober realm of education and improvement; such is the role of many museums, some television documentaries and popular publications, including magazines about history. It is no coincidence that within the burgeoning museum industry, a notably fast-growing sector is educational activities. Naturally it is understood that these are to be, if at all possible, pleasurable and entertaining; nonetheless their main concern is with conveying views of the past. Historical documentaries can be understood in a similar manner. We can see the diversity of public history particularly clearly if we think about its less clearcut forms, especially in the media and popular publishing. In doing so it is vital to remember that it is the past's perennial usefulness in the present that underpins these phenomena.

USABLE PASTS

The idea of a usable past is hardly new, but it is probably more prominent now than it ever has been before. If the past is usable, then history is an open field that is available to be put to very different, even conflicting ends. History as entertainment uses the past for commercial purposes. History as consciousness-raising uses the past for political ends. History as public education uses the past to inform audiences (selectively) about political and social trends. But what about organisations, such as Britain's National Trust, the widespread erection of war memorials, the maintenance of public cemeteries and so on? What kinds of usable pasts are being deployed here? The National Trust was founded in 1895, 'to preserve places of historic interest or natural beauty permanently for the nation to enjoy' – a heritage ticket, designed to preserve what was construed as simultaneously precious, of historical importance, and under threat.[9] It was, and remains, a complex and contested project, as must

8 Their author, Mrs Montagu Barstow, published under the name Baroness Orczy: see J. Neild, *A Guide to the Best Historical Novels and Tales*, London, 1911. The most famous film was made in 1934 and remade in 1950, and there have been several television versions.

9 The statement about the Trust's aims is printed in their annual handbook. Its holdings include 'over 200 public houses, 230 gardens and 25 industrial monuments'.

necessarily be the case given that they have acquired a house associated with the Beatles while promoting the grand country house. Clearly there is an educational dimension, but objects in the Trust's properties are not labelled as they would be in a museum; that is, the displays are not openly or conventionally didactic. Visitors are entering a world as close as possible to the 'original', and thereby their fantasies about the past are engaged. The very notion of an original state is problematic, it hardly needs saying. Houses evolve; there is unlikely to be one single time that they genuinely evoke, although the period of the main building plays an important part in perceptions of the whole. Displays tend to gloss over such questions, so that the main effect, from the point of view of visitors, is of unspecified historical 'authenticity'.

However, it would be a mistake, and a serious over-simplification, to present visits to country houses or palaces only in terms of 'education'. For example, visitors may have a craving for nostalgic experiences which country houses meet. Nostalgia is a longing for a past state, for something by definition unobtainable – it concerns conventionalised forms of fantasy. It is striking how, in recent times, film and television shape the specific forms such nostalgia takes. We could think of this as the *Brideshead* phenomenon, following the huge success of a television adaptation of Evelyn Waugh's 1945 novel about the English aristocracy earlier in the century, and seen in many countries.[10] Self-evidently, the country houses open to the public *now* are not at all as they *were*. As we see them today, they have been sanitised – of smells and backbreaking work, for example. So when the kitchens of large houses, often among the most popular attractions, are viewed now, they convey little or no idea of what they were like when in use. Rather they offer a special kind of fiction, which visitors agree to treat as 'history'. Ironically, since more of us are descended from servants than masters, a full recognition of the conditions in domestic service, say a hundred years ago, is potentially quite disturbing. Yet there is ample evidence that country houses are satisfying a range of popular curiosities, which are woven into a collective sense of the past. The simple fact that there are marked *national* variations in this kind of behaviour reinforces the point. The folk museums found in most European countries, are, except in Wales, rare in Britain, where there is huge interest in the country house, while 'theme-park' history has been most extensively developed in the United States. In many, many places there is a huge appetite for the past, which needs to be understood and respected in its myriad forms. It is met by displays of

10 The full title of the novel is *Brideshead Revisited: The Sacred and Profane Memories of Captain Charles Rider*. F. Scott Fitzgerald's *The Great Gatsby* (1925), and the film version of 1974 have had a comparable effect.

'history' and by ways of approaching the past that are not narrowly academic, but are more akin to tourism, especially in their open appeal to fantasy.

If we turn for a moment to memorials, especially war memorials and cemeteries, the matter becomes even more complex.[11] Typically, war memorials affirm the values upon which the war in question was based. This is a matter of rhetoric, of presenting a persuasive, publicly acceptable face. The complicated conditions – diplomatic, military, political – leading up to the conflict are hardly the main issue, which is rather giving an account that bestows honour on the instigators and the personnel involved. Memorials are built to endure but have not mainly been designed as 'history'; they become so the moment they are erected. They constitute in fact a public record (and a representation) of events that are of general interest. But the very nature of the record gives them a particular set of characteristics and that is why they are, like all cultural products, representations. Like most memorials, they cannot be critical of those they commemorate, they have to present a positive image, which is artfully constructed and apt for their moment of creation. What is their purpose? They celebrate events of public significance, for governments and for large swathes of the population. They pay respect to those who lost their lives in the process. They provide a location and object for mourning for those left behind, and are, in their own right, historical documents. Furthermore, they are likely to be visually pleasing or at least markers of some kind, and hence may be visited for 'pleasure' as well as for edification, for historical interest as well as for the expression of grief and consolation. All this is part of public history, indeed it is history *in* public.[12]

These brief examples are designed to open up the meanings of 'public', such as, 'for a mass audience', 'popular', 'non-specialist', 'of concern to an entire polity' or 'available for anyone to see'. This range of meanings that can be carried by the term 'public' and the diverse uses to which the past is put are closely related issues. 'Public' also refers more specifically to the government, to the concerns and interests of the state, which may be researched in public or state record offices. Such archives are used by numerous groups, both amateur and professional, and they contain many of the raw materials for public

11 J. Gillis, ed., *Commemoration: The Politics of National Identity*, Princeton, 1993; Winter, *Sites of Memory, Sites of Mourning*, ch. 4.
12 M. Agulhon, *Marianne into Battle: Republican Imagery and Symbolism in France: 1789–1880*, Cambridge, 1981, brings out just these points. The study of public sculpture is an important area for historians, although such research is generally undertaken by specialists in art history. On war memorials, see A. Borg, *War Memorials: From Antiquity to the Present*, London, 1991; and A. King, *Memorials of The Great War in Britain: the Symbolism and Politics of Remembrance*, Oxford, 1998.

RIBA

6.2 The Great War Stone for the Imperial War Graves Commission; design by Lutyens, October 1918

Lutyens designed many memorials to commemorate the First World War and held elaborate views on the form such memorials should take. The inscription here is taken from Ecclesiasticus and was chosen by Rudyard Kipling. It may be taken as speaking to, even commanding, those left behind. Remembrance becomes a kind of universal obligation.

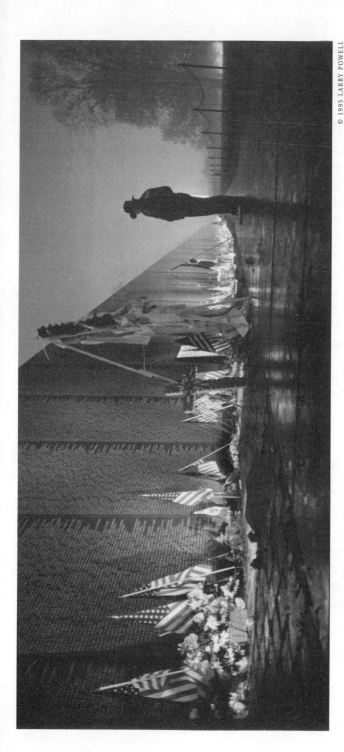

© 1995 LARRY POWELL

6.3 The Vietnam War Memorial, Washington, D.C.

The commemoration of recent events is particularly difficult, especially when views of them are as heated and diverse as those elicited by the Vietnam War have been. This particular war stands out because it has been so extensively discussed in the press and represented in the media. It is equally noteworthy because people across the world recoiled against the weapons deployed – napalm, for example – and the ruthless intervention of the United States government in distant territories. Yet those who died were to be mourned, those who were damaged to be consoled. War memorials have not lost their significance, even when the morality of the war in question is fiercely contested.

history, however this is defined. The *creators* of much public history tend to be drawn from small cadres with highly specific agendas, even if they claim to be acting in the name of wider groups. This is in stark contrast with what can be termed amateur history, undertaken by those who are not paid for their historical labour. Although what it produces could rarely be called public history, history as a hobby, an activity for amateurs, is an important phenomenon, usefully seen in the context of usable pasts. Local and family history, for example, are hugely popular and often practised by enthusiasts with refined skills in genealogy or charting the history of houses, for instance. Tracing origins, making lineages that serve particular purposes, are important themes in many parts of public history. Spin offs include local exhibitions and clubs – this is very much history being used for present purposes. One important point to emerge from thinking about the nature of amateur history is the types of concern that motivate people to undertake historical hobbies – remember that 'amateur' originally meant 'doing something for love', not 'lacking in skill', as is sometimes supposed. The difference between professional and amateur historians is probably not as clear-cut as the former think. It may be worth recalling here that the majority of historical bestsellers are by people who write, outside the university system, for money. Hence what constitutes a professional historian, a historical writer, or an amateur historian is somewhat fluid, as reflection upon public history demonstrates.

GENRES AND AUDIENCES

However they are to be defined, professional and amateur historians tend to work within different historical genres. By 'genre' I mean a recognisable type of representation, whether in the form of words, displays, pictures or film, that is governed by literary, artistic or institutional conventions, such as the novel, the monograph, the diorama, the local history lecture and so on. Inevitably there are huge variations within genres, and their conventions are far from static, but the concept is nonetheless a useful one. Genres are historically specific. Indeed, genre is a notion of central importance for understanding public history, and vice versa. Let me explain why. Because genres always involve elements of convention, they are recognised, often intuitively, by audiences and readers. There are certain expectations on both sides that are, in effect, informal rules of engagement. Historical fiction is a genre with many subgenres, including historical romances. Readers of these expect closure, romantic resolution between hero and heroine, especially in ones written by popular novelists such as Georgette Heyer, who, writing between the 1920s and the 1970s, specialised in eighteenth- and early nineteenth-century England.[13] Other sorts of historical novels may culminate in an adventure successfully completed or the death of the hero(ine). These are narrative types and they deploy easily recognised *topoi*. I want to insist on the importance of genre (and other literary conventions) for any understanding of the practice of history. All writings have a generic context, and being aware of the point enables one to evaluate any given piece more effectively. Recognising genres and analysing instances of them depends precisely on understanding conventions and their implications. This is particularly important in thinking about *public* history. Public history uses a wide variety of genres, which are different from those of the academic discipline – a fact that shapes the content of the type of history we are designating 'public'. If we can identify and reflect upon this generic range, the whole phenomenon, including the means by which publics develop their sense of the past, can be appreciated more fully.[14]

One thing is certain, the audiences for history are wide, diverse and in places extremely well informed. Thus 'public', which covers so much, is slippery and ambiguous, but nonetheless useful. One historical account, by Jürgen Habermas, the German sociologist and philosopher, which has become hugely influential, charts the development of a so-called 'public sphere' over the eighteenth century.[15] 'Sphere' here is a metaphor, which unfortunately carries the misleading connotation of watertight areas. Many historians refer, rather unselfconsciously, to a gendered distinction between the public (male) and the private or domestic (female) spheres, which is also supposed to have developed over the eighteenth century in concert with the economic and social shifts summed up in the phrase 'the industrial revolution', and with a political conservatism about female roles in the wake of the American and French

13 See J. Hodge, *The Private World of Georgette Heyer*, London, 1984.
14 Although not primarily about (public) history, the following works are useful:
    G. Levine, ed., *Realism and Representation: Essays on the Problem of Realism in Relation to Science, Literature, and Culture*, Madison, 1993; L. Cooke and
    P. Wollen, eds., *Visual Display: Culture Beyond Appearances*, Seattle, 1995; D. Haraway, *Primate Visions. Gender, Race and Nature in the World of Modern Science*, New York, 1989, ch. 3 (about the New York Museum of Natural History).
15 J. Habermas, *The Structural Transformation of the Public Sphere: An Inquiry into a Category of Bourgeois Society*, Cambridge, Mass., 1989. Cf. D. Castiglione and L. Sharpe, eds., *Shifting the Boundaries. Transformation of the Languages of Public and Private in the Eighteenth Century*, Exeter, 1995.

revolutions.[16] Habermas's approach is rather different, in that it focuses on the generation of 'public opinion' – a concept and a set of practices – and on arenas for debate within which matters of wide interest could be discussed in a liberal and tolerant fashion. Emblematic of this shift is the development of newspapers, which Habermas finds particularly marked in eighteenth-century England. We might note with interest that public museums developed in Europe at this very time – the British Museum, for instance.[17] Although the growth of print culture was gradual over the sixteenth and seventeenth centuries, and certainly subject to considerable local variation, the eighteenth century does mark a significant turning point in relation to the history of communications, of audiences, and of the idea of 'the public'.[18] Benedict Anderson summarised the point particularly eloquently in his influential book *Imagined Communities* (1991). His purpose was to identify the preconditions for a modern sense of nationhood, in the development of which citizens all over a nation reading simultaneously the same or similar news, played, he claims, a significant part. He was concerned with mechanisms through which what is essentially an abstract idea – 'nationhood' – can be communicated to large numbers of people. Part and parcel of this idea was a sense of their nation's history, shared by a significant proportion of the population, and incorporated into their lives and identities. So, the concept and practices of 'the public' are themselves historical phenomena, and more specifically what I am calling public history has been bound up with nation-formation for nearly three centuries. Tracing the uses that governments, professions and other interested parties make of 'the public sphere' and of the past and charting the ways in which the results have become part of each society's imaginary, helps to explain the origins and current importance of public history.

I am suggesting that there is a helpful model here for understanding the development of the phenomenon 'public history'. People in far-flung places encounter historical displays and publications that are relevant to them, and through which they construct their identity. Political structures, such as nations and their administrative infrastructures, mediate the processes involved, which are thereby value-laden. These days the public can visit

16 On the gendering of public and private, see J. Elshtain, *Public Man, Private Woman: Women in Social and Political Thought*, Oxford, 1981; A. Vickery, 'Golden Age to Separate Spheres? A Review of the Categories and Chronology of English Women's History', *Historical Journal*, 36, 1993; L. Davidoff, *Worlds Between: Historical Perspectives on Gender and Class*, Cambridge, 1995, ch. 8; J. Landes, *Women and the Public Sphere in the Age of the French Revolution*, Ithaca, N.Y., 1988.

17 E. Miller, *That Noble Cabinet: A History of the British Museum*, London, 1973.

18 Cf. Castiglione and Sharpe, *Shifting the Boundaries*.

museums and see films that have similar effects. They use what they read and see in other bits of their lives, they become parts of imagined communities, often through the nation which, Anderson suggested, exists in part through having a shared, publicly available history. Memorials to leaders and to events of symbolic importance are, like dynasties of rulers, visible signs of a nation's shared history, even if that past has been subject to the equivalent of creative accountancy. While education systems put in place the building blocks of collective identity, it is further shaped and sustained, occasionally radically altered, by public history. It follows that one of the most important insights the phenomenon of public history affords, is that collective understanding of the past is imbibed by *all* the senses, and worked upon in the imagination.

It will be evident by now that in discussing 'public history' I have in mind three principal issues – the non-academic audiences for history, the general cultural uses of the past, and specific displays that relate to history broadly defined. 'Public', then, indicates a wider interest and participation in history than simply professional historians and specialised publications. The past is essentially open-ended, and accounts of it are public property, available for numerous uses. Recognising this should help historians to see their own activities in a wider perspective and to raise broad questions about the practice of history. In particular, it should be possible to focus more clearly on those issues that are central to public history, but that are frequently neglected in professional practice. Shortly I shall briefly pursue one of these, which has elicited widespread interest: who, if anyone, *owns* the past? Raising the question involves thinking less about the raw materials of history, although ownership of these is certainly a matter of some significance, than about who is entitled to represent the past authoritatively. I understand this to be a political issue, so it is important to be clear about the ways in which this is so.

PUBLIC HISTORY AND POLITICS

We should remember that the state, which in many countries plays a major role in funding institutions such as archives and museums, lies at the very heart of public history. Public history is a political matter in at least two further respects. First, since it represents the past to the public, the 'displays' that make up public history contain and promote particular interests. Second, they depart from specific vantage points, although the precise nature of these varies from case to case. These are indeed political matters; they concern alignments and representations of power. For example, understanding the role of the state in funding, and of elites in shaping, historical displays, is a vital part of examining public history. The representation of political winners and losers, whether these are classes, religious alliances, political factions or ethnic group- ings, is an obvious example. Furthermore, much public history is sponsored, especially in museums, and when it comes to galleries on the history of food production or nuclear power in which the related industries have a hand, then there are complex political forces to contend with.

There is a related and looser sense in which public history is political in that it weaves moral discourses around objects displayed. We are familiar with the idea that history is composed of narratives. For most people, historians tell stories, not in the sense that they make things up, but in the sense that their accounts of the past are structured and gain plausibility in the same manner as other narratives. We are equally familiar with the idea that historical sto- ries are morally charged. Everyone can laugh at *1066 and All That*, the comic account of British history, or the Asterix stories, cartoon strips about Roman Gaul, because they recognise that judgements about, for example, kings, polit- ical leaders and whole nations being 'good' or 'bad' are absolutely everywhere, including among professional historians.[19] This should come as no surprise, and I am certainly not suggesting that historians either can or should refrain from moral discussions altogether. The point about history that reaches wider audiences is that the moral judgements can be crude, implicit or concealed, making them (sometimes) hard to discern and to be held up for critical inspection by those not 'in the know'.

The political nature of history for the public becomes exceptionally clear when there are fierce controversies, as there were over the plans to put the *Enola Gay*, the aeroplane that dropped the bomb on Hiroshima, on display at the National Air and Space Museum in Washington, D.C. in 1995, 50 years after the end of the Second World War. Its proposed mode of presentation caused an uproar, especially among veterans. The resulting controversies have been extensively documented and debated, providing an exceptional range of insights into public history in the United States.[20] This was a political matter in that it revolved around how objects associated with one of the most highly charged events of the twentieth century should be presented to the public, the

19 W. Sellar and R. Yeatman, *1066 and All That. A Memorable History of England*, London, 1930 and Goscinny and Uderzo, *Asterix the Gaul*, Leicester, 1969. Samuel, 'One in the Eye: *1066 And All That*' in *Island Stories: Unravelling Britain*, pp. 208–13.

20 Particularly useful is the special section in *Technology and Culture*, 39, 1998, pp. 457–82, which discusses not only the *Enola Gay* fiasco but also broad issues around public history. The Allied bombing of Dresden in 1945 has raised similar issues.

© 1999 LES ÉDITIONS ALBERT RENÉ / GOSCINNY-UDERZO

6.4 A page from Asterix in Spain

History reaches the public in many forms. In the case of Asterix cartoons, the past is a source of fun and especially of word play; readers are expected to have some familiarity not only with the Roman world, but also with literary representations of it. Note here the reference to Shakespeare's Julius Caesar.

Key: H = loan from Hiroshima Peace Memorial Museum
    N = loan from Nagasaki International Culture Hall

6.5 *Proposed (and abandoned) exhibition layout for 'The Last Act: The Atomic Bomb and the End of World War II' (1995)*

Since 1945 the world has had to live with nuclear power, but has found no easy ways either of coming to terms with the bombs dropped on Japan or with the integration of nuclear energy into everyday life. Telling the story of how this particular form of energy was developed, used at the end of the Second World War and deployed subsequently, inevitably provokes violent reactions since there can be no neutral, purely factual account. Hence any version of the story will be controversial because it will contain both implicit and explicit assumptions about politics broadly defined. There is nothing unique about this issue, but the polarised responses are particularly dramatic, as the Smithsonian Institution's National Air and Space Museum discovered when they tried to mount an exhibition built around the Enola Gay.

balance between commemoration and historical interpretation, and the soundness of received accounts that the bombs 'saved' lives in the end. Many people now think that the Allies were simply wrong to drop the bombs on Japan and that their motives for doing so were decidedly mixed. For others the Allies were right, and the event may legitimately be celebrated. It is impossible to present these issues 'neutrally', and it could be argued that it is improper to do so, given the huge destruction of civilian life and the long-term effects of the bombs. Yet, publicly funded institutions are subject to a range of forces and constraints, which have nothing to do with academic history. A critical analytical view of the end of the war proved threatening both to veterans and to the United States government.

Other institutions besides governments and museums are involved in public history, however, which remains a loosely political issue even in its more commercial forms. History is part of many industries that sell the past in one form or another. Reproduction clothes, jewellery, furniture and decorative objects in effect present views of particular historical periods to the general public, thereby creating and maintaining an image of distinct eras – the eighteenth century was elegant, the nineteenth ornate, the twentieth streamlined and so on – based on notions of style. This may sound innocuous, such clear fictions that they are hardly significant, but, as I have argued earlier in the book, aesthetic responses are a powerful force in shaping attitudes to the past. Although there appear to be no political elements here, it is vital to remember what dramatic forms of selection are involved. To see the eighteenth century in terms of elegance, for instance, depends on giving priority to aristocratic lifestyles and to their cultural hegemony. It further depends upon particular readings of the *ancien régime*, which buy into the ideologies of the time.[21] The huge growth of retailing in museums, which involves items related to the collection, has greatly contributed to this trend.

Another significant element in public history is the *commissioning* of books by commercial enterprises, such as those designed to celebrate a business's history, that is to construct a particular kind of public face for it. The whole question of commissioned histories has become a rather vexed one. Professional associations and political organisations, like departments of government and other organisations, frequently buy in the services of historians, who

21 The chain of shops that retails 'historical' items, Past Times, demonstrates
the point. The idea that the eighteenth century was 'elegant' is
commonplace, e.g. in relation to clothes and music. Other public,
marketable images co-exist, which are equally politically freighted, e.g. the
'romp', bodice-ripping view of the eighteenth century, which totally ignores
class tensions, and is based on a selective reading of fiction from the period.

HISTORICAL COLLECTIONS GROUP PLC

6.6 Pages from the Past Times catalogue

These pages are from the catalogue of a successful company that sells goods related to the past in its chains of shops and by mail order. Note the associations between periods and styles and also the videos of a dramatisation of a series of historical novels.

become dependants, losing a measure of intellectual freedom. Such relationships are never unproblematic. One major issue is whether historians are given unfettered access to the relevant archives and allowed to make what they will of them, or whether they will be expected to write a history that is constrained from the very beginning, by the restricted materials to which they have been given access. Then there is the question of interpretation – are commissioned historians able to pass whatever judgements they think fit, or is the account to be written in order to show the company or organisation in a good light? I have stated the issue rather crudely and no doubt in practice it is less clear-cut than this. But it is as well to be aware of the possible pitfalls – he who pays the piper . . . Although some commissioned histories are written mainly for other historians, and thereby contribute, for example, to the growing field of business history, they also have wider publics. Potential audiences include those who work for or support the commissioning body. Here, the writing of history is being used for purposes determined by the commissioners, making tensions between commemoration and analysis almost inevitable.[22]

The difficulties of commissioned histories remind us of a theme that runs throughout this book and that is especially important for public history. It is generally accepted that historical accounts are, unavoidably, implicitly moralising. Some historical accounts are commissioned specifically to make the subject look good, precisely because history is deemed to have moral authority and people with power try to make themselves, and those with whom they identify, appear worthy of respect by these means. This is a particularly important issue in the case of biographies, which, for living or recently dead subjects, are often commissioned by families, colleagues and friends. Readers may be surprised that I mention biography in the context of public history, yet as one of the most popular and enduring of historical genres, biographies bring history to a broad public and are themselves widely discussed. They make an interesting comparison with official, commissioned histories. It is worth remembering that *un*authorised biographies can cause a fantastic stir. How a life is publicly valued *is* significant – the actions of significant figures and their interpretation are morally charged.[23]

22 C. Webster, *The Health Services Since the War*, 2 vols., London, 1988 and 1996, was commissioned by the government. Cf. his *The National Health Service: A Political History*, Oxford, 1998. Business history is a growing field: see, for example, the journals *Business History* (1959) and *Business History Review* (1926).
23 Figures such as the steel magnate and philanthropist Andrew Carnegie exemplify the point: H. Livesay, *Andrew Carnegie and the Rise of Big Business*, Boston, 1975; J. Wall, *Andrew Carnegie*, New York, 1970; L. Hacker, *The World of Andrew Carnegie 1865–1901*, Philadelphia, 1968. Cf. *Autobiography of Andrew Carnegie*, Boston, 1920, and J. Wall, 'A Second Look at Andrew Carnegie', in S. Baron and C. Pletsch, eds., *Introspection in Biography: The Biographer's Quest for Self-Awareness*, Hillsdale, N.J., 1985, pp. 209–22.

The reputations of major historical actors are of public concern. Since many biographers need special permission to use private papers, their relationships with the guardians of those papers is vital. Let us be clear that the issue is rarely that of 'the truth'. Families may know things about relatives but still prefer biographers not to publicise them – indeed, this could be a condition of granting access. The biographer who agreed to such terms would not so much be distorting the past, as this phrase is generally used, but deftly omitting material that is in some way problematic. Selection is a central historical skill, and its evaluation is exceptionally tricky, since much of it is rendered invisible in the final account. The presentation of historical figures in a positive light is not as simple as it might appear. To write a convincing biography the author needs a certain measure of sympathy with their subject, and they are likely to identify more or less strongly with that person – this is true of all historical projects. A few biographies are written out of dislike, disapproval or hatred, but they are relatively rare.[24] If family members are still alive, the historian may get close to them too, and inevitably emotional bonds are set up. Unconsciously, then, historians tell their stories in particular ways that could be seen as 'flattering', but are not necessarily intentionally so. All such accounts are necessarily selective. Naturally a historical training involves raising one's consciousness about such matters, but the unconscious is a powerful force, never completely mastered.

In the very process of writing a biography, the historian's responses to and evaluations of their subject are expressed. Readers, who already think in terms of praise and blame, of innocence and guilt, will pick this up. All historical accounts contain moral judgements, either implicit or explicit. History written for a general public is, by its very nature, likely to bring such judgements into prominence. In other words, although all historical activities raise questions about morals, responsibility and ethics, public history does so with special urgency. This is partly because public historical discourses tend to be condensed and simplified, bringing out such issues in a pristine form. Biographies make the point particularly clearly, but they are hardly the only genre of historical writing where we run across debates about the moral judgements of historians – debates that are at once about the emotional and political dimensions of history. The content of public history – wars, genocide, dictators, national and international crises, for instance – places moral issues in the foreground. Moral and political dimensions are inseparable.

---

24 Jesse Foot's defamatory life of the celebrated surgeon John Hunter who died
    in 1793, is a good example: *The Life of John Hunter*, London, 1794.

WHO OWNS THE PAST?

I have described the past as 'public property', which brings us back to the question of who owns the past?[25] Property and ownership are potent metaphors. I am less interested in the issues around public access to historical sources, although these are important matters, than in the investment in and identification with aspects of the past, which, somehow, make them our own. The notion that the past is public property can be used to stress the openness of the past, its availability for diverse purposes. But its implications need to be followed through. For example, the past is routinely deployed for openly manipulative ends. The claim all too commonly made by racist groups that their country began to decline with increasing rates of immigration would be a case in point. This claim depends upon people believing a specific, highly interested account of two past trends ('decline' and 'immigration'), positing a causal relationship between them, and drawing a political inference from it. To say that the past is public property certainly implies that there will be diverse, competing accounts; hence developing a critical perspective upon them is essential. Yet, beyond personal preference, it remains unclear how, in the case of public history, competing accounts are to be evaluated. Both historical sources and the ability to construct historical accounts cease to be the exclusive domain of a professional cadre, and the ubiquity of history is affirmed.

'Public property' implies thinking about the past in the idiom of ownership. In order to pursue these matters further, two preliminary points need to be made. First, in drawing attention to the language of ownership I am not implying approval of it. Rather I am spelling out common assumptions and encouraging critical reflections upon them. Second, if history is popular because people identify with aspects of it, then the question of ownership is bound to come up one way or another. Ownership is not only an exceptionally powerful metaphor, it is totally bound up with identity – this has *not* been true always and everywhere, but it definitely is here and now.[26]

A familiar example, women's history, makes the point.[27] During and as a result of second-wave feminism, a distinctive brand of historical heroine was

---

25 I. McBryde, ed., *Who Owns the Past?*, Melbourne, 1985.
26 I am emphatically not making a global statement here. Notions of ownership are historically specific. I refer to the political and intellectual traditions that I, and most of my readers, have been shaped by, whether we like it or not.
27 Cf. B. Anderson and J. Zinsser, *A History of Their Own: Women in Europe from Prehistory to the Present*, 2 vols., London, 1989. More generally, we should note periodical publications such as *Our History* (1956) and *Our History Journal* (1977).

sought and celebrated. The notion of role models began to be widely used at that time. Women *readers* of history were encouraged to identify with women *makers* of history through the *writers* of history, and to applaud, and emulate, past achievements, which embraced all women. In this sense women's history was not just *about* women, but *for* women, to use in their own lives. And for some it was 'our' history, that is, a story with special relevance for one group – women – who were its rightful possessors. But who was part of that 'our'? Black women were quick to point out that a false inclusiveness had been implied by generalisations about women in the past, and the extent to which there are common threads in female experience across classes and races at a given time and place remains a contested issue. Some of the pioneers of women's history in the 1970s were men, and this gave rise to considerable comment – they were muscling in on the act, 'using' women for their own career ends, since this was a trendy new field. All this implies assumptions about relationships between subjects and interpreters of history most familiarly expressed in the language of ownership. To say 'my' or 'our' history is to evoke the past of a group with which the speaker is strongly identified. It is essential to remember, however, that each speaker is likely to have a number of possible identities; hence, in practice, it is never self-evident which one is dominant. Histories, especially popular ones, find multiple identities difficult to negotiate, often because political imperatives dictate that *one* should be paramount. There are those who would say that only women can write women's history, because only they can know the subject from the inside. While I happen to think this argument is fallacious – it has to assume that woman is a timeless category – it is not hard to feel its emotional tug, and for 'women' we could substitute a number of ethnic, racial or religious categories.

I wish to draw attention both to the assumptions about the practice of history upon which arguments about who may practise what we could call identity history draw, and to their implications for history presented to the public.[28] In fact, these arguments about identity history are quite widely believed in, especially in the United States, where it is commonly assumed that black history should be written and taught by black people, Jewish history by Jews and so on. Similar questions are raised about museums and exhibitions – should a non-Jew, for instance, be appointed director of a Jewish museum? For the case in favour of such restrictions to be plausible, two conditions have to

28   The phrase 'identity politics' is widely used in the United States, and it has helped to shape the type of history I am discussing here.

obtain. First, the insider point has to work. There has to be some privileged insight that is afforded by belonging to the category in question. However it is unclear just how this privilege works, especially for historians interested in much earlier times: can enough continuity across centuries reasonably be assumed to make the insider argument plausible? What kind of continuity is involved? Second, a political assertion has to be made, so that even if the historian has no privileged insights, it would somehow be wrong for them to study a group unless they were part of it. An ethical cum political argument would be required about who is entitled to study the past and by virtue of what characteristics.

To my mind, all historians, whatever their professional status, have ethical obligations, to be humane, accurate, self-aware and judicious, for instance, but these are mobilised in the actual practice of history and not by virtue of those aspects of the historian's person over which they have little or no control. Indeed the best historians excel precisely because they can understand conditions that are *not* part of their own immediate experience. This capacity is central to the historian's imagination. My position is consistent with one aspect of public history that I am presenting in this chapter. The past is everywhere, it is constantly being used and re-presented, and ideally should not to be appropriated by special interests. Yet my position is in manifest tension with another aspect of public history to which I have also drawn attention. Public history by and large is interested history, and the closer it is to the state and its concerns, or indeed to any powerful faction with a strong identity and plentiful resources, the more insistent those interests are likely to be. Displays concerning the history of nuclear power, which are invariably controversial, are an excellent example of the point. This is precisely why those who are alienated from dominant interests have developed oppositional strategies to bring their histories into the public eye. This has resulted, in the museums and heritage world at least, in a proliferation of museums representing the concerns of different groups. Curators within what could be called establishment museums are working extremely hard to present divergent views within their institutions. There is a vital distinction to be made between the urgent need for oppositional public history, and assessments of who is best qualified to carry it out. To locate those qualifications in the race, gender, class or religious background of the historian is dangerous. It misplaces historical authority by putting it in biological or social attributes over which their possessors have little or no control rather than where it should be – in carefully acquired skills and experience.

MORAL JUDGEMENTS

One theme that has been running through this chapter is the importance of public history for any understanding of general attitudes towards the past and of beliefs about history among communities. The centrality of public history has two facets. First, public history reaches mass audiences; its capacity to penetrate into everyday life is formidable. In the way I have defined it, 'public history' includes many phenomena, including television and fiction. My hunch is that these two forms of culture have done more than anything else to shape popular historical mentalities. It follows that professional historians need to understand them and appreciate their complex effects. Second, in mobilising potent feelings that can loosely be described as 'moral', public history works with the emotions. There are thus powerful investments in a significant proportion of historical accounts. Some events in the human past are disproportionately dense in these respects. I want to explore these questions a little further, while insisting that they are not unique to *public* history; it just throws them into sharper relief.

The twentieth century has witnessed, and is currently witnessing, a number of events that appear so terrible we flounder in the face of them. It is unclear to me whether they are completely without precedent in human history, and in any case the intellectual challenge they present would not be lessened if precedents could be found.[29] Their terribleness consists partly in their proximity to us, which has less to do with how recent they are than with their *sensual* immediacy through film, television and fiction, as well as through radio, newspapers and oral transmission. Although the Holocaust and the dropping of the bombs on Hiroshima and Nagasaki are extreme in their horror, the responses they elicit have a lot to tell us about public history, and hence about the practice of history in general.

In memorials to the millions who died in the 1930s and 1940s, and in museums on related subjects, a limited number of quotations are repeatedly used. They concern the importance of remembering in order to learn from the past, and in particular they stress that those who forget the past are destined to repeat it.[30] Indeed for many people this would be one of the most important goals of public history: we remember in order to learn. But what precisely can

29 Charles Maier addresses just this question in *The Unmasterable Past*, Cambridge, Mass., 1988. See also, A. Rosenbaum, *Is the Holocaust Unique? Perspectives on Comparative Genocide*, Boulder, Colo., 1996.
30 E.g. the Museum of the Resistance, Lyon, and the Memorial to the Deported, Paris. See also, J. Young, *The Texture of Memory: Holocaust Memorials and Meaning*, New Haven, 1993 and J. Young, ed., *The Art of Memory: Holocaust Memorials in History*, Munich, 1994.

be learnt? What are the lessons of history and how are they to be applied to other times and places? Are there clear, unambiguous inferences to be drawn from past events that can be transformed into recipes for doing it better? We should note that 'doing it better' would necessarily involve an entire society, so historians would somehow have to become politically effective conduits between past and future. It is certainly a problem that historians draw extremely diverse conclusions from the materials they study. The notion of 'lessons from history' is so glibly invoked that the difficulties behind it are often missed. These are extraordinarily difficult questions, and people easily misunderstand each other because feelings about them run so high. The result is a desire for simple answers and for clear moral polarities. One of the most important insights historians can bring to wider audiences is that there are no such things, however clear-cut the moral issues appear. And saying this is emphatically not the same as claiming that the historians can or should be neutral.

At the heart of these difficulties lie guilt and blame. Obviously historians evaluate the competing claims of historical actors, they piece together accounts of how decisions and actions were taken, and they form ideas about responsibility. Once responsibility is assigned, it is a tiny step into the territory of guilt and blame. The need to find culprits for terrible deeds is deep-rooted: it is emotionally satisfying to have hate-figures, it brings clarity and simplicity, and, most important of all, it clears others of blame. And there will always be prior emotional preferences about where blame should lie. I believe it is impossible to explain fully where those prior commitments come from, but historical controversies bear witness to them. For example, in recent years, as events in Germany that led up to the Second World War have been re-evaluated (and how far back do you go in explaining the rise of Fascism?), there have been huge public debates about the role of the German population as a whole. To what extent did they know what was going on? If they did know and were complicit or even willing participants, what kind of responsibility do they bear? Whose fault was the Holocaust?[31]

These questions spawn another set. If responsibility is successfully assigned, what follows? Should the perpetrators make reparations, and if so, how? Is literal or symbolic compensation being sought, or both? Will justice be achieved by saying 'sorry', demanded by those who suffered in Japanese prisoner of war camps; by returning property, which is being asked of museums and banks who

---

31 The ferocity of responses to D. Goldhagen's *Hitler's Willing Executioners: Ordinary Germans and the Holocaust*, London, 1996, makes the point. See also C. Browning, *The Path to Genocide: Essays on Launching the Final Solution*, Cambridge, 1992, and J. Stern, *Hitler, the Führer and the People*, Glasgow, 1975.

hold Jewish possessions; or by paying compensation, a fairly frequent request to governments, banks and businesses? Should aged Nazis be prosecuted so long after the relevant events took place, and, if found guilty, punished? What punishments are appropriate – imprisonment, execution, public shame? Naturally the intensity of these debates is fuelled by many of the participants still being alive, and the practical consequences of prosecutions are hardly straightforward. It is possible to reflect upon many of the questions just posed in an abstract manner; more concrete responses have to be based on national and international law. Legal cases demand extensive historical evidence. Furthermore each case, each issue, must be seen in context, its particularities examined. This is, at least in part, the historian's province, a point which explains why many of the protagonists in the on-going consequences of the Holocaust are employing historians to undertake archival work. Much of the sorting out involves trying to determine who knew what and when, because only then can responsibility, blame and guilt be assigned in a more secure manner. The Holocaust and its aftermath involve historians in a number of ways – historians are doing research upon which judgements are based, they participate in wider debates about what happened and why, they bear responsibility, especially to survivors, for accounts that go out in the name of history. Historians are thoroughly implicated then in the history that reaches the public. It follows that they carry special responsibilities by virtue of the stakes in historical accuracy and the moral authority that the discipline of history enjoys. But what counts as authoritative 'history' here is just what is at issue. Not all accounts of the horrors of the 1930s and 1940s are equally authoritative. Popular discourse, which is rather unreflexive about moral polarities, and scholarly history need each other, yet they march to different beats.

It is widely known that there are revisionist historians around who believe that a distorted view of, for example, Nazi concentration camps has been disseminated in order to exaggerate the suffering of the Jews. This is anti-Semitic history and its existence reinforces many of the points made earlier in the chapter. If the past is open, available, usable, public property, what is to stop revisionist historians, such as David Irving, telling stories that could be regarded as deeply malicious, unethical and completely irresponsible, especially when they claim to have evidence to back them up?[32] In earlier chap-

---

32   D. Irving, *The Destruction of Dresden*, London, 1963; *Hitler's War*, London, 1977; *Nuremberg: the Last Battle*, London, 1996. For a critical view of this work, see Harris, *The Media Trilogy*, esp. pp. 374–9. A defence of Irving is N. Jackson, *The Case for David Irving: The Selective Censorship of History and Free Speech*, Cranbrook, Western Australia, 1994. Holocaust denial is a criminal offence in Germany.

tcrs I argued that the apparatus of scholarship, and the ability to scrutinise other historians' sources, methods and arguments, are the solution. In the context of public history and debates about the Holocaust, this response appears naïve and inadequate. It does so precisely because public discourse is not scholarly discourse. Given that many people do not possess the materials or the tools to evaluate radically different accounts of a morally charged event, they will turn to their emotions for guidance. It is in the interest of many groups to present the past in simplified moralistic and didactic terms, which play upon intense feelings. The problem is that feelings are not always a very good guide because, by their very nature, they make people uncritical. And since there is never unanimity on matters of the heart, who is to say whether one person's emotions are 'better' or more justified than another's?

At this point we have reached the hub of concerns about relativism.[33] A simple definition of relativism would be 'the rejection of absolute standards of judgement'. In the eyes of critics, however, the term implies a repudiation of any standards at all, a lack of discrimination in seeing everything as equally acceptable. However tricky or emotive a subject, 'relativism' sums up a cluster of concerns that historians have to consider. On the one hand, it has been part of educational philosophy for some time that different opinions are to be respected; seeing the world through the eyes of diverse groups has come to be preferred over passing judgements based only on our own perspective. It seems to me that the recent growth of interest in environmental history is a striking example of this trend. Changes to the management of natural resources are no longer seen in terms of necessary and inevitable economic progress but from the vantage points of natives, poor labourers and so on. This example further illustrates the close relationships between politics, public policy and the practice of history, given the rise of environmental movements over the same period.[34] Many recent trends in the discipline depend on this orientation towards other ways of life and belief systems, which is partly due to the huge influence of anthropology.

On the other hand, we have been encouraged to respect (some types of) interested history. Committed history puts one particular perspective and may not be terribly sympathetic to other, competing ones. This, rather different, form of relativism, sanctions value judgements, usually so long as they are on

33 See, for example, P. Finney, 'Ethics, Historical Relativism and Holocaust Denial', *Rethinking History*, 2, 1998, pp. 359–69.
34 W. Cronon, *Changes in the Land. Indians, Colonists, and the Ecology of New England*, New York, 1983; R. White, *Land Use, Environment and Social Change: The Shaping of Island County, Washington*, Seattle, 1980.

the 'right' side. For example, it was only relatively recently that left-leaning historians have turned with some confidence and pleasure to writing about the history of the aristocracy. While there are diverse ways in which the history of the aristocracy can be approached, the 1960s and 1970s witnessed a surge of interest in less privileged groups. Since then the ideological climate has shifted and the rich materials left by aristocrats have exercised an allure over historians, who are approaching their research with the agendas of social and cultural history in mind.[35] There are a number of possible responses to the resulting dilemmas. One could say that all history departs from a specific viewpoint, so that identifications and preferences are inevitable, they are not objectionable in themselves so long as they are avowed, and the scholarly apparatus is in clear view. However, this works better in scholarly than in public history. Or, one could say that the positions taken should depend upon the situation studied. This implies that historians need to be open and flexible, rather than coming to research with fixed ideas. For example, the assertion that history should, on principle, be written from the servants' rather than the masters' viewpoint, could be criticised as too abstract, ungrounded in the materials. It seems that many servants exploited their masters, for instance through blackmail, while in other cases masters exploited their servants, for example sexually.[36] Indeed even in a single household the situation might vary, so that to take *one* position as *the* starting point fails to do justice to the historical complexities. Thus it could be argued that the framework should always be grounded in the historical problem it is designed to elucidate, and not in abstract positions.

Yet another response to the complexities of relativism in relation to public history might be to attempt to change the terms in which history is debated in public, so that the genuine ambiguities can be acknowledged and more generally appreciated. But does this mean that a historian has the right to publish a book 'sympathetic' to Hitler – to take an extreme case?[37] I feel the answer

35 Work on the aristocracy has included, L. Stone, *The Crisis of the Aristocracy, 1558–1641*, Oxford, 1965, and *The Family, Sex and Marriage in England*, London, 1977; D. Lieven, *The Aristocracy in Europe, 1815–1914*, Basingstoke, 1992; S. Tillyard, *Aristocrats: Caroline, Emily, Louisa and Sarah Lennox, 1750–1832*, London, 1994 and a TV series; P. Mandler, *The Fall and Rise of the Stately Home*, New Haven, 1997.

36 On servants, see C. Fairchilds, *Domestic Enemies: Servants and their Masters in Old Regime France*, Baltimore, 1984; A. Kussmaul, *Servants in Husbandry in Early Modern England*, Cambridge, 1981; J. Hecht, *The Domestic Servant Class in Eighteenth-Century England*, London, 1956. Similar issues are raised by any kind of historical research on unequal power relationships where one side is widely castigated.

37 Irving, *Hitler's War*, cf. Kershaw, *Hitler: 1889–1936: Hubris*.

must be 'yes', so long as they abide by the rules for the responsible use of evidence and for the production of an authoritative historical account. They should also declare the nature of their commitment to their approach, and justify it on *intellectual* rather than emotional grounds. It needs to be made clear that analysing something is not the same as approving of it, a mistake that is all too commonly made. In any case, the censorship of historical publications is inherently undesirable, and diversity of opinion is healthy, so long as the results can be critically evaluated, in *both* scholarly *and* public history.

BRIDGE

The moral commitments of historians and the nature of their human values need to be made explicit whenever possible and tempered by evidence that is open to scrutiny. But, because of their professional obligations, historians must be willing to mount arguments about their commitments and values rather than just asserting them, and to explain more openly to a wider public the processes through which historical judgements are reached. As I have argued, public history raises exceptionally complex issues upon which all historians must reflect. We cannot dismiss public history as 'mere' popularisation, entertainment or propaganda. We need to develop coherent positions on the relationships between academic history, institutions such as museums, and popular culture. One way in which this can be done is by addressing the misleading notion of lessons from history. The study of the past is indeed inspiring and instructive but it is not a fount of clear, unambiguous lessons or recipes. Rather it is an arena for contemplation and thought. Certainly the past is the context for the present, but it does not by that token generate simple instructions. Historians do well when they raise awkward questions and unsettle received views. To imagine that the general public could not appreciate these points is patronising, and they should, at the very least, be given alternatives to tabloid history. My vision of a world where scholarly and public history work more closely together depends not only on collaboration between constituencies too often kept apart, but also upon the widest possible dissemination of the skills and insights that historians possess. These are too often veiled in public history. An array of skills is the foundation of the historian's craft and the subject of the culminating chapter of the book.

7 Historians' Skills

WHAT ARE SKILLS?

'Skills' sounds like something basic, a starting point, the tools that enable their possessor to get on and do more interesting things. Hence it may seem odd that I have left the topic until the end of the book. In this final chapter I want to examine the skills that historians can reasonably be expected to have, and to assess whether they are in any way distinctive – does a particular combination of skills help to define the discipline of history? The key point about such skills, whether they are definitive of the discipline or not, is that they are built up over time, as one practises as a historian. They are not mechanical, like the skills required to operate machinery, change a plug and so on. These can be taught, and then the pupil can go off and exercise them right away, without the need for change unless the technology itself alters. Historians' skills are completely different; they are developed and refined over a lifetime, becoming an integral part of the person. They are enhanced by the ability to write well and to grasp the complexity of situations. Naturally there is much that can be taught, but there is a great deal else that relates to more subtle human qualities, which are not so amenable to direct instruction.

The issues around skills are less straightforward than they might appear. For example, they reflect notions about a discipline's priorities, and about its proper relationship with cognate fields. As a result, they are a site of conflict. Skills have come into new prominence in recent years, partly because in many countries higher education policies are laying particular emphasis on 'transferable skills', which can be used in a variety of contexts. In some ways this is positive, since being a historian involves diverse skills, which can indeed be extremely useful in a variety of settings. Hence the study of history can be presented as having general value. However, the political emphasis on transferable skills does also tend to emphasise what could be described as a mechanistic approach to learning – a model that is unsuited to historical work, and that can give the misleading impression that there are finite things to learn. As a concept, transferable skills gives more weight to the similarities than to the differences between disciplines. For many people, historians are those who have acquired a lot of *information* about the past, so how does this fit in with the idea of skills?

At first sight, the term 'skills' implies techniques that can be generally applied, hence it appears to be more about methods than about content. The point is reinforced when we add the word 'transferable'. Although I will be trying in the rest of this chapter to specify and evaluate the specific skills historians need, I want to state at the outset that it is unhelpful to draw too firm a distinction between skills and the matter to which they are applied. Historians' skills are refined through use, that is, through their application to concrete historical problems. In this way a fund of knowledge and experience is built up, and it is meaningless to divide it into techniques and substance, since the two are blended through constant interaction. Let us be clear that knowing lots of historical facts without any sense of how to use and interpret them is pointless – perhaps the most common lay assumption about what characterises a professional historian is that they know lots of facts, and especially dates. I would suggest that the important skills are tracking down information and knowing how to deploy it rather than remembering it.

I am arguing against a polarity between skills and substance because I see these two aspects of the historian's craft developing together in mutual dependency. Skills need to be applied to something, and that something, which has a number of facets, helps in refining skills. The *substance* of history is important because it provides concrete information through which to construct historical arguments. It is a source of comparisons without which no case study can be interpreted, it suggests the broad patterns of change within which specific phenomena need to be seen, and it offers insights into the fundamental structures of human societies. So, having a sense of the main contours of at least bits of the past is absolutely vital. I am emphasising experience as a blend of knowledge and skills. It is hard to generalise about such matters, but there is a 'feel' that comes from familiarity with a subject, even if it is unwise to romanticise or idealise it.

TYPES OF SKILLS

A number of skills are fundamental to historical work, most of which are used in other humanities or social science disciplines. We can divide these skills into three types. The first can be called technical skills, such as palaeography and diplomatic, cliometrics and prosopography, and I shall discuss these fairly briefly. The second could be called source-based skills, and they relate to the finding and evaluating of sources, whether primary or secondary, *once* a historical problem has been identified. The third are interpretative skills, in which I include the ability to construct a plausible argument. These three types of skill are insepaɪable, and are being treated here under distinct headings simply for clarity of exposition. I will take each type in turn, but first I want to draw attention to perhaps the most important skill of all – identifying and shaping a historical problem. This does not fit neatly into any of the three categories, it is even more fundamental than they are, and without it no decent history can be produced.

A historical problem is not simply a topic, a piece of the past. Studying something just because it is there leads to unfocused, empirically driven accounts. Of course it is very tempting to turn to a place, a person, an institution or an archive and study them because no-one has done so before. But the results tend to be intellectually unsatisfying. The way into any historical work – whether undergraduate essays or the most advanced research – must be through a question, a puzzle, a conundrum, an anomaly, a surprise, a hypothesis. These can take many different forms, but most often they involve some kind of comparison, which provides a context for the question. Historical work is based on the idea that there is an issue requiring explanation; it therefore depends upon existing explanations. Thus comparison is at the heart of historical practice. Historians constantly compare sources, case studies, secondary accounts, and theories – it would be impossible to develop a historical problem without making comparisons, and, in comparative history, the method is made the explicit centrepiece of the field.[1]

Historians ask many different kinds of questions, and why they do so follows from what I have already said. Questions are shaped mainly by scholarly traditions and by the concerns historians find around them. Thus fields build up their own traditions and by that very process spawn questions; these questions are less in the sources than in the minds of those who study them. Let me give a couple of examples. I am writing this book in Norwich, a city that was for several centuries the most heavily populated in the country after London. By the eighteenth century, patterns of regional development were changing decisively with the growth of Bristol and Liverpool as ports, and Birmingham and Manchester as industrial centres. Nowadays Norwich is a lovely provincial city, but is, in a number of respects, 'out on a limb', a fact reflected in the limited transport links in and out of Norfolk. This situation prompts a historian to ask a number of questions. Why was Norwich so impor-

---

1   See, for example, the journal *Comparative Studies in Society and History* (1958), and also E. Acton, *Nazism and Stalinism: A Suitable Case for Comparison?*, London, 1998.

tant before? What caused its relative decline? How is the importance of urban areas best measured? What effects have these changes had on the city and on the region in which it is located? Even an elementary answer depends on the understanding of long-term economic trends, including types of industry and agriculture, patterns of trade, including overseas, and the distribution of wealth. Norwich needs to be put in a context, in fact in many contexts, to answer these questions and the production of historically sophisticated answers depends on comparisons between Norwich and Norfolk and other *comparable* areas. Areas would be comparable if they shared some features – cathedral cities with agricultural hinterlands, for example – while differing in others – patterns of population growth, for instance. Hence the choice of cases for comparison is highly significant, because it will weight the research in certain directions simply by virtue of which features are shared, which are not. Indeed questions about Norwich only arise because there are accumulated ideas and explanations of urban and regional development across Europe to draw upon. Furthermore, we might want to set up the historical problem quite differently, by questioning whether the analysis should be primarily economic and considering other possibly relevant dimensions, such as the institution of the church local elites, and religious practice. Of course these all have economic dimensions, just as economic questions have social, political and cultural ones.[2] The important point is that there are a number of ways of thinking about an issue such as regional decline, and that selecting and formulating a problem also involves making choices about the sorts of answers one wants, and expects, to find. Historians' choices are shaped by existing work and by their views on regional development. Setting up a problem for historical research thus involves subtle skills; these choices always possess a comparative dimension.

Let me take another example, which is considerably more tricky – the history of illegitimacy, a relatively new subject for historians. Its trickiness resides in two of its aspects – it is an extremely emotive and topical subject, and it is amenable to quantitative treatment. Although largely studied by demographers, illegitimacy would not arise as a topic without legal structures governing marriage and inheritance, and without administrative procedures for recording such matters. So, how does one formulate historical questions about illegitimacy? These might be prompted, for example, by perceptions that its incidence has changed markedly. Changes, especially increases, are perceived

2   J. Pound, *Tudor and Stuart Norwich*, Chichester, 1988; B. Ayers, *English Heritage Book of Norwich*, London, 1994; F. Meeres, *A History of Norwich*, Chichester, 1998.

to be problematic, particularly for social welfare provision. Indeed the history of illegitimacy has direct relevance for current debates, and the terms in which current debates are being conducted can therefore affect the way in which historical inquiries are set up. It is to be hoped that, conversely, historical work might inform current discussions. The association between single parenthood (mainly mothers) and poverty has become a major area of concern because in welfare states these are pressing matters for public policy. Links between infanticide and illegitimacy have attracted the attention of historians, since it seems that unmarried mothers were more likely to kill their children than married women were.[3] Furthermore, illegitimacy bears on the status of marriage and thereby on the maintenance of social order. Attempts during the French Revolution to abolish bastardy as a legal category suggest how much had been invested in legitimacy in the *ancien régime*.[4] Closely connected was a much more permissive notion of marriage and divorce, which was rather short-lived.[5] This example reveals how politically significant marriage and the legal status of children can be. Many societies stigmatised the women who bore children out of wedlock, hence the phenomenon of illegitimacy raises questions about the position of women and responses to female sexuality. In some cases tremendous moral pressure and severe punishments were brought to bear upon 'bastard bearers'.[6] There must be complex historical forces at work because there have been societies with a high average age of marriage, low illegitimacy rates and no mechanical forms of contraception. Hence far from being 'natural', sexual behaviour varies markedly, being bound up with a wide range of historical conditions.

Illegitimacy continues to be an emotive subject, frequently mentioned as an indicator of social trends, but just what do figures about illegitimacy indicate? Answers offered have included: changes in family structure, decreasing social control, increasing economic independence of women, enhanced mobility, which allowed men to escape their responsibilities, and changing moral frameworks.[7] So, formulating a historical question about illegitimacy is challenging precisely because the topic is so morally freighted. And the fact

3   See, for example, R. Schulte, *The Village in Court: Arson, Infanticide and Poaching in the Court Reports of Upper Bavaria, 1848–1910*, Oxford, 1994; M. Jackson, *New-Born Child Murder: Women, Illegitimacy and the Courts in Eighteenth-Century England*, Manchester, 1996; L. Rose, *The Massacre of the Innocents: Infanticide in Britain 1800–1939*, London, 1986.
4   C. Brinton, *French Revolutionary Legislation on Illegitimacy, 1789–1804*, Cambridge, Mass, 1936.
5   R. Phillips, *Family Breakdown in Late Eighteenth-Century France; Divorces in Rouen 1792–1803*, Oxford, 1980.
6   P. Laslett et al., eds., *Bastardy and its Comparative History*, London, 1980.
7   On illegitimacy see the works by Jackson, Brinton and Laslett cited above.

that it is amenable to quantitative analysis compounds the problem. Is it appropriate or meaningful to study such a topic quantitatively? Are the sources reliable enough to justify the exercise? How long a time-span is needed to reveal significant trends? Might a quantitative study give a false sense of precision and allow the results to be used in a misleading manner by policy-makers? In order to place illegitimacy figures in context, what sort of comparisons are appropriate across time and place? Is it reasonable, when a topic is so *culturally* complex, to use case studies that are disparate temporally and geographically? The list of questions illustrates the difficulties surrounding research on this topic. This example reveals some of the diverse and complex issues that are packed into the formulation of a historical problem.

TECHNICAL SKILLS

One thing is crystal clear – when it comes to formulating a problem, we depend hugely on the work of other historians. For a problem to be a really good, juicy one, a researcher needs the sources, the time, the framework, and a sense of how their project fits into larger patterns of scholarship. They also need an acute sense of whether any special technical skills will be required. I used the example of illegitimacy above in order to suggest that what I am calling technical skills relate to the entire way in which a historical problem is conceptualised. A quantitative study of illegitimacy requires a sound and critical understanding of demographic methods. In this sense skills and framework are inseparable. While I will not discuss technical skills at length, it is worth giving them careful consideration, because they are more integral to the practice of history than may be apparent. In carving out a historical problem for study it is essential to consider and then evaluate the range of ways of approaching it that the sources permit. Thus, to return to illegitimacy, it would be possible to think about the topic in terms of the history of the family and of attitudes of female sexuality, which is in effect to recast it as an issue in social and cultural history. 'The family' is exceptionally hard to define, because it embraces so many historical phenomena.[8] Some of the concerns of demography relate to family phenomena, especially through the study of birth and death rates, and marriage patterns. Demographers also use tax, poor relief and

---

8 *Journal of Family History* (1976), *Journal of Marriage and the Family* (1939),
   *Continuity and Change: A Journal of Social Structure, Law and Demography
   in Past Societies* (1986). A useful introduction is J. Casey, *The History of the
   Family*, Oxford, 1989.

census records to reconstruct households in past times.[9] Yet household composition and 'the family' are hardly the same, since family members are not necessarily co-resident, and the numbers of children, age at marriage and so on do not necessarily shed light on the *quality* of personal relationships. There is a gap between demographic patterns and cultural ones, one cannot be extrapolated from the other, and historians therefore need to be clear about what their chosen techniques can or cannot reveal. So, the techniques of demography may have to be mastered for some kinds of historical research to be pursued, but they also have to be evaluated, and the decision to deploy them brings entailments with it.

It would be unfortunate if readers supposed that demography was the principal part of history in which quantitative methods are used. Measurement is, as Roderick Floud pointed out some time ago, everywhere in the practice of history: 'the measurable areas may help us in our interpretation of the immeasurable'.[10] It would be impossible to provide a brief summary of where quantitative issues come up within the discipline, but two general points, that reinforce the ones already made about technical skills, are in order. First, statistical methods involve aggregates; they bring together sets of data that are processed according to standardised procedures. This is significant, not just because the methods are transparent, but because it becomes necessary to think about collective phenomena. When, for example, information about individuals is brought together under categories such as occupation, income, marital status, class and age, historians need to reflect upon the historical meanings of those very categories. There are issues concerning groups that can only be rigorously studied using quantitative methods, which will, if used well, become integral to the conceptual framework being deployed. Second, quantitative methods have their own history. It is helpful if those who deploy them understand their origins. Such insights reveal why and how phenomena are measured and the assumptions and values that are built into the process, all of which should raise historians' awareness of their own procedures. The flow-

9 On demographic methods, see J. Willigan and K. Lynch, eds., *Sources and Methods in Historical Demography*, New York, 1982; D. Reher and R. Schofield, eds., *Old and New Methods in Historical Demography*, Oxford, 1993.

10 R. Floud, *An Introduction to Quantitative Methods for Historians*, second edition, London, 1979, p.3. On quantitative history see also, J. Le Goff and P. Nora, eds., *Constructing the Past: Essays in Historical Methodology*, Cambridge, 1985, chs. 1, 2 and 5; O. Handlin, *Truth in History*, Cambridge, Mass., 1979, ch 8; C. Harvey and J. Press, *Databases in Historical Research. Theory, Methods and Applications*, Basingstoke, 1996.

ering of studies of the *history* of statistics in recent years is thus warmly to be welcomed.[11]

If we are interested in skills that assist us in analysing collectivities, then prosopography, the study of collective biographies, should be mentioned. Its origins lie in the piecing together of fragments of information that ancient historians undertook in order to overcome the dearth of more complete sources. More recently the technique has been taken up by historians who study communities that are relatively easy to define. By 'community', I do not just mean people living in the same location, but those voluntarily associating together or linked in some significant way, that is, groups likely to have values and aspirations in common. It is no coincidence that historians of science have been drawn to the technique, since organisations of like-minded men (*sic*) – scientific and medical societies, for instance – can be fruitfully approached in this way. The aim is not so much to select variables and treat them according to rigorous quantitative techniques, as to discern patterns, for example, in religious affiliation or social background, that will promote deeper historical understanding.[12]

Other technical skills may be more straightforward: they are principally palaeography, diplomatic and languages. Although we think of palaeography as principally concerned with handwriting, the whole array of issues connected with the authenticity of documents comes within its remit. Historians who work on periods prior to the late nineteenth century have to become comfortable with styles of handwriting, which vary markedly with space and time. Sometimes this is principally a matter of familiarity, so that getting plenty of practice is the prime requirement. At others special instruction may be required for handwriting in Gothic script or in secretary hand, for instance. Many important medieval documents are available in printed editions, but the ability, at postgraduate level and beyond, to go back to the originals is essential. In fact, for medievalists much more than deciphering handwriting is

---

11 M. Cullen, *The Statistical Movement in Early Victorian Britain: The Foundations of Empirical Social Research*, Hassocks, 1975; T. Porter, *The Rise of Statistical Thinking: 1820-1900*, Princeton, N.J., 1986, and *Trust in Numbers: The Pursuit of Objectivity in Science and Public Life*, Princeton, N.J., 1995; A. Desrosières, *The Politics of Large Numbers: A History of Statistical Reasoning*, Cambridge, Mass., 1998.

12 *Medieval Prosopography* (1980); K. Keats-Rohan, *Family Trees and the Roots of Politics: The Prosopography of Britain and France from the Tenth to the Twelfth Century*, Woodbridge, 1996. Arnold Thackray has been a promoter of prosopographic approaches in the history of science. His joint book with J. Morrell, *Gentlemen of Science: Early Years of the British Association for the Advancement of Science*, Oxford, 1981, explores the nature of scientific communities.

OPPOSITE: *7.1 Signatures deciding Louis XVI's fate (1793)*
There is something inexplicably exciting about seeing a document so
directly associated with a dramatic historical turning point. The fact
that it is relatively easy to read and that it contains the signatures of
several famous historical figures adds to the thrill. The human drama
to which this document bears witness is immediately apparent.

involved, since every aspect of a document has the potential to yield up rich insights, including the ink, parchment and paper. The complexity of manuscript illuminations is well known, although the historical insights they afford are matters of debate. Of particular importance are the formulae according to which documents were drawn up; the ability to recognise them and spot variations that may be significant is therefore a fundamental skill for those working on the Middle Ages. Indeed since this period saw a profound transition 'from memory to written record', the nature and role of those documents that became part of everyday life over the thirteenth century are the way into broader social questions.[13]

The arguments for working in other languages, despite the availability of some primary sources in printed translations, are similar: historians need to engage with all aspects of their original sources.[14] All these technical skills involve thinking more deeply about the period under scrutiny and about how records were generated at that time. I am totally against mystifying archives and original documents.[15] Nonetheless, experience of working with such materials is indispensable. One advantage is the total range of sensory experiences available to historians, which raise overall levels of historical awareness – format, style and size of handwriting can all help build up a picture of the past. It is necessary to go back to originals in any case since it is always possible that

13 M. Camille, *Images on the Edge: The Margins of Medieval Art*, London, 1992, and *Mirror in Parchment: The Luttrell Psalter and the Making of Medieval England*, London, 1998; R. Gameson, ed., *The Early Medieval Bible: Its Production, Decoration and Use*, Cambridge, 1994; M. Clanchy, *From Memory to Written Record: England 1066–1307*, London, 1979; B. Bischoff, *Latin Palaeography: Antiquity and the Middle Ages*, Cambridge, 1990.

14 E.g. G. Vernadsky, *A Source Book for Russian History from Early Times to 1917*, New Haven, 1972; B. Szczesniak, ed., *The Russian Revolution and Religion: A Collection of Documents Concerning the Suppression of Religion by the Communists, 1917–1925*, Notre Dame, Ind., 1959; and S. Page, compiler, *Russia in Revolution. Selected Readings in Russian Domestic History since 1855*, Princeton N.J., 1965.

15 Cf. M. Lindemann, 'Confessions of an Archive Junkie', in P. Karsten and J. Modell, eds., *Theory, Method, and Practice in Social and Cultural History*, New York, 1992, pp. 152–80.

Paris

12 130 Robespierre ——— La mort.
    131 Danton ——— La mort.
    132 Collot=d'herbois — La mort
        Manuel ——— La détention dans un fort ailleurs
                    qu'à Paris, jusqu'à ce que l'intérêt
                    public permette la déportation.
    133 Billaud-Varenne] — La mort dans 24. heures
    134 Camille Desmoulin — La mort.
    135 Marat ——— La mort dans 24. heures.
    136 Lavicomterie ——— La mort.

C 11   137 Legendre ——— La mort.
314   138 Raffron ——— La mort dans 24. heures
    139 Pariar ——— La mort.
    140 Sergent ——— La mort.
    141 Robert ——— La mort.
        Dubayet ——— Le bannissement à la paix.
    142 Fréron ——— La mort dans 24. heures
    143 Beauvais ——— La mort.
    144 Fabre d'Églantine — La mort.
    145 Osselin ——— La mort.
    146 Robespierre, jeune — La mort.
    147 David ——— La mort.
    148 Boucher ——— La mort.
    149 Laignelot ——— La mort.
        Thomas ——— La détention jusqu'à la paix, et la
appel nominal des 16 & 17 janvier 1793. mort dans le cas d'un rétablissement du
B. 17.   territoire français ... par les
                                          puissances étrangères.

    150 L.J. Egalité ——— La mort.

                Pas de Calais.
    151 Carnot ——— la mort
    152 Duquesnoy ——— La mort.
    153 Leban ——— La mort.
        Thomas Payne ——— La détention, le bannissement à la paix.
        Personne ——— La détention. Le bannissement à la paix.
    154 Guffroy ——— La mort dans le délai de la loi, sauf
        Carlard ——— la déportation dans ... dans ... jolie, pour
                    y être détenu, et le bannissement de
                    toutes les terres de la République à la
                    paix.
    155 Bollet ——— La mort.

mistakes have been introduced in transcription and translation. There is no substitute for reading sources in their original language. Each language has its own flavour deriving from its grammar, the history and size of its vocabulary, and its historical traditions. Picking up these resonances is an important part of historical work. Thus we can re-affirm that apparently technical tools relate to the whole way in which sources are approached.

The skills required to construct footnotes are also, to a degree, technical ones. But this example illustrates yet again how intertwined a historian's various types of skill are. Footnotes naturally require accuracy; the idea behind them is the transparency of scholarship. But it remains a challenge to translate this into concrete terms. Clearly not everything can be footnoted – that would be cumbersome – so selection is required. It is generally agreed that all direct quotations require footnotes of sufficient detail that any reader would be able to consult the original, although popular works frequently dispense with such supports altogether. There is also consensus that the writer's intellectual debts should be acknowledged. Furthermore, footnotes should give a sense of other work in the field, as well as substantiating the broad approach taken in a specific piece of writing. All these tasks, except giving details of quotations, involve selection, anything else would be impractical. So, although footnotes require a certain technical competence, they also involve judicious selection and rhetorical skills: footnotes help to convince readers of arguments, and hence are an important part of historians' persuasive strategies.

I have suggested that groups of people working in an academic field can usefully be thought of as communities of belief. The purpose of putting it this way has been to highlight the centrality of the social context within which intellectual work is done. The peer group is audience and judge. Footnotes are a significant element within the system of communication between members of a peer group, a field, a community of belief. Two points follow from this. Footnotes reveal lineages, alliances, lines of power within a field, and it is best to be aware of this. In this respect, footnotes are not neutral pieces of information, but social signals. If people feel their work should have been acknowledged in a publication but is not, they can take serious offence. Thus footnotes are also tools of diplomacy. The second point is closely connected. When similar materials are used by different fields and sub-fields, their manner of footnoting is likely to be correspondingly distinct. Earlier I mentioned the history of the family, which nicely illustrates the point about footnotes. Let us take the example of widowhood, which can be studied in a variety of ways – demographically; using legal records, especially wills; economically, in terms of poverty and poor relief; culturally using representations of widows in literature, art, music and so on; or through case studies of particular families.[16] These approaches, even if they use material from the same place and time, will produce writings with very different footnotes. This is not just because they will emphasise different sources and different traditions of scholarships, but because their implied audiences are different. They may also display different assumptions about evidence and about what constitutes a convincing argument. Hence the whole way in which they make their writings persuasive is likely to be different too. This point is particularly important because of the trend towards inter-disciplinary history. Bringing together sources and perspectives from different disciplines poses a number of challenges. These include technical ones, some of which I shall discuss shortly. Footnotes are an issue for inter-disciplinary work because they are means for establishing convincing arguments when you are talking to and drawing upon a number of scholarly communities. Many of those now publishing historical work have been trained in other fields, for example, literary studies, and they are likely to establish their points in their own ways, drawing on work that is literary in orientation, and on conceptual frameworks rooted in literary theory.

While it is often assumed that historical research starts with the sources, I have argued that many tasks need to be performed before one even gets to the primary sources, because some context within which to place them is required. It is unhelpful to think about historical research in terms of a simple sequence of tasks that should be performed in a given order; the whole tenor of this book suggests so. It suggests, in fact, that historians constantly move between the main types of activity they perform, namely, engaging with the sources, delineating a problem, setting it in broad contexts, developing a framework, and constructing arguments in written form. This is a more dialectical way of imagining historical work. Unfortunately, it does not fit particularly well with the norms implicit in the practices of grant-giving bodies, which are based on an idealised view of scientific research, according to which one proceeds in a logical sequence from initial questions to research with sources, and then to written-up conclusions. Many historians return time and time again to their sources, finding different things in them at each return journey and using them to illuminate a range of problems. The idea that you can 'gut' a source, take away what you want and then move on, seems to me to promote an overly mechanistic view of the subject, and to lessen the complexities of the interpretative process that engaging with the sources necessarily involves.

16 E.g. C. King, *Renaissance Women Patrons: Wives and Widows in Italy c.1300–1550*, Manchester, 1998; S. Cavallo and L. Warner, eds., *Widowhood in Medieval and Early Modern Europe*, New York, 1999.

SOURCE-BASED SKILLS

The nature of the source-based skills that historians use can be described quite briefly, although their execution is by no means straightforward. It is necessary to identify the relevant sources, to read them accurately and critically, to evaluate them and then to integrate them into a historical account. This last step forms the transition into interpretative skills. Deciding which are 'relevant' sources is rarely straightforward, and often it is a question of thinking laterally, even of finding oblique sources that provide unexpected insights into a problem. Making judgements about the value of sources cannot be done in a vacuum. Sources need to be compared with one another, and their value will depend on the research project in question. Sources have no *absolute* value, however enchanting they may be. Every time a source is examined, a set of questions runs through the historian's head – who, what, why, where, when, how . . . ? Asking these basic questions has two purposes – to understand the source as a *text*, and to reconstruct the circumstances of its generation. Every text used by a historian can be analysed somewhat in the manner of a literary critic. The vast majority of the 'raw' materials historians use have been knowingly made by people, who leave, unknowingly, traces of both themselves and their circumstances behind them. The purpose of close, critical reading is to reveal as much as possible, to allow a source to yield up its riches. Of course the manifest content has to be clearly understood, but so do any hidden agendas. In the case of written sources, the precise language used has to be probed, along with sentence constructions and the organisation of the whole text. Thus, an awareness of metaphor, for instance, including historically specific resonances, is an important part of the historian's tool kit. It is important not so much for its own sake as because it enables the reader to think laterally, to move in their imagination from text to text and from texts to contexts. It is a great skill to be able to reconstruct the circumstances of a given source's production. Careful textual analysis is necessary but by no means sufficient for doing so. The source's maker, their situation, including the pressures and structural constraints upon them, all need to be considered. Legal historians, for example, have been assiduous in pointing out that court records need to be critically assessed in just this way. All one's knowledge of a specific historical situation is mobilised in setting the source in its context of production, which has to be done in order to appreciate both its fruitfulness and its limitations for a particular project. These skills come from practice, from constantly checking and comparing different sources, and from familiarity with the particular historical situation that gave birth to them. In this way, yet again, we see that skills and content are closely connected.

Most sources are, as I have already emphasised, mediations, that is, they have been made by human beings, they are the products of complex minds, composed of conscious and unconscious dimensions. No sources are transparent records of a past situation, not even archaeological fragments. So historians need to be able to imagine the kinds of mediations at work in any given artefact, and I have suggested some of the means – textual and contextual – by which they do so. The problem is that there are a number of different possible approaches here, some of which are simply incompatible: there is no one 'historical method', just as there is no single method of textual analysis. The differences stem from fundamental assumptions, for example, about human nature. The language I have used and the examples I have given – metaphor, unconscious, mediation and so on – already indicate a particular view – one I happen to think well grounded. But many historians feel uncomfortable with talk of the unconscious, a situation which exposes profound disagreements about human nature and its study which cannot be resolved. Nonetheless, it is worth being open about these disagreements and noticing exactly how they affect historical work. Taking notice and critically evaluating are *skills*, whereas claims about human nature are *beliefs*. Thus we can agree that an ability to analyse texts and objects critically is a fundamental historical skill, but we fail to agree on precisely what the analysis should consist of, or on what its founding assumptions should be. Are human beings the same at all times and places or not? Is self-interest their main motivating factor? Do historians need to think about the unconscious? On the answers to such questions will depend the detailed manner in which sources are interpreted. Skills and worldviews are intimately entwined but by no means identical.

INTERPRETATION AND SKILL

If this seems complicated, questions of interpretation are yet more so, although again it is possible to summarise the skills required fairly briefly.[17] They include: using historical materials and ideas in a coherent argument, showing their significance, especially in the light of other accounts, making convincing, plausible claims based upon research findings, and employing concepts, theories, frameworks appropriately. These are dependent on other skills: clear, logical and evocative writing, critical reading, making connections,

17 A stimulating account of the concept of interpretation is S. Sontag, *Against Interpretation*, New York, 1966. See also R. Nelson and R. Shiff, eds., *Critical Terms for Art History*, Chicago, 1996, pp.87–100; Lentricchia and McLaughlin, eds., *Critical Terms for Literary Study*, part 2, esp. pp. 121–34.

and the ability to see patterns and links, that is, to think laterally, integrating different kinds of materials. These are complex and subtle skills and in so far as they can be taught, it is by the power of positive and negative examples. Yet interpretation is largely a matter of taste, and I use the word 'taste' advisedly to indicate that personal preferences are involved. These can partly be explained by the interpreter's training, politics and past experience, and they need not be completely idiosyncratic – a preference for a certain style of history can be shared by a number of people. The skills required for generating compelling historical interpretations are intricate, and cannot be presented in terms of formulae. It does not follow, however, that they are mysterious. What follows is that they are embedded in the practice of history, not set apart from it, and can best be evaluated through results.

Perhaps the idea that there exists *a* historical method, along the lines of scientific method, is appealing because it appears to simplify questions of interpretation. Indeed the very notion of a method emphasises the gathering rather than the interpretation of materials. As we know, 'scientific method' is something of a fiction, since there are many methods used in the production of the special kind of knowledge called 'science'. And so there are in history. It seems implausible in any case that a field as complex and diverse as history could have one unifying method. I would argue that the most important act historians perform is that of writing, because it is through writing that their disparate ideas are integrated into a single whole. Historical ideas, accounts, claims are apprehended by others via the written, and to a lesser extent the spoken, word. Writing is the foremost act of interpretation. As we saw in Chapter 6, a sense of the past may be communicated by many means, yet, *within* the discipline of history, texts are the principal means of communication. It is curious then that the practice of history has been identified much more with the archive than with its results: with a privileged repository of sources rather than with historical interpretation. This displacement requires careful consideration.[18]

THE CULT OF THE ARCHIVE

There is no doubt that there is a considerable cult of the archive among many historians. It is where one cuts one's teeth, develops identifications with the 'raw' materials, lodges claims to originality, and, to a degree, inhabits another

18 See the two special issues of *History of the Human Sciences* on 'The Archive', vol. 11, no. 4, 1998 and vol. 12, no. 2, 1999.

world. What is implied by invoking this notion of 'the archive'? It certainly involves the authority of collections of unpublished sources, which are imagined as closer to their originating situations, that is, less mediated, when they are in an archive. 'The archive' implies a kind of intimacy with particular aspects of the past that are more personal, individual, private, and hence worth looking at precisely because they concern 'real life'. After all, by and large what is in the archive has not been placed fully in the public domain, whether the archive relates to a person, a government or a region. The love letters of a famous person, the confidential minutes of high-level political meetings, witness statements to a court, all share the qualities I have described, despite being distinct types of sources and typically located in very different kinds of archives. Many archives bear witness to the manner in which major areas of administration functioned and interacted with their constituencies. In these contexts quite separate social groupings come together – colonial administration would be an excellent example – and touch each other at pressure points, such as death, crime, political insurrection, dire poverty and so on. Furthermore, much archival material can be understood in terms of stories. This is especially true of legal records, and hence they seem to offer a seduction into past worlds. Such narratives are recognisable types, they follow the patterns of contemporary fictional work, and hence they are particularly appealing. The use of familiar, seductive narratives becomes an issue for historians if, in writing up their research, they seek to trade on or reconstruct stories uncritically. However delicious, they should not be glamorised, or used as substitutes for analysis. The entrancing stories in the archives are quite distinct from the historical arguments in which they will be deployed. Evidently there are many different kinds of archives: local, regional and national, personal, institutional and so on; using them requires a wide range of skills and of background knowledge, above all about the processes that led to the generation, selection and cataloguing of their materials. 'The archive' further implies materials not looked at by anyone else or only by a few – the very idea nurtures historians' fantasies about their privileged access to the past.

I have presented the archive as enjoying a privileged place in the practice of history. In itself this is neither bad nor good, it is simply a feature of current historical practice. Naturally, like all other aspects of that practice, it needs to be held up for critical, yet sympathetic inspection. These complexities of the archive have clear implications for historians' skills. As I have already said, it is an absolutely basic skill to reconstruct the means by which materials were originally produced and have come into archives. We need to know how the archive has been managed and classified, whether items have been lost, destroyed or altered. Just as crucial is an insight into one's own responses to the material – the skill, if you like, of self-analysis. And, at another conceptual level altogether, there needs to be a critique of how and why historical achievement is still understood as being derived from the supposed quality of the primary sources. I have argued that this draws our attention away from interpretation and towards 'research', away from the historian's mind and towards historical actors and past states. While this move may be salutary in that it forces historians to engage deeply with other worlds, to recognise their difference, it may just be that it is also safer. If so much rests on the sources, we shift responsibility away from historians and towards their materials. I am not denying the myriad delights of archival sources, but I am giving priority to what is done with them by historians.

Historical achievement, then, derives from the manner in which sources are handled; it is not located in the sources themselves, however enchanting these may be. The skill of finding unusual, little-known or previously neglected sources is certainly valuable, and it reinforces my point, since the accomplishment is the historian's. I am stressing writing as a major historical skill because that is how achievement has to be judged. The transition from primary sources to historical account involves many steps, and is not a simple journey from document to book or journal article – typically there is much doubling back, many twists and unexpected turns. The quality of the resulting narrative, itself a composite, is what counts. Inevitably there are many different ways in which the final result is arrived at. The writer's choice of the theoretical framework, given there are so many possibilities, is an obvious example – and this further reminds us that skills inform every part of historical practice. A less obvious example would be the selection of historical genres. I have laid great emphasis on the skills required to delineate a historical problem, but this is not independent of the genres through which it is given expression. It is vital to choose the right genre for the problem and vice versa. A journal article can only cope with certain kinds of problems: the genre has strict word limits and fairly rigid conventions and demands an exceptionally clear focus. In a book, by contrast, which requires distinctive writing skills, such as the ability to keep a conceptual or narrative thread going, it is possible to explore issues that are more ramifying and wide-ranging, possessed of different facets. Choosing a genre and using it well also involves decisions about the level of detail required, and where it should be located – in the main text or in the footnotes. We cannot legislate about such matters, since so many variables are involved. The way forward is to bear these issues in mind every single time we read a historical account. It is less a matter of having a formal checklist than of understanding the implications of the seemingly mundane elements that make up published historical work. The skills involved are inferred, backwards as it were, by comparing a range of practices, and evaluating their effectiveness. Such an evaluation must take into account the chosen genre and its aptness, and place the work in the context of other similar accounts. We could summarise these points about the centrality of writing in historical practice by stating that all historical texts need the power to convince others. This is the art of rhetoric, which is an important historical skill, or rather a blend of skills, and is not to be understood pejoratively.

SKILLS AND NON-TEXTUAL SOURCES

So far, this chapter has presented historians as both users and producers of *texts*, but what about other kinds of sources and the skills needed to use them? Non-textual sources include items of visual and material culture, such as seals, maps, photographs, drawings, prints, paintings, jewellery, costume, tools and machines, archaeological remains, buildings, town plans, films – indeed any artefact. They also include music – compositions, libretti, performances, instruments, stage designs for operas and so on. Non-textual sources tend to elicit one of two responses from general historians, and both are unproductive. According to the first, they require very special, almost arcane skills. As a result such sources are mystified and their differences from texts reinforced. In fact we can approach them in a *similar* manner, by thinking about the technical, the source-based and the interpretative skills required. According to the second response, visual sources are privileged as transparent windows onto past times rather than artful constructions in their own right, which implies that no skills at all are required in their use!

I want to pursue a little further the suggestion that non-textual sources are similar but not identical to textual ones, by taking the example of the skills required for the use of visual materials. Thinking about technical skills first, prints provide a useful example, and they are especially popular among historians.[19] It is emphatically not necessary to be a connoisseur of prints to use them in historical work, but it is essential to be able to identify the type of print – engraving, etching, mezzotint, lithograph and so on – and to have some understanding of its mode of production, its cost and likely audiences. These are relatively 'technical' issues, which form the basis for any work with such

19 For example, *Print Quarterly*, (1984); R. Porter, 'Seeing the Past', *Past and Present*, no. 118, 1988, 186–205; D. Jarrett, *England in the Age of Hogarth*, St Albans, 1976; L. Colley, *Britons: Forging the Nation, 1707–1837*, New Haven, 1992; D. Donald, *The Age of Caricature: Satirical Prints in the Reign of George III*, New Haven, 1996.

sources. The source-based skills would take these points further in a given historical context. For example, the print makers and sellers should be considered – where did they practise, did they work with particular artists, what were their political affiliations, how does their output compare with others'? Prints are rarely studied independently of other types of evidence; hence another set of source-based questions would place prints into the context of other comparable sources on related *themes* – fashion excesses, politics, scandals, for example. Whereas a traditional art historian might be especially interested in prints that were the creations of a master, such as Dürer or Rembrandt, a historian will want to integrate prints with a wide range of other materials and to evaluate their status as historical evidence. This involves moving away from the print itself and into its context. Historians will still need to pay careful attention to the visual conventions of artistic genres and to the way in which any given image is working. The print becomes a form of evidence only by meticulous analysis, just like any other document, and the distinctive kinds of mediation it represents must be taken account of.

When it comes to interpretation, historians will certainly need to read accounts given by those with an art-historical training. Disciplines, as we know, have their own habits of mind, so a certain amount of translation is certainly involved. Nonetheless the procedures are not so very different from the interpretative ones required in all historical work – a clearly shaped argument, the apt use of visual 'quotation', a well-chosen framework, a good fit between materials, arguments and conclusions. So, non-textual sources have distinctive logics and conditions of existence and they have been interpreted in particular ways by other disciplines, which have their own scholarly traditions. The principles behind the skills needed to use them well are the same as those applied to texts. The problem comes when we use unfamiliar materials and want to endow them with a special status. I have already referred to one of the most problematic examples, namely what could be called reflection or window history. This is the surprisingly widespread claim that (some) art offers a window onto past worlds, so that by looking at it historians can see directly what it was like then. Or, to put it differently, art reflects life. This is certainly not what working historians assume about written sources, which are recognised as mediations. Art too is a mediation, but of a distinctive kind. Historians writing illustrated books often fail to recognise this point. The pictures become decorative add-ons: they are not integrated into historical arguments, but are treated as unproblematic illustrations of insights arrived at by conventional means. The images are not contextualised in the way any written source would be. This is a kind of double standard and has rightly been criticised, for example, by Michael Baxandall in his *Painting and Experience in*

Fifteenth Century Italy, a beautifully conceptualised and highly accessible discussion of what pictures are, and are not, evidence of.[20]

I want to insist on the need to treat images, or indeed any item of visual culture, critically. This is necessary because they have repeatedly been used unthinkingly by general historians to evoke a mood or emotion and attach it to a specific time and place, to encourage readers to identify with particular categories of historical actor, and to convey 'authenticity'. All of these are at work in the use historians make of documentary photography, of Hogarth's *oeuvre*, of Dutch genre painting and of Victorian domestic scenes, to give some obvious examples. These are manipulative and *un*skilful uses of non-textual sources, precisely because the procedures I am discussing in this chapter have not been followed. I want to insist equally vigorously on the advantages to be gained from acquiring the skills needed to use non-textual sources. A wider range of evidence will provide richer insights. An argument will be stronger if it can be shown to apply to a larger number of examples. A theme will be understood better if we can trace more of its modulations and variations. Each type of source affords its own kinds of insight. People in the past did not experience the world in the compartments into which sources are conventionally divided, still less did they think in terms of divisions between kinds of history such as economic and political. Many of the skills demanded by non-textual sources are in any case part of everyday life. In scholarly contexts they need to be brought up for conscious inspection and deliberately refined, and, if approached in this spirit they can only add to a historian's strengths.

Admittedly, historians' use of some types of musical evidence demands skills with a high technical component. One problem with music is that to the extent it may be said to be representational at all, it is so in a quite different sense from, say, figurative art. This accounts for the fact that it is much easier for historians to use music with an accompanying text than 'abstract' music, much easier for them to approach the subject via patronage, institutions and performances than through scores. However, with the right skills these limitations can be overcome, and in general similar arguments apply to the case of music as to other non-textual sources – all carry historical traces if we know how to capture them.[21] The goal is a balance between respecting the logics of

20 M. Baxandall, *Painting and Experience in Fifteenth Century Italy*, Oxford, 1988, p. 152.
21 For some very different examples of the use of music, see E. Said, *Musical Elaborations*, London, 1991; R. Leppert, *Music and Image: Domesticity, Ideology and Socio-Cultural Formation in Eighteenth-Century England*, Cambridge, 1988; J. Brewer, *The Pleasures of the Imagination*, London, 1997, ch. 14.

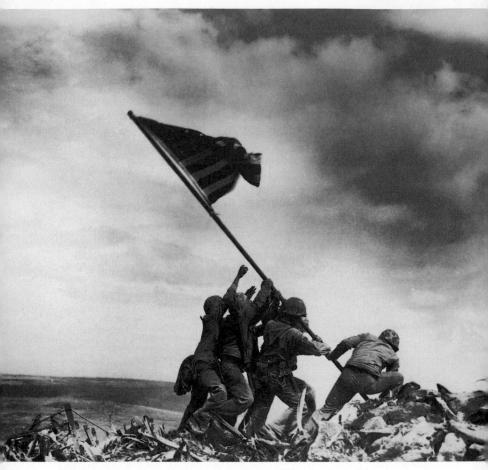

AKG, LONDON

7.2 *US marines planting the flag on Iwo Jima, February 1945; taken by Joe Rosenthal for Associated Press*
This photograph has become extremely well-known. Its powerful composition is both pleasing and dramatic. This evocative image looks spontaneous; it suggests triumph. Viewers place special faith in photographs, especially those designated 'documentary' and we tell ourselves that the camera never lies. Yet this is demonstrably false. So what trust can be placed in a photograph? Can it be treated as reliable evidence?

different media, while integrating them into historical arguments, not leaving them as decorative extras. If done well the result is a more holistic view of the past, and a greater awareness of the critical skills needed to use, evaluate and integrate any type of source. Using materials that are seen as the property of other disciplines raises questions that are best described as political, and I shall come to them shortly. But first I want to trace out the implications of my arguments for the teaching of history.

TEACHING HISTORY

The pedagogical implications of my arguments about skills are totally straightforward and can be stated succinctly. There are core skills that every historian needs, and the main one is critical reading – the ability to dismantle any piece of writing as fully and rigorously as possible, no matter when or how it was produced. The purpose behind critical reading is certainly not to treat texts in isolation, but to develop the basic analytical tools that will reveal their composition and mode of production. The result will be an understanding of the skeleton of a given piece of writing, as well as of its outward appearance, its core assumptions, its use of evidence, metaphor and footnotes. In order to apply this particular skill to secondary sources, students need to have a familiarity with what I have called scholarly traditions. They need to be able to navigate around their discipline, to have a sense of its history, the main changes it has undergone, the important journals in the field, influential approaches and relations with neighbouring domains. Navigation involves not just recognising signposts, but the capacity to evaluate the main contours of a field and current trends within it. Historians depend on their ability to write, and hence need to be taught about authorial skills. They also require plenty of historical cases through which to develop a sense of patterns, and these should be cases of different types – focused case studies, large-scale surveys, thematic courses, source-based studies and so on. These cases will form a repertoire, a fund, resources to think through and with. It follows then, that an undergraduate course, which allows students to specialise in, say, nineteenth- and twentieth-century Europe, or the history of their own country, is providing an overly narrow education. I know of no history department that teaches its students to write. And too few teach 'historiography' as anything other than dry 'philosophy of history' or 'methods and approaches', which are almost universally loathed by students.

The key then to a good history education is to marry a wide variety of substantive courses with skills-based ones, which should include what I have called 'navigating the field'. Ideally, skills, in the way I have presented them here, would be fully integrated into *all* historical teaching. The advantage of naming and drawing attention to them is that awareness of their significance is thereby raised, so that they can be practised and refined quite explicitly. Styles of teaching should also encourage students to take notes effectively and to develop their oral and aural techniques, since these reinforce the other central skills – selection, evaluation and argumentation. None of this is possible if students cannot undertake critical analysis, which is the foundation of all scholarly work in the humanities. This is not an end in itself, but a way of opening up wider intellectual perspectives.

Professions reproduce themselves through teaching their skills and transmitting their knowledge to others. As a result, what constitutes the core skills and the way in which they should be transmitted become political issues within the profession, because they affirm views of the discipline in which those who seek dominance have huge stakes. They are also political in a wider sense, by virtue of the phenomenon of public history, from which it is both impossible and wrong for academic historians to disengage themselves. There is little consensus today about how to teach history at university level, and there has been a noticeable move away from the idea that curricula should have a core and towards a modular, 'supermarket' approach that offers students what they want, like and find relevant. And since historians differ greatly in their attitudes to related disciplines and to what defines 'history', both of which are significant issues in shaping the curriculum, no consensus about a core can be arrived at by these means. Unfortunately, claims that there *is* a core to the subject are widely perceived as old-fashioned, even reactionary. They seem fundamentalist, and are often associated by their critics with an interest in reasserting the centrality of traditional forms of history, such as 'high' political history. My argument in this *chapter* has been that there is a core – an assemblage of skills and substance. We can think of it in terms of a portfolio of skills, which are learnt most effectively through being applied to a wide range of historical situations. My argument in this *book* has been that this core has an ethical dimension since historians have obligations to their sources, their readers, the past and the public at large.

Some of the most heated debates about the history curriculum concern the nature and range of topics covered. Since I advocate giving students a variety of historical fare, I consider an emphasis on world history, on going beyond the history of one's own nation, to be healthy. This is not because nation-based history is *ipso facto* 'bad'; everything depends on how it is presented. It has been subjected to savage criticism as a vehicle for promoting conservative and elitist values, for marginalising minority voices, and for providing self-justifying teleological narratives that pre-empt political dissent. It is possible and indeed desirable to teach a nation's history in a critical fashion. The same arguments apply to larger geographical areas. 'Europe', like 'the west' and 'the east', is an invention: the very idea has become and continues to be central in shaping identities and practices. Hence the history of Europe needs to be taught critically and with these points in mind. It does not follow that, because these types of history carry baggage, they should not be taught. They should be for two reasons. First, being able to locate oneself and one's own community or communities historically is intrinsically important. It builds on people's own experience, as much radical history advocates. It is therefore a vehicle through which a great deal can be learnt, for example, about patterns of identification (involving religion, the workplace, the family and so on), about the methods and sources best suited to this specific type of history, and about the past of an immediately available situation. Second, it illustrates the different analytical *levels* of which historical work is composed. To study the history of a town or an ethnic group, a nation, a continent, and then to think in terms of world history is to move through analytically distinct levels, which are complementary to one another, not mutually exclusive. This is the repertoire point – historians need the *range* of levels precisely because it illustrates different types of historical problem. It would be entirely wrong to think of some of these levels as 'better' than others. Here is the point about contexts in another guise. Historians need to see their chosen level or levels in the light of others: regions have national settings, continents global ones and so on. Obviously levels do not only concern geographical scale, they also involve types of generality (individuals, families, villages, occupations, classes, political parties), and the point about contexts also holds for these cases too.

Throughout the book I have strenuously resisted the idea that some forms of history are better or worse than others and suggested that such terms should be applied instead to the quality of the historical knowledge. I raise these moral terms because that is how, in the light of debates about political correctness, these matters have come to be considered, so that using the suffix '-centric' is a criticism on both political and moral grounds. Thus, it is often said that much history teaching, including in the United States, is 'eurocentric', which is to say that it privileges a European perspective on the world. Such a criticism has bite if one viewpoint is presented as unquestionable when other viewpoints are potentially relevant but actually neglected, and if Europe is, inappropriately, taken in isolation from other parts of the world. As it happens, I am sceptical about whether there is *a* single European point of view, in which case, if such a thing were claimed to exist, that would be wrong because it would be a distorting simplification. The problem is that once a notion such as 'eurocentrism' or 'orientalism' exists, it gets bandied about rather freely, becoming an unthinking term of criticism and thus pre-empts critical thinking. As I suggested earlier, effective teaching about 'Europe' would subject the very term to scrutiny, ask what work it does, think about relationships between regions both within and outside 'Europe' and hence eschew a single viewpoint. The eastern borders of 'Europe' have long been especially problematic – where does Europe end and Asia begin, and what is at stake in where the line is drawn? Such an approach draws creatively upon what students already know about Europe, whether a little or a lot. Since every historian comes from a particular background, it is necessary to build upon it, not pretend it does not exist. Thus, world history is always and inevitably written from particular standpoints because it cannot be otherwise. Yet, by consciously varying the level of focus, it is possible to raise one's awareness about what is taken for granted, to imagine other ways of cutting the historical cake, and to enhance intellectual flexibility.

SKILLS AND THE DISCIPLINE OF HISTORY

The discipline of history has been subjected to a number of critiques, especially over the last ten years. In the course of this book I have alluded to many of them. They are important in relation to skills, because they contain implications for the manner in which the discipline should be taught. Many if not most of these critiques have their roots in intellectual paradigms that are outside the discipline as this is customarily defined. As a result some historians feel attacked from outside. Equally they have brought to historians' attention hitherto unfamiliar perspectives and insisted on their relevance for contemporary historical practice. If, for instance, history is simply one type of narrative, whose claims to intellectual authority are fragile because based on stories that serve particular, limited interests, then claims about the distinctiveness of the discipline are also fragile, and there are important consequences for its pedagogy. So I want now, finally, to turn to the question of how the discipline of history may be distinctive.

Taken individually none of the skills I have described define the discipline of history. If we put them all together, and think of them as closely related to substance, we may get closer. It is vital to remember that there can be no firm boundaries around 'history' – there are no watertight definitions for any humanities or social-science discipline, and the boundaries have definitely become more permeable in recent years. It is possible to think of the discipline as a capacious umbrella – people choose to come under it, and to call what they do 'history', and others can agree or not as the case may be. These matters are in any case socially negotiated. 'History' has never been and cannot be a stable category. Those who shelter there have a sense of being 'a historian', they construct a professional identity around the label. It may be possible to get slightly closer to what is distinctive about 'history' if we think about the *assemblage* of skills involved. It is not possible to define history simply as the study of the past, because other disciplines do that too. While they share some features, archaeology and history are very different fields. Furthermore, there is contemporary history, a fast-growing area – the very name suggests that past and present are brought together in its practice. Nonetheless, for the most part history is concerned with a past for which there are extensive written records and with accounting for continuities as well as changes.

It is possible to be a little more specific. For example, we can say what history is *not*. History does not involve one specific category of human activity or production, such as music, dance, dress, leisure, procreation, literature or travel. Specialised sub-branches have a narrower focus, but these are only fully *historical* if they set such activities in a broader context. Historians study human nature in operation. They do not observe this directly as anthropologists, sociologists and psychologists have the chance to do, but mediated through sources. They are interested in both the abstract and the concrete features of past societies, and in the connections between them. They want to make statements of a fairly high level of generality about the past, to speak of phenomena that encompass many of its facets. General trends are always illustrated in particular instances, which, reciprocally, contribute to the delineation of broad features – history involves intricate dialogues between the specific and the general. Any given text, image, activity or experience is set in context*s* – the plural is important since historians typically consider a range of contexts, including those in which their sources were produced, received and used and those in which complex phenomena take place and are given meaning. Customarily such contexts involve structural elements, that is, the systems through which a given society functions – the distribution of wealth and of power, forms of social difference, institutions, administration, governance and so on.

A correspondingly wide range of historical explanations results, but they carry the features I have just described, with certain variations, according to the type of history in question. So, it would be possible to say that history is simply what historians do, which helps to recognise the huge diversity of practice. It would follow that skills were anything people who call themselves historians deploy in their work. Yet this is too bland. The rather abstract account

I have just given of what may be distinctive about the discipline indicates some of its specific habits of mind and we can be a bit more precise by examining some of the ways in which history is *unlike* related disciplines.

There is no single concept around which the discipline of history is organised in the way that sociology is predicated upon the concept 'society' or anthropology upon 'man'. Similarly there is no set of master theories, or of founding fathers in the way that sociologists and anthropologists can turn to Durkheim and Spencer, Marx, Mauss and Malinowski. There were great and influential historians in the past, but their legacy was much looser, and their writings are relatively neglected except by specialists. Whereas sociology students still read Weber, for instance, to familiarise themselves with his ideas and assess their usefulness, no comparable figures exist in history. Sociologists and anthropologists are expected to know the gist of the theories upon which their fields have been constructed in a way that no history student would be expected to do for the great historical writings of the nineteenth and early twentieth centuries. The field has become more theoretical over recent years, but this difference remains: there do not exist in history a limited number of thinkers, about whose status as founding fathers, practitioners, whatever their theoretical predilections, agree. In other words, history is inherently an eclectic discipline and the skills it requires are correspondingly diverse. And therein lie its strengths. Eclecticism is sometimes treated as a dirty word. At the very least it sounds untidy – just so: if historians treat the past in too tidy a manner they lose a great deal. Hence the discipline is rightly pragmatic, including in its methods and the skills these demand. It is precisely the ability to embrace complexities while making sense of them, and to think flexibly about diverse phenomena at distinct analytical levels, that characterises historians' purchase on the past.

HISTORY'S FUTURE: A PERSONAL STATEMENT

I hope it is clear to readers that this book has been written in a spirit of passionate enthusiasm for the study of the past. While it is not a requirement for the job, the majority of historians love what they do. I say this because it is essential to understanding the discipline as a whole, which possesses a paradoxical identity. It demands intimate involvement with one's objects of study, which, precisely because it is a form of love, can lead both to sympathetic identification and to the myopia that comes from being too close. The discipline has another complex face: a self-aware intellectual distance, that makes analysis possible, but which can be impersonal, stolid and frankly pompous. It is extremely difficult to say at all briefly what the defining characteristics of history as a field are, but I want to reiterate the point made in the last chapter that knowing eclecticism and analytical flexibility are major features. Thus I believe that integrating apparently diverse sources and approaches to produce more holistic accounts is an important goal of the discipline. For me, this is bound up with what is often meant by 'cultural' history. Cultural history is pretty hard to define too, but it always gives priority to mental processes, to what I have referred to as mediations, in any historical study.

When scholars articulate their aspirations, they naturally reveal their personal visions, and by 'personal' I do not mean 'idiosyncratic', since these visions may be shared by many practitioners, but 'close to the heart', integral to a given biography. Let me give a specific example. It was only in the course of writing this book that I realised how deeply permeated my view of historical practice has been by the history and philosophy of science in which I was trained, and by an approach to scientific and medical knowledge that is often called social constructionist. As a result I have stressed the social construction of historical knowledge and its production within communities, now of a fairly structured kind, that are rooted in institutions, nations, political groupings and so on. What counts as successful history depends, then, on the context in which it is being judged, and the most helpful way of thinking about such matters is in terms of trust, not truth.

Because of persistent misunderstandings on the matter, it is crucial to be clear about what does *not* follow from this position. I am not suggesting either that there are no clear standards by which historical work can be judged, or that history as a discipline cannot engage with the material, embodied worlds of past times. What I have counselled against is a smooth, thoughtless, naïve transition between the sources and the claims historians make, just as I have counselled against taking the sources themselves at face value. Behind the work done in this vein in the history and philosophy of science was a desire to unsettle received views of science. So long as this is done well, that is, within a sophisticated intellectual framework, such unsettling is all to the good – and so it is with history. In both their teaching and their research, historians should, responsibly, unsettle their audiences, provoke them to think harder and deeper about the human condition.

Since historical knowledge is produced socially within communities and because that knowledge is given some status, those who produce it have ethical obligations. We are not free to say whatever we like about the past, because historical claims have entailments, for which their makers are responsible. These responsibilities are a complex matter, and a full discussion of them is beyond the remit of this book, but I have tried, in discussing public history, to sketch in some of the main issues.[1] If I have one wish for the future of the discipline it is that it embrace the possibilities for which 'public history' stands as a shorthand. This would involve, for example, a greater willingness to write for the general public and to collaborate with museums and the media. No group is better placed than historians to demonstrate to the public how fatuous and dangerous the crude moral polarities are that are so often invoked in history's name and how simplistic it is to think that unambiguous lessons from history exist, which provide simple formulae according to which present policies can and should be formulated. Taking account of history is quite different from claiming to draw 'lessons' from it. As I have been writing this postscript, notions of a 'just war' in the Balkans are being tossed about. Where does the notion of a 'just war' come from and how has it been used previously? The answers will not give governments recipes, but they will give their citizens a greater level of understanding of how things come to be and of the manipulative uses of history, and that it is the first step towards change.

One possible sceptical response to my position on the importance of public history is that my arguments are unsound because they do not take account of *differences* in historical opinion. Historians, as I have constantly

---

1   F. Bédarida, ed., *The Social Responsibility of the Historian*, Providence, R. I., 1994.

stated, are subject to the same forces as everyone else, although their professional and scholarly training encourages them to temper their emotions, to channel their commitments and to be as balanced as possible when making judgements. Nonetheless they see the world in diverse ways; there is indeed no consensus on matters of substance, and historians will never speak with one voice. I do not see their wider role as being one where they are saying, as it were, the 'right' things, or the same things. Rather historians should foster informed debate about the past, and encourage people to think critically about evidence and what it does and does not reveal. In other words, political pluralism is essential, and in this sense I am against 'political correctness' in one of its meanings. So, diversity of opinion among historians is not a problem.

Healthy pluralism is built upon openness. I have not concealed my own interests and preferences, so readers will have perceived that my sympathies lie more with the left than with the right. However, my position does not make me automatically uninterested in or disapproving of conservative history, so long as it, like its radical counterpart, is done well. I may not always 'like' it, but I can certainly respect it. Indeed, it is important to be stimulated into deeper reflection by views that challenge one's own. One of the things that most enrages me is styles of women's history that make simplistic, universalist claims about the oppression of women. This is poor history and it is also poor politics, and these shortcomings are not forgivable just because we might be 'on the same side'. Disagreement should not be solely about ideological conflicts – it should also be about the *quality* of scholarship and about the uses to which that scholarship is put. Ideological conflict is inevitable, although it is important to be open and constructive about it. Never, ever, should such disagreements be personalised or allowed to get nasty, leading to the blocking of jobs or publications, for instance. Most historians will witness some such behaviour over the course of their careers: for example, at seminars and conferences. It is wholly to be condemned, and conveys to young historians the impression that besting people, putting them in their place, is acceptable. Passions can be lived and expressed in vigorous debate without such destructiveness. I am not implying that historians are worse than others, but since this part of the book is about history's future it seems reasonable to make the point here.

Another point, which requires explanation, follows from my position. It is sometimes thought that to study a historical phenomenon is to approve of it. While this is not an entirely unreasonable assumption – I have, after all, stressed historians' identifications with what they study – it is too crude. Intellectual curiosity is aroused in all manner of ways, including by concern as well as by approval. So to study, let us say, Fascism in Britain in the inter-war period, does not imply that historians share the value system they are examining. Another way of making the same point is to say that people often mistake *de*scription and analysis for *pre*scription and advocacy. Giving an account of a state of affairs is not to advocate it. When historians write they cannot do so without 'bias' or 'objectively', but it does not follow from the fact that they are interested parties that they are being advocates or prescribers. And, if historians do indeed use their historical research inappropriately, they must be censured for it. By 'inappropriately' I mean *without* due regard to evidence and other scholarly work and a transparent apparatus, or for dishonest ends. I accept that providing a full apparatus is a problem in popular works, but if publishers and their referees are responsible this should not cause overwhelming difficulties.

Historians' differences are inevitable, but the mere fact of their existence should not undermine the discipline's capacity to be active in public debate, so long as the points I have just made are taken fully into account. I can restate my position using different words in order to tackle another problem that the discipline is currently facing. It must be pluralist in terms of the topics and approaches that are pursued. Fashion is a real problem here. I would not say that fashion is a bad thing – that would be a waste of breath – but I would say that it is in the interests of the discipline to keep a wide range of activities going, including ones that may seem obsolete to some practitioners. For example, there has been a trend towards placing ever greater emphasis on the history of the last 150 years or so, with the result that students have often studied a rather narrow chronological range. This limits them intellectually, and curricula that offer all students a wider chronological range are highly desirable. It is of course ironic that at a popular level ancient civilisations, such as Egypt,[2] exercise wide appeal and that areas with continuing allure, such as medieval history, are not taught at all by some history departments. By the same token, whilst it is obviously good for newer forms and styles of history to be available to students, it should not be at the expense of traditional ones. In my opinion, economic history is particularly vulnerable in this respect. It is always hard to work out how it is that fields change in the image and value they are given, but it is evident that they do. Rather than capitulating and agreeing that students should get whatever they want, we need to mount clear intellectual arguments about why a given area or approach is important.

2   The popularity of exhibitions and museum displays, like fiction and films on ancient Egypt and its archaeology, are well known. Cf. B. Waterson, *Ancient Egypt*, Stroud, 1998, part of the series Sutton Pocket Histories.

Economic history (like some others fields) is a fundamental part of the discipline, of which every student *ought* to have some understanding. This is because the subject matter of economics, which studies the generation and distribution of resources, is intrinsic to the manner in which every society functions. There are only a limited number of such 'structural' phenomena and they lie at the heart of history, which, as a discipline, aspires to make general statements about past societies. Faced with a choice between courses on the history of sport or the history of animals and those on economic, political, social or intellectual history, I would hope students would be able to see that the latter are likely to be of more *general* use than the former. This is not at all to diminish the interest of the former, it is simply to recognise that their role in the discipline is different. A course on the history of dress will not afford the same kinds of insight as one on the history of government. One is not 'better' than the other, but they do occupy different positions within the discipline. However, one *is* more fundamental and general than the other. We would not insist that, *instead* of studying sonata form, musicologists should look at, say, paintings of performers, or the history of subscription concerts, inherently interesting though they are. The latter simply would not give them the basic tools they need to go on to other topics in the field, although they could be useful extensions once some kind of groundwork was in place. Cultural history and the history of intellectual traditions are integral parts of this groundwork because they provide insights into the way the world is experienced in other times and places. Thus they help in relation to phenomena, such as religion, that many students find increasingly baffling.

Inevitably there is no consensus on what such historical groundwork should cover, in which countries and over which centuries, but, in a given context, it is essential to debate what that groundwork would look like. For me, it should cover economic, social and political history, together with major intellectual traditions in several countries (including the student's own), at least two continents, and over more than three centuries. It should do all this in a fairly systematic fashion, through core courses, which act as a kind of spine onto which flesh is put in options. I have already said that I would like to see skills integrated into all history teaching. I would also like to see an understanding of the discipline itself integrated in the same manner. It has always puzzled me why historians are not more 'historical' in relation to their own professional practices. It is not hard to train students to ask basic questions of any item they read, including secondary sources. 'When was it written and in what circumstances?' should be asked of all secondary sources without exception, and by systematically doing so we can build up a sense of changing historical practices and of where we have come from in intellectual terms.[3] This would be a logical extension of both the critical reading and the placing of phenomena in contexts that are basic historical skills.

Curiosity about where 'we' have come from is an important aspect of the historical enterprise. When I used the word 'we' at the end of the previous paragraph, I meant those who identify themselves as historians, including those studying history at university level. But broader groups are also addressed by historians. It is generally recognised that curiosity about the past is a widespread phenomenon, met in an amazing variety of ways, of which the discipline of history is just one. I have found the idea of conversation useful here. Thus, we could say that, although historians are constantly in conversation with each other, with their predecessors and with their sources, they also talk to other interested parties, on behalf of whom they write and teach. These matters are rarely made explicit, although I would argue that they become more visible in relation to some utterly exceptional historical phenomena, such as the Holocaust. I would go further and claim that these 'interested parties' include the societies in which historians function. This is not to say that every person at a given time and place is consciously interested in history – if only. But it seems that, as a collectivity, we depend in our public discourse on claims about the past; hence my stress on the ethical dimensions of historical practice.

The argument about the centrality of history in public discourse suggests to me that historians have the function of bearing witness. They do not do so directly, but they operate where direct witnessing is not available. The notion of bearing witness has strong religious connotations, including the idea that direct observation of divine powers has a special status in the transmission of beliefs. I would like to invoke another aspect of the idea – doing something on behalf of others. It seems to me that historians have been given considerable privileges and rights, even if people do not always listen to them. The contemporary role of historians is especially significant given the general recognition of the emotional and social value of memory and commemoration. Our historical practice should reflect these functions and responsibilities, which have come about precisely because what actually happened is

---

3 A good example is Bryce Lyon's historiographical essay, 'Henri Pirenne's *Réflexions d'un Solitaire* and his Re-Evaluation of History', *Journal of Medieval History*, 23, 1997, 285–99, which examines Pirenne's changing attitudes towards German historiography in the light of his experiences during the First World War. Such insights into how history is written are a fundamental part of the discipline. Cf. M. Berg, *A Woman in History: Eileen Power 1889–1940*, Cambridge, 1996.

constantly being used and called into question. If history were solely fiction, *and* universally recognised as such, we would hardly care so much about its practice. An awareness of history as a made narrative is perfectly compatible with recognising both its genuine significance and its capacity to speak meaningfully about past times. The future of history lies in practitioners and their publics possessing *both* an awareness of its limitations *and* a confidence in its intellectual strengths and achievements.

While I accept that historians need and want to be highly specialised, I hope we never lose sight of major 'structural' elements, of broad sweeping themes, of motifs that persist for centuries. I also hope we can be inclusive with respect to sources and approaches and creatively cultivate wide audiences. The goal of inclusiveness requires careful consideration, however. Let me give a concrete example. I have argued that the disciplines should be keeping alive and actively promoting areas, such as economic history, because they contribute not just to the substance of history but to thinking about structural issues within societies. In this sense, as in others, I have argued for inclusiveness. At the same time this book has not engaged with traditions of history writing that have developed over many centuries in, say, China or India. In this sense it is not inclusive. To be inclusive in the sense of embracing many cultures presents challenges to any individual historian. Writing about such complex matters without having studied and thought about them deeply would be impertinent. Ways of writing history are inseparable from language, literary and cultural traditions, political formations and so on. For the majority of historians, global inclusiveness is simply not feasible, and tokenism is, to my mind, offensive. Yet it would clearly be totally wrong to pretend other traditions did not exist. A useful analogy comes from the history of science. Nonspecialists are frequently astonished to learn how ancient and sophisticated were the forms of natural knowledge developed outside what is too frequently reified as 'the west'. Joseph Needham's life's work was to bring the riches of Chinese scientific and medical traditions to a wider audience.[4] Similarly, we need, and will certainly profit from, work on other ways of doing history provided by people who are genuinely steeped in them, as Needham was in the civilisation of China. Thus the goal of inclusivity should go hand in hand with a humble appraisal of each historian's limitations.[5] I am vividly aware of mine; hence I have written out of what I know and have experienced, and make no

---

4   See the multi-volume *Science and Civilisation in China*, Cambridge, 1954 onwards, which Joseph Needham initiated.
5   M. Bentley, *Companion to Historiography*, London, 1997, chs. 24–27 and 29 on historiographical traditions outside Europe and North America.

pretensions to have done otherwise. If inclusivity is interpreted mechanistically, as an obligation to mention something because it is there, the results will be intellectually shallow. Openness, together with a sense of historical practice as provisional and limited, might be a better way of thinking about these issues.

While no historian can ever be totally open, they can encourage this trait in themselves and in others. Openness is about emotional and intellectual receptivity, whether this concerns the types of sources used, their content, the ideas of others or methods and approaches. I could go further and say that, in setting up historical problems for research, a degree of open-endedness is essential, otherwise there is a risk of simply confirming what was already thought. It is in this spirit that parts of the world hitherto unfamiliar to particular communities and new perspectives are best approached. The underlying motive should be generating fresh historical insights. It would be possible to think about this issue in terms of comparative approaches to history, which involve taking a range of cases for comparison, because doing so will shed light on a specific historical problem. In this way, historians can expand the areas they work on in a realistic fashion, and the selection of regions is driven by tough intellectual considerations. Furthermore it should be axiomatic that excellent language skills and first-hand familiarity with countries being studied are part of this more open approach to historical practice.

An individual's reasons for working on the areas they do are bound to be mixed. They generally include an assessment of what others are likely to be interested in over the coming years. Since historians depend on their audiences, they have, it seems to me, always had an eye on the future. Far from being immersed in a fusty past, and unaware of what is going on around them, historians stand firmly in the present as mediators between past and future. The notion of usable pasts is now common currency. Hence it is fitting that historians come to see their field as helping to create understanding and identities that are future-orientated. If I seem to be constantly giving priority to public history this is because it is a logical extension of what goes on inside the discipline. Throughout *History in Practice* I have mentioned six features of the discipline that seem to me to be of paramount importance. First, its modes of operation should be transparent; second, eclecticism is acceptable and desirable; third, historians need to be judicious; fourth, they must embrace a range of approaches and subjects; fifth, rigid polarisations, such as that between those who are for and those who are against theory, should be eschewed; and, finally, consciousness-raising is crucial, so that practitioners understand their own traditions and procedures better. All these features suggest to me that there cannot and should not be rigid boundaries around the particular set of academic practices named 'history'. The public implications of historical practice are profound, whether academic historians like it or not. Most of us practise history not just because we love doing so but because we believe it matters to *everyone* precisely what accounts are given of the past. An integral part of being a historian is having a fair and honest sense of one's own practices, which should be reflected in every single piece of speaking, teaching and writing one undertakes. *History in Practice* has attempted to bring some of the key issues of historical practice to a wide audience. In this respect it is a modest contribution to public history.

Further reading

Health warning: the English-language works cited below illustrate a variety of perspectives. No attempt has been made to produce a comprehensive or exhaustive list. This section is designed to provide suggestions for going further into matters mentioned in the text, and includes items that are often referred to in debates about the nature of history. Many are available in cheap paperbacks, some have been published in a number of editions, others are out of print.

General works

Appleby, J., Hunt L., and Jacob, M., *Telling the Truth about History*, New York, 1994

Arnold, J., *A Very Short Introduction to History*, Oxford, 2000

Berkhofer, R., *Beyond the Great Story: History as Text and Discourse*, Cambridge, Mass., 1995

Bloch, M., *The Historian's Craft*, New York, 1953

Braudel, F., *On History*, London, 1980

Burke, P., ed., *New Perspectives on Historical Writing*, Cambridge, 1991

Butterfield, H., *The Whig Interpretation of History*, Harmondsworth, 1973

Carr, E. H., *What is History?*, London, 1961

Collingwood, R. G., *The Idea of History*, Oxford, 1946

Elton, G., *The Practice of History*, London, 1969 (first published 1967)

Evans, R., *In Defence of History*, London, 1997

Galbraith, V. H., *An Introduction to the Study of History*, London, 1964

Gardiner, J., ed., *What is History Today?*, Basingstoke, 1988

Gay, P., *Freud for Historians*, New York, 1985

Jenkins, K., *Re-thinking History*, London, 1991

———, *On 'What is History?'*, London, 1995

Marwick, A., *The Nature of History*, London, 1970

Ritter, H., *Dictionary of Concepts in History*, New York, 1986

Smith, B., *The Gender of History: Men, Women and Historical Practice*, Cambridge, Mass., 1998

Southgate, B., *History: What and Why?*, London, 1996

Stanford, M., *A Companion to the Study of History*, Oxford, 1994

Stern, F., ed., *The Varieties of History from Voltaire to the Present*, London, 1970 (first published 1956)

Tosh, J., *The Pursuit of History*, third edition, London, 1999 (first published 1984)

Tuchman, B., *Practicing History*, New York, 1981

Vincent, J., *An Intelligent Person's Guide to History*, London, 1995

White, H., *Metahistory: The Historical Imagination in Nineteenth-Century Europe*, Baltimore, 1973

Williams, R., *Keywords*, second edition, London, 1983

Chapter 1 Introduction
Bentley, M., ed., *Companion to Historiography*, London, 1997
Burke, P., *The French Historical Revolution: The Annales School 1929–89*, Cambridge, 1990
Hewison, R., *The Heritage Industry*, London, 1987
Levine, P., *The Amateur and the Professional: Antiquarians, Historians and Archaeologists in Victorian England*, Cambridge, 1986
Samuel, R., *Theatres of Memory*, 2 vols., London, 1994 and 1998

Chapter 2 Mapping the discipline of history
Burke, P., ed., *New Perspectives on Historical Writing*, Cambridge, 1991
Chartier, R., *Cultural History: Between Practices and Representations*, London, 1988
Coleman, D., *History and the Economic Past. An Account of the Rise and Decline of Economic History in Britain*, Oxford, 1987
Gay, P., *Freud for Historians*, New York, 1985
Gottschalk, L., *Understanding History: A Primer of Historical Method*, New York, 1963 (first published 1950)
Hunt, L., ed., *The New Cultural History*, Berkeley, 1989
Porter, R., *Gibbon*, London, 1988
Renier, G., *History: Its Purpose and Method*, New York, 1965 (first published 1950)
Ritter, H., *Dictionary of Concepts in History*, New York, 1986
Wilson, A., ed., *Rethinking Social History: English Society 1570–1920 and its Interpretation*, Manchester, 1993

Chapter 3 History and other disciplines
Abrams, M., *A Glossary of Literary Terms*, sixth edition, Fort Worth, Tex., 1993 (first published 1941)
Bentley, M., ed., *Companion to Historiography*, London, 1997, esp. part 5.
Bruce, S., *Sociology: A Very Short Introduction*, Oxford, 1999
Burke, P., *History and Social Theory*, Ithaca, N.Y., 1993
Douglas, M., *Natural Symbols: Explorations in Cosmology*, London, 1970
Geertz, C., *The Interpretation of Cultures*, New York, 1973
Haskell, F., 'Visual Sources and *The Embarassment of Riches*', Past and Present, no. 120, 1988, pp. 216–26.
Haskell, F., *History and its Images: Art and the Interpretation of the Past*, New Haven, 1993
Hastrup, K., *Other Histories*, London, 1992
Leff, G., *History and Social Theory*, London, 1969
Lentricchia F., and McLaughlin, T., eds., *Critical Terms for Literary Study*, second edition, Chicago, 1995.
Lodge, D., ed., *20th Century Literary Criticism: A Reader*, London, 1972
Nelson R., and Shiff, R., eds., *Critical Terms for Art History*, Chicago, 1996
Pointon, M., *History of Art: A Student's Handbook*, fourth edition, London, 1997 (first published 1980)
Rabinow, P., ed., *The Foucault Reader*, New York, 1984
Rotberg R., and Rabb, T., eds., *Art and History: Images and their Meaning*, Cambridge, 1988
Smith, D., *The Rise of Historical Sociology*, Cambridge, 1991

Thomson, E. P., *Customs in Common*, London, 1993
Tilly, C., *As Sociology Meets History*, New York, 1981

Chapter 4 The status of historical knowledge

Fay B., et al., eds., *History and Theory: Contemporary Readings*, Oxford, 1998
Gardiner, P., ed., *Theories of History*, New York, 1959
Lemon, M., *The Discipline of History and the History of Thought*, London, 1995
Lloyd, C., *Explanation in Social History*, Oxford, 1986
Mandelbaum, M., *The Status of Historical Knowledge: An Answer to Relativism*, New York, 1967
Schlink, B., *The Reader*, London, 1997
Stanford, M., *An Introduction to the Philosophy of History*, Oxford, 1998
Tosh, J., *The Pursuit of History*, London, 1999, ch. 7.

Chapter 5 Periodisation

Best, G., ed., *The Permanent Revolution: The French Revolution and its Legacy*, London, 1988
Briggs, A. and Snowman, D., eds, *Fins de Siecle: How Centuries End 1400–2000*, New Haven, 1996.
Hunt, L., The Challenge of Gender', in H. Medick and A.-C. Trepp, *Geschlechtergeschichte und Allgemeine Geschichte*, Göttingen, 1998, pp. 59–97.
Kubler, G., *The Shape of Time: Remarks on the History of Things*, New Haven, 1962
Roberts, J., *The Penguin History of the World*, London, 1995
Williams, N., *Chronology of the Modern World 1763–1965*, revised edition, Harmondsworth, 1975

Chapter 6 Public history

Benson, S., et al., eds., *Presenting the Past: Essays on History and the Public*, Philadelphia, 1986
Friedländer, S., ed., *Probing the Limits of Representation: Nazism and the 'Final Solution'*, Cambridge, Mass., 1992
Gillis, J., ed., *Commemoration: The Politics of National Identity*, Princeton, 1993
Horne, D., *The Great Museum: The Re-presentation of the Past*, London, 1984
Lowenthal, D., *The Past is a Foreign Country*, Cambridge, 1985
Maier, C., *The Unmasterable Past*, Cambridge, Mass., 1988
Nora, P., *Realms of Memory*, 3 vols., New York, 1996, 1997, and 1998
Samuel, R., *Theatres of Memory*, 2 vols., London, 1994 and 1998
Tosh, J., *The Pursuit of History*, London, 1999, chs. 1 and 2
Vergo, P., ed., *The New Museology*, London, 1989

Chapter 7 Historians' skills

Abbott, M., ed., *History Skills: A Student's Handbook*, London, 1996
Bédarida, F., ed., *The Social Responsibility of the Historian*, Providence, R. I., 1994
Clanchy, M., *From Memory to Written Record: England 1066–1307*, London, 1979
D'Aniello, C., *Teaching Bibliographic Skills in History*, London, 1993
Floud, R., *An Introduction to Quantitative Methods for Historians*, second edition, London, 1979
Hockett, H., *The Critical Method in Historical Research and Writing*, New York, 1955

Karsten, P., and Modell, J., eds., *Theory, Method, and Practice in Social and Cultural History*, New York, 1992

Le Goff, J., and Nora, P., eds, *Constructing the Past: Essays in Historical Methodology*, Cambridge, 1985

Lloyd, C., *The Structures of History*, Oxford, 1993

Seldon, A., ed., *Contemporary History: Practice and Method*, Oxford, 1988

Tuchman, B., *Practicing History*, New York, 1981, esp. part 3, 'Learning from History'

Vansina, J., *Oral Tradition: A Study in Historical Methodology*, London, 1985

Postscript

The following list contains two types of publication: first, a small number of my own writings that relate to the themes of this book, and, second, a selection of works I have found important and helpful.

L. Jordanova, 'Resisting Reflexivity', *History of the Human Sciences*, 5, 1992, 59–67

——, 'Gender and the Historiography of Science', *British Journal for the History of Science*, 26, 1993, 469–83

——, 'The Social Construction of Medical Knowledge', *Social History of Medicine*, 8, 1995, 361–81

——, 'Cultural Effort: An Introductory Essay', chapter 1 of *Nature Displayed: Gender, Science and Medicine 1760–1820*, London, 1999, pp. 1–18

Appleby, J., 'Locke, Liberalism and the Natural Law of Money', *Past and Present*, no. 71, 1976, 43–69

Baxandall, M., *Patterns of Intention: On the Historical Explanation of Pictures*, London, 1985

Crow, T., *Emulation: Making Artists for Revolutionary France*, New Haven, 1995

Davidoff, L., *Worlds Between: Historical Perspectives on Gender and Class*, Cambridge, 1995

Douglas, M., *Purity and Danger: An Analysis of Concepts of Pollution and Taboo*, London, 1966

Figlio, K., 'The Metaphor of Organisation: A Historiographical Perspective on the Bio-medical Sciences of the Early Nineteenth Century', *History of Science*, 14, 1976, 17–53

McManners, J., *Death and the Enlightenment: Changing Attitudes to Death among Christians and Unbelievers in Eighteenth-Century France*, Oxford, 1981

Pointon, M., *Mulready*, London, 1986

Porter, R., *Health for Sale: Quackery in England, 1660–1850*, Manchester, 1989

Schaffer, S., 'States of Mind: Enlightenment and Natural Philosophy', in G. Rousseau, ed., *Languages of Psyche: Mind and Body in Enlightenment Thought*, Berkeley, 1990, pp. 233–90

Strathern, M., *After Nature: English Kinship in the Late Twentieth Century*, Cambridge, 1992

Glossary

(All words are nouns unless otherwise stated.)

anachronism: something that is out of its own time; specifically historians using ideas that are alien to the period under discussion.

bricolage: a French term for something that is assembled from disparate pieces.

canon: an authoritative body of writings or art works that are deemed of special value and worthy of academic study.

citation index: a list of where a particular publication is made reference to, i.e. cited, by other scholars.

cliometrics: the application of mathematical and statistical methods to historical data.

counterfactuals: speculative claims that are contrary to known facts and deployed to examine alternative, hypothetical sequences of events. This is generally undertaken to clarify issues of causation.

critical theory: a set of approaches to knowledge loosely indebted to Marxism, which is sympathetic to **social constructionism** and develops politically informed critiques of the uses to which knowledge is put.

discourse: a more or less coherent body of statements that can be analysed using approaches deriving from linguistics, and underlying which is a particular view of the world.

documentary (noun and adjective): a cultural artefact, such as a photograph, film or television programme, which purports to report actual events, persons and circumstances.

episteme(s): the dominant mode of knowledge of a specific era, common to many, even all, forms of knowledge produced at the time.

epistemology: theories of knowledge; how we know what we know.

exoticism: infatuation with or admiration for what is exotic, foreign, unfamiliar.

genre: a type of text or cultural product with its own conventions; a way of classifying works of art and literature.

hagiography: literally, lives of saints and martyrs written to glorify their subjects; more loosely, uncritical, reverential accounts of a life.

hegemony: all-embracing dominance, especially of a political and/or ideological kind, wielded by states, classes, or, by extension, other groupings.

heritage industry: the marketing of the past for leisure purposes; the development of forms of tourism that promote 'historic' places, such as old towns, villages, museums, rural activities and so on. Associated with this is the selling of objects, for example, in museum shops, that evoke past times.

heuristic device: an assumption that assists in taking research further, a useful tool to think with.

histoire totale: a French term meaning history written so that a number of levels or aspects of the past are thought about together.

historiography: the writing of history and the study of historical writings. More broadly an awareness of different ways of doing history.

history from below, see **people's history**

holistic (adjective): the tendency or ability to perceive wholes, that is, to see how the parts of a historical situation are related to one another, and to embrace apparently disparate phenomena.

human sciences: a name for all the fields of knowledge that focus on human beings, principally psychology, anthropology and sociology. It is possible to see history and philosophy as human sciences.

hypothesis: an untested proposition, used as a basis for argument and research, which will be (or ought to be) empirically tested.

ideology: a set of ideas, held with deep commitment by individuals or groups, which shapes their view of the world, and which serves their material interests, if only indirectly.

imaginary: originally a psychoanalytic term, used loosely to suggest a way of imagining the world that is widely held at a given time and place.

keywords: those words in any language that carry special weight because they are contested, highly value-laden, ideologically fraught or unusually emotive. As a result they are exceptionally revealing historically.

linguistics: the systematic study of the elements of language and of the principles governing their organisation; the science of language.

longue durée (adjective): a French term to describe a piece of historical writing or research that covers a long period of time.

mediation: in everyday use the term 'mediators' refers to go-betweens, who bring together two groups, but remain separate from them. Mediation is the name given to the whole process. 'Mediation' the noun, and 'mediate', the verb, can also be used metaphorically in relation to ideas and the transformations they undergo, which is how I use them in this book. Behind these terms is a strong conviction that ideas perform major social work. Scholars who deploy them have generally been influenced by Marxian traditions.

medicalisation: the process of making phenomena medical, that is, under the control of doctors, which were not so previously. The term implies criticism of this process.

mentalités: a French word for which there is no precise English equivalent, but 'attitudes' and 'outlook' come fairly close. It is used of a kind of history that is concerned with people's mental lives, and especially those aspects of it that remain tacit, but which nonetheless shape daily lives; child-rearing, for example.

meta- (prefix): when attached to nouns it indicates a higher, more abstract or general level of the noun in question.

micro-history: a level of social analysis that is concerned with everyday life; historical research, often of a single community, on a small scale.

modernism: a western artistic movement usually associated with the late nineteenth and early twentieth centuries and with a repudiation of settled, traditional approaches; especially evident in literature, music, architecture and art. More broadly, the cult of what is modern, self-consciously innovative and dismissive of traditional ways.

modernisation: the processes whereby supposedly traditional societies become modern ones; and the ways in which these processes are conceptualised. Modernity is the state of being modern, where modern can be defined in a variety of ways.

monograph: a piece of writing, generally a book, on a specific historical phenomenon, person, place or event and the result of specialised research.

myth: stories, often involving supernatural or exceptional persons, actions or events, that are endowed by a society with special significance, and that speak to its most cherished concerns, such as its origins, leadership or destiny; a fictional account; a view that is deeply ingrained and resistant to contradictory evidence.

narrative: an account, or narration of events, in the form of a story or tale.

orientalism: the cult of the orient; the development of an aesthetic based on (imagined) ideas of the east; the term now implies a criticism of such attitudes on the grounds that they distort and homogenise 'the east' inappropriately.

other/otherness: that which is not the self, and which possess the quality of being different; the tendency of dominant groups to see and exploit the differences they find between themselves and subordinate groups.

palaeography: the study of documents, generally ancient or old ones, with special attention to the handwriting and to their authenticity, including accurate dating.

paradigm: a model or pattern, sometimes a coherent worldview or set of theories.

pedagogy: the art or science of teaching; the principles according to which instruction is given.

people's history: history for and about the majority of the population; the serious and committed study of non-elite groups; historical writing that is highly accessible and relevant to the people as a whole; history from below that rejects elite perspectives.

post-modernism: a reaction to modernism that is both dependent upon and highly critical of it; a scepticism of totalising explanations, an insistence on the impossibility of objective knowledge, and an acceptance of what is partial and fragmentary, both in human experience and in accounts of it; sometimes an amorphous term for recent cultural trends.

prosopography: the study of collective biography; a historical method involving the examination of significant numbers of lives, for example, in a given occupation, institution or place.

quadrivium: the division of knowledge into four parts, current in medieval and early modern times.

relativism: the view that there can be no objective standards, for example, of historical truth, hence theories, values and so on must be understood as relative to the circumstances that produced them.

research assessment exercise: the periodic review and assessment of the quality of research produced in universities, the results of which are sometimes used to determine the amount of government money each department receives for its research activities.

rhetoric: using language effectively, for instance, so as to persuade or influence others; the systematic study of how this can be achieved. Sometimes used pejoratively to suggest merely superficial verbal effects with no underlying substance.

second-wave feminism: the forms of feminism that developed over the 1960s and that have been continuously developing both intellectually and politically since then.

semiotics: the systematic study of signs; analysis of the wider meanings and social functions of sign systems, both verbal and non-verbal.

sign: a basic element of communication, not objects or referents themselves but the device, whether verbal or non-verbal, that refers to them.

social construction(ism): theories that emphasise the socially created nature of collective life; the idea that human existence is made up not of natural givens but of social products or constructs.

structuralism: an approach in the social sciences that studies the structures that underlie and generate observable phenomena; these structures are often thought to be rooted in the basic characteristics of the mind. **Post-structuralism** is a set of influential cultural theories that departs from structuralism but that refuses the possibility of a scientific study of structures. Instead they stress the indeterminacy of meaning.

subaltern (adjective): subordinate or inferior; in the phrase 'subaltern studies', it involves looking at colonial situations from the vantage point of the colonised.

teleology: explanation in terms of goals or purposes; the assumption that ends or outcomes are present in and/or explain earlier stages of a process.

topos (plural, ***topoi***): a motif or theme in a literary or artistic composition, a convention or formula.

Whiggish (adjective): history that is written either from the point of view of the winners or from an unthinking commitment to progress. The term implies criticism of such an approach.

Bibliography

Abercrombie, N., Hill, S,. and Turner, B., *The Penguin Dictionary of Sociology*, third edition, London, 1994

Abrams, M., *A Glossary of Literary Terms*, sixth edition, Fort Worth, Tex., 1993

Baldick, C., *The Concise Oxford Dictionary of Literary Terms*, Oxford, 1990

Bullock, A., and Trombley, S., eds., *The New Fontana Dictionary of Modern Thought*, London, 1999

Marshall, G., ed., *A Dictionary of Sociology*, second edition, Oxford, 1998

Ritter, H., *Dictionary of Concepts in History*, New York, 1986

Weigall, D., 'Historical Terms', in Abbott, M. ed., *History Skills: A Student's Handbook*, London, 1996, pp. 107–16

Williams, R., *Keywords: A Vocabulary of Culture and Society*, revised edition, London, 1983

Index